PERSPECTIVES ON WRITING
Series Editor, Susan H. McLeod

PERSPECTIVES ON WRITING
Series Editor, Susan H. McLeod

The Perspectives on Writing series addresses writing studies in a broad sense. Consistent with the wide ranging approaches characteristic of teaching and scholarship in writing across the curriculum, the series presents works that take divergent perspectives on working as a writer, teaching writing, administering writing programs, and studying writing in its various forms.

The WAC Clearinghouse and Parlor Press are collaborating so that these books will be widely available through free digital distribution and low-cost print editions. The publishers and the Series editor are teachers and researchers of writing, committed to the principle that knowledge should freely circulate. We see the opportunities that new technologies have for further democratizing knowledge. And we see that to share the power of writing is to share the means for all to articulate their needs, interest, and learning into the great experiment of literacy.

OTHER BOOKS IN THE SERIES

Charles Bazerman and David R. Russell (Eds.), *Writing Selves/Writing Societies* (2003)

Gerald P. Delahunty and James Garvey, *The English Language: From Sound to Sense* (2009)

Charles Bazerman, Adair Bonini, and Débora Figueiredo (Eds.), *Genre in a Changing World* (2009)

David Franke, Alex Reid, and Anthony Di Renzo (Eds.), *Design Discourse: Composing and Revising Programs in Professional and Technical Writing* (2010)

Martine Courant Rife, Shaun Slattery, and Dànielle Nicole DeVoss (Eds.), *Copy(write) : Intellectual Property in the Writing Classroom* (2011)

Doreen Starke-Meyerring, Anthony Paré, Natasha Artemeva, Miriam Horne, and Larissa Yousoubova, *Writing in Knowledge Societies* (2011)

CHINESE RHETORIC AND WRITING: AN INTRODUCTION FOR LANGUAGE TEACHERS

Andy Kirkpatrick and Zhichang Xu

The WAC Clearinghouse
wac.colostate.edu
Fort Collins, Colorado

Parlor Press
www.parlorpress.com
Anderson, South Carolina

The WAC Clearinghouse, Fort Collins, Colorado 80523-1052
Parlor Press, 3015 Brackenberry Drive, Anderson, South Carolina 29621

© 2012 by Andy Kirkpatrick and Zhichang Xu. This work is licensed under a Creative Commons Attribution-Noncommercial-No Derivative Works 3.0 United States License.

Printed in the United States of America

Library of Congress Cataloging-in-Publication Data

Kirkpatrick, Andy.
  Chinese rhetoric and writing : an introduction for language teachers / Andy Kirkpatrick and Zhichang Xu.
     p. cm. -- (Perspectives on writing)
  Includes bibliographical references.
  ISBN 978-1-60235-300-8 (pbk. : alk. paper) -- ISBN 978-1-60235-301-5 (alk. paper) -- ISBN 978-1-60235-302-2 (adobe ebook) -- ISBN 978-1-60235-303-9 (epub)
  1. Chinese language--Rhetoric--Study and teaching. 2. Report writing--Study and teaching--China. I. Xu, Zhichang. II. Title.
  PL1129.E5K57 2012
  495.1'82421--dc23
                     2012005609

Copyeditor: Don Donahue
Designer: Mike Palmquist
Series Editor: Susan H. McLeod

This book is printed on acid-free paper.

The WAC Clearinghouse supports teachers of writing across the disciplines. Hosted by Colorado State University, it brings together scholarly journals and book series as well as resources for teachers who use writing in their courses. This book is available in digital format for free download at http://wac.colostate.edu.

Parlor Press, LLC is an independent publisher of scholarly and trade titles in print and multimedia formats. This book is available in paperback, cloth, and eBook formats from Parlor Press at http://www.parlorpress.com. For submission information or to find out about Parlor Press publications, write to Parlor Press, 3015 Brackenberry Drive, Anderson, South Carolina 29621, or e-mail editor@parlorpress.com.

CONTENTS

Introduction. *3*

1 Rhetoric in Ancient China *13*

2 The Literary Background And Rhetorical Styles *31*

3 The Rules of Writing in Medieval China and Europe *51*

4 The Ba Gu Wen（八股文）. 75

5 *Shuyuan* and Chinese Writing Training and Practice *93*

6 Principles of Sequencing and Rhetorical Organisation: Words, Sentences and Complex Clauses *107*

7 Principles of Sequencing and Rhetorical Organisation: Discourse and Text *125*

8 The End of Empire and External Influences *143*

9 Party Politics, the Cultural Revolution and Charter 08 . . . .*163*

10 A Review of Contemporary Chinese University Writing (Course) Books *189*

Conclusion. *203*

Works Cited. *207*

Notes *221*

CHINESE RHETORIC AND WRITING

INTRODUCTION

The primary aim of this book is to give teachers of writing, especially those involved in the teaching of English academic writing to Chinese students, an introduction to key stages in the development of Chinese rhetoric. The book will make Western readers familiar with Chinese rhetorical styles and Chinese scholarship on Chinese rhetoric.

Chinese rhetoric is a wide-ranging field with a history of several thousand years. This book is concerned with what might be loosely termed non-fiction or "academic" writing and the writing of essays. It therefore does not deal in any depth with the Chinese poetic tradition. While the focus is on writing, principles of persuasion in Chinese oral texts will also be considered.

Why is such a book necessary? For some forty years, it has been customary to argue that Chinese students' academic writing in English has been influenced by traditional Chinese writing styles. Many scholars, both Chinese and Western, have long argued that Chinese rhetorical norms and traditions are somehow unique to Chinese and that these, when transferred into academic writing in English are a source of negative interference (cf. Kaplan; Jia and Cheng; J. Chen). The underlying assumption is that the English writing of these students is, in some way, inappropriate to academic writing in English. The view is that Chinese students bring with them culturally nuanced rhetorical baggage that is uniquely Chinese and hard to eradicate.

In this book we shall argue that these views stem from an essentially monolingual and Anglo-centric view of writing and that, given the exponential increase in the international learning and use of English, there needs to be a radical reassessment of what English is in today's world. It is no more than a truism to point out that there are many more speakers of English who have learned it as an additional language and use it, either as a new variety of English, such as Indian English, or as a lingua franca, than there are native speakers of it. Kingsley Bolton has estimated that there are some 800 million users of English in Asia alone. In China, it has been estimated that there are currently more than 350 million people who are learning English (Xu, *Chinese English*). This means that there are more speakers of English in China than the total population of the United States. If we also consider the number of English speakers in Europe and other parts of the world—bearing in mind, for example, that when people who belong to the so-called BRIC group, which comprises Brazil, Russia, India and, China normally communicate through English—it becomes clear that English is now a language far more used by multilinguals than by native speakers.

To date, the native speaker and Anglo-American rhetorical styles have remained the benchmarks against which other English users are measured, although many scholars have argued for some years that this needs to change. John Swales suggested that it was time "to reflect soberly on Anglophone gate-keeping practices" (380) and scholars such as Ammon have called for a new culture of communication which respects the non-native speaker (114). Canagarajah (*A Geopolitics of Academic Writing*) has pointed out that, in this age of globalisation, we need to be able to accommodate and respect people who are moving between different cultural and rhetorical traditions. Likewise we shall here argue that, in today's globalising and multilingual world "we need to be sensitive to rhetorical traditions and practices in different linguistic and ethnic communities" (You, Writing, 178).

We shall describe the Chinese rhetorical tradition in order to illustrate its rich complexity and show that Chinese writing styles are dynamic and change for the same types of reasons and in the same types of ways as writing styles in other great literate cultures. In particular, we will argue that the socio-political context is a main driver of change in Chinese writing styles. To argue, therefore, that Chinese students bring with them culturally determined and virtually ineradicable rhetorical traditions to their English writing is to overlook the contextual influences of writing styles and the rich and complex Chinese rhetorical tradition. It also overlooks the value of different rhetorical traditions. The aim of the teacher of writing should not be to gut the English of the Chinese writer of local cultural and rhetorical influences, but to look to see how these can be combined with other rhetorical "norms" to form innovative and effective texts. This will require the writing teacher to have some knowledge of Chinese rhetorical practices. This book will provide writing teachers with a reference to the ways Chinese writing styles have developed over time and a clear understanding of how writing styles change and develop.

An example may help illustrate this point. Chapter 3 includes a summary of the *Wen Ze* or *Rules of Writing*. This was written by Chen Kui in 1170. The *Wen Ze* is an important text, being commonly referred to by Chinese scholars as China's first systematic account of rhetoric (Zheng; Zong and Li; Zhou).

The rhetorical principles that *The Rules of Writing* promulgates include the importance of using clear and straightforward language, the primacy of meaning over form, and ways of arranging argument. These principles were, in large part, determined by the needs of the time (Kirkpatrick, "China's First Systematic Account"). *The Rules of Writing* was written at a time of great change in China. Two changes were of particular importance. The first was the development of printing (Cherniack). This made texts much more accessible and affordable than they had been before. The second change was that the Song dynasty sought to increase dramatically the number of men entering the civil service through merit, as opposed to privilege (Chaffee). The role of the civil service exams in ensuring only men of merit entered the civil service increased significantly. We have argued that *The Rules of Writing* was written as a guide for men who wanted to enter a career in the civil service and who needed to pass the strict series of civil service exams in order to do so. As such, it can be compared with contemporary "Anglo" texts on rhetoric that aim to provide university students with advice on the correct way of writing academic texts.

This book also aims to encourage debate about the "primacy" of Anglo-American rhetoric. While it is indisputable that English is the primary language of research and publication and that this English is a specialised variety based on Anglo-American rhetorical principles, this encourages a one-way flow of ideas. We need to create an environment in which the ideas of others can flow through to the Anglo-American world. We need to debate the proposition that ideas and research which do not conform to Anglo-American rhetorical principles might be presented and published in varieties of English (cf. Canagarajah; Swales). As the world of education becomes increasingly international, the more we know about the rhetorical traditions of different cultures the better. And, of course, as China becomes increasingly powerful and influential, the world needs to understand Chinese culture; and we cannot understand China "without also understanding what it says, how it says things, how its current discourses are connected with its past and those of other cultures" (Shi-Xu 224–45).

The book also aims to make a contribution to the debate over the link between language, thought and culture. Chinese has commonly been seen as a prime exemplar of the Sapir-Whorf hypothesis, as scholars (cf. Graham, *The Disputers of the Dao*) have argued that the Chinese language determines Chinese ways of thinking and seeing the world. This view has recently been challenged (Wardy), and the book will provide further evidence that it is the socio-political context, rather than underlying thought patterns determined or influenced by language, which provides the major impetus for the arrangement of texts and argument.

The two authors of this book have both had to cross the Anglo-Chinese rhetorical divide. Xu is originally from Liaoning Province in the northeast of China and did his undergraduate and master's degrees at a leading university in Beijing, where he also taught English and Applied Linguistics. One of the courses he taught was "English for Academic Purpose (EAP): Academic Writing" to engineering master's and doctoral students. Throughout the course, he was constantly aware of the cultural differences in the writing of his students in relation to the Anglo-American academic texts he had read in his own research field. Some differences could be as subtle as the use of "we" instead of "I" for single-authored essays and papers by his students. However, while he was aware of the cultural differences, he still became a "victim" of the rules of Anglo-American writing discourse. For example, his first submission for a conference in Australia was rejected partly because of the "inconsistent use of single and double quotation marks." Although his submission was eventually published in the online version of the proceedings, he came to realise the different conventions even in the use of punctuation marks between Chinese and English for academic writing. Xu did his doctoral study at a university in Australia, then worked there before spending five years teaching in the department of English at the Hong Kong Institute of Education, where he taught applied linguistics courses to language and education major students, and led a project on English academic writing (cf. Xu et al. *Academic Writing*). He is now lecturing in world Englishes at Monash University in Melbourne, Australia.

As far as Xu's experience of learning to write Chinese is concerned, he went through local Chinese primary and secondary schools in which he acquired Chinese literacy (reading and writing) and studied both modern Chinese texts and selected Classical Chinese texts. He achieved high grades in both Chinese and English in the *gao kao* (College Entrance Examination) in 1985. As a result, he majored in English education and Chinese English translation for his BA degree. Apart from the English language course, he also took compulsory Chinese courses (primarily reading and writing) in the first two years of his BA degree studies. The textbook for the Chinese course was entitled *Daxue Yuwen* (University Chinese). This contained classical Chinese texts, for example, selected verses from the Book of Poetry, and prose from the Tang and Song dynasties. There were also contemporary Chinese texts, for example, by Lu Xun, and Zhu Ziqing, and translated texts of overseas authors, for example, Anton Chekhov, Mark Twain, Nikolai Gogol, and William Shakespeare. The Chinese lecturer would periodically assign some writing tasks based on the genres of the reading texts. Writing was only tested through summative assessments during the course, while examinations which tested knowledge of Chinese comprised the major formative assessments. We provide a summary of contemporary Chinese writing textbooks such as *Daxue Yuwen* in Chapter 10.

Kirkpatrick did his first degree in Chinese Studies at the University of Leeds before doing a postgraduate diploma in Chinese literature at Fudan University in Shanghai, which is where he was made aware of different rhetorical requirements of academic writing. As part of the diploma he had to write a thesis (in Chinese) which he proudly handed in by the due date. Two weeks later, the thesis was returned with instructions that the first part would have to be rewritten if he was to receive the diploma. The examiner was happy with the content but could not pass it as it stood because there were no references to authority to buttress the arguments that had been put forward. As this took place in 1977, the references to authority actually meant references to Chairman Mao. Kirkpatrick then spent the next week looking for suitable quotes from the Chairman which he could insert in appropriate places towards the beginning of his thesis. Once his thesis had been correctly framed by quotes from authority, it was passed. We recount a rather more serious case of urgently needing to find the appropriate reference in Chapter 9.

Both authors, then, have direct but different experiences with learning the rules of academic writing in different cultural traditions which we hope will provide useful insights to readers of this book, the framework of which is briefly summarised below.

Roughly speaking the book takes a chronological approach in tracing the development of Chinese rhetoric and writing. While noting that such comparisons can be dangerous, we nevertheless also attempt to compare the origins and essence of Chinese and "Western" rhetoric at various stages throughout the book.

Chapter 1 provides a brief overview of rhetoric in Ancient China. It is important to establish here that one reason why it is difficult to be precise about tracing the origins of rhetoric in China is that there was no distinct discipline of rhetoric in ancient China in the same way that there was in the West (Harbsmeier). There were, however, important works which touched on rhetoric and, of course, incorporated it. In Chapter 1, we review some of these important texts and try and dispel several "myths" (see Lu, X., Ancient China) about Chinese rhetoric and show, for example, that it was not monolithic and represented only by the Confucian school. In fact, as we show, Confucian style only received state sanction during the period of the Western Han dynasty (206 BCE-9 CE).

In Chapter 1 we also introduce the common Chinese sequencing pattern of "because-therefore" and "frame-main," showing how this operates in an argumentative text of the Western Han. We will argue that this rhetorical sequence has become a fundamental principle of sequencing in Chinese and is one reason why so many Western scholars have classified Chinese rhetoric and writing as indirect. We shall argue that this is not so much a case of "indirectness" but one of a preference for inductive reasoning. We also stress, however, that deductive and "direct" reasoning was used by Chinese writers.

Chapter 1 also demonstrates how aware Chinese rhetoricians and writers were of the importance of audience–in particular the relative status of speaker/writer and listener/reader–on the choice of rhetorical style and the way in which a speaker/writer sequenced argument. We cite examples from classical texts to demonstrate how a subject who was trying to persuade his emperor had to be careful not to ruffle the "dragon's" scales. This, naturally enough, also encouraged an inductive method of argument.

As noted above, rhetoric did not develop as a discrete discipline until the twentieth century, but many early texts discussed topics directly relevant to rhetoric and Chapter 2 provides a summary of some of these key texts. These texts include the famous *Wen Xin Diao Long (The Literary Mind and the Carving of Dragons)*, thought by some to be the first Chinese text on rhetoric itself. We also compare and describe two major Chinese literary styles, namely *guwen* (classical prose) and *pianwen* (adorned prose) before reviewing ways of reasoning in Chinese. In this, we provide a number of examples from written texts which show how the Chinese writers arranged their arguments and we discuss their motivation for sequencing their arguments in the ways that they did. Again, we show that a frame-main or inductive style was the preferred methods, and suggest reasons for why this was so.

Chapter 3 is devoted to a summary of the work that most Chinese scholars describe as China's first systematic account of rhetoric, the *Wen Ze (The Rules of Writing)* by Chen Kui. The Rules of Writing was published in 1170. Chen Kui's aim was to summarise the rules and techniques of writing, using classical texts for his examples and source materials. Five main topics make up the book: genre, "negative" rhetoric, "positive" rhetoric, syntax and style (Liu). Negative rhetoric deals with such aspects of rhetoric as text structure and argument sequencing. Positive rhetoric deals with rhetorical tropes. As a fervent advocate of the *guwen* or classical style, Chen Kui identifies the general overriding principle that language should be simple, clear, succinct and contemporary (Kirkpatrick, Systematic, 115). By giving a summary of the book, we feel that some of the advice Chen Kui gave to Chinese student writers on topics such as the arrangement of ideas will be familiar to teachers of writing in American universities today.

As the *Rules of Writing* was more or less contemporaneous with the *Ars Dictaminis* treatises of Medieval Europe–themselves also manuals on how to write appropriately–we provide a brief summary of two of these and compare the advice in them with the advice provided in the *Rules of Writing*. We also compare the times at which the *Rules of Writing* and the *Ars Dictaminis* treatises were written. We argue that the comparable needs of empire and bureaucracy were important factors in explaining some of the rhetorical similarities.

The *ba gu wen* or eight-legged essay, probably the most (in)famous of all Chinese text structures, is the topic of Chapter 4. Several Western scholars have argued that this structure influences the writing in English of Chinese students (e.g., Kaplan, *The Anatomy of Rhetoric*). In disputing this, we provide the historical background to this essay style and its role in the imperial civil service exams. We summarise the critiques Chinese scholars have recently made of it. We also provide a detailed historical example of a *ba gu wen*, along with the rhetorical analysis of it. This chapter concludes with a very rare example of a modern *ba gu wen*, written in 2005 by the famous Chinese scholar Zhou Youguang, and a discussion on whether a reincarnation of the *ba gu wen* is likely or not.

In Chapter 5 the focus shifts from rhetoric and text to the institutions in which these were taught. The *shuyuan* academies originated during the Tang dynasty (618-907) and lasted right up until the end of the Qing in 1912. The *shuyuan* have been defined as "essentially comprehensive, multi-faceted cultural and educational institutions, serving multiple functions, as a school, a library, a research centre or institute, and others including religious and spiritual functions" (Yang and Peng 1). They played a key role in Chinese education, in particular in the teaching of writing. This chapter will describe the *shuyuan* curriculum and how writing was taught. *Shuyuan* also prepared students for writing the *ba gu wen* essays, the topic of the previous chapter. The chapter ends with a discussion of the reasons for the suppression of the *shuyuan* in the twentieth century.

Chapters 6 and 7 review and describe fundamental principles of rhetorical organisation in Chinese. Chapter 6 looks at these principles and how they operate at the level of words, sentences and complex clauses. Chapter 7 looks at these principles and how they operate at the level of discourse and text.

In chapter 6, the principles or rhetorical organisation which we discuss include: topic-comment; modifier-modified; big-small; whole-part; the principle of temporal sequence and the "because-therefore" or "frame-main" sequences found in complex clauses in Chinese. The chapter includes a discussion of parataxis and hypotaxis in Chinese and English, and shows that Chinese is traditionally a more paratactic language in that clauses follow a "logical" order and that therefore the use of explicit connectors which signal the relationship between the clauses are not required. For example, in Chinese, the sequence, "He hurt his ankle, he fell" *must* mean, "Because he hurt his ankle he fell." We argue that these subordinate clause–main clause sequences represent the unmarked sequence in Chinese, but point out that, through influence from the West, caused in large part by the translation into Chinese of Western texts, the alternative main clause–subordinate clause sequences have become more common, along with the explicit use of connectors to signal the subordinate clause and its relation to the main clause. That is to say, sentences of the type, "He hurt his ankle because he fell" are now common in Chinese.

In chapter 7 we show that these principles of rhetorical organisation and sequencing also operate in extended discourse and texts. We exemplify this using naturally occurring data of extended discourses and texts, including a university seminar, a press conference and an essay which compares Hitler with the first Chinese emperor, Qin Shihuang. We conclude chapter 7 by summarising the principles of rhetorical organisation and sequencing we have identified.

Chapter 8 describes how ideas from the West started to enter China and become influential in the early part of the twentieth century. We look at the language reform movement and how this was influenced by Chinese scholars who had studied overseas in Japan and the West. This includes an account of Hu Shi's proposal for promoting the use of the vernacular language as the medium for educated discourse. As we show, Hu Shi had studied at Cornell and Columbia universities and was particularly influenced by the ideas of the American pragmatist philosopher, John Dewey. As American influence was important at this time, we also give a brief account of changes in attitudes towards rhetoric and writing in the United States during this period. We also argue, however, that Hu Shi was at least equally influenced by the Chinese rhetorical tradition as by American rhetorical practice.

Along with Hu Shi and his contribution to language reform in general, the Chinese scholar who made the most significant contribution to the study of rhetoric and its establishment as a discrete discipline in China was Chen Wangdao, the author of *An Introduction to Rhetoric*. This became an important book because Chen combined key concepts of Western rhetoric along with ideas from the Chinese rhetorical tradition. Chen Wangdao was himself a powerful figure, being appointed president of the prestigious Fudan University in Shanghai in 1952, a position he held for 25 years (Wu H.). Fudan remains a leading Chinese centre for the study of rhetoric.

The final section of Chapter 8 summarises two important comparative studies into paragraph organisation and arrangement in Chinese and English (Wang C.; Yang and Cahill) and we argue that the findings of these two studies support the operation of the principles of rhetorical organisation we have identified as fundamental to Chinese rhetoric and writing.

In Chapter 9, we turn our attention to the influence of Communist Party politics and the Cultural Revolution upon contemporary Chinese rhetoric and writing and the ways in which these influences have radically altered Chinese rhetorical style. Using texts from Mao and from dissidents, including the controversial Charter 08, we argue that Chinese rhetoric has developed a strikingly confrontational style and that this is seriously undermining civic discourse and constructive criticism in today's China. We argue that Chinese rhetoric needs to return to its fundamental principles if it is to provide an effective medium of civic discourse and constructive criticism.

Chapter 10 provides an in-depth review of contemporary Chinese academic writing textbooks and shows that these books display influence both from Chinese traditions and from Western theory and practice. We also show that there is more focus in many of these textbooks on *yingyong* or practical writing, as opposed to academic writing as such and consider possible reasons for this. The final chapter, the Conclusion, summarises the main points we have made in the book.

We hope that, after reading this book, readers will have gained both an understanding and interest in the Chinese rhetorical tradition, and that this will help those readers who are teachers of writing by giving them insights into a different rhetorical tradition. This, we hope, will, in turn, help them help and better understand writers who come from different rhetorical traditions.

1 RHETORIC IN ANCIENT CHINA

In this chapter we provide a brief overview of rhetoric in ancient China. The chronology of Ancient Chinese dynasties and periods is (Lu X.):[1]

21-16 centuries BCE:	The Xia Dynasty (a legendary dynasty about which little is known)
16 –11 centuries BCE:	The Shang Dynasty (aka Yin)
1027-770 BCE:	The Zhou Dynasty (which Confucius looks back on as the golden age)
722-481 BCE:	The Spring and Autumn Period (Chun Qiu)
475-221 BCE:	The Warring States Period (Zhan Guo)

Rhetoric is most commonly perceived as "the art of persuasion, the artistic use of oral and written expressions, for the purpose of changing thought and action at social, political and individual levels" (Lu, X., *Ancient China* 2). However, the notion of rhetoric has many different meanings within the Chinese tradition, as it does within the Western one, some of which are reviewed in Chapter 8. Chinese rhetoric has enjoyed an extremely long history, but did not enjoy the status of a distinct discipline until the early twentieth century (Harbsmeier 115–16). Thus "rhetoric" has been known under a variety of different terms. The ancient Chinese (up to 221 BCE) had a well-developed sense of rhetoric but called various branches of it by different names. Lu (5) provides the meanings of key Chinese rhetorical terms as used in classical Chinese texts.

Yan (言)	speech, talks and the use of language
Ci (辞)	modes of speech, types of discourse, eloquence, style
Jian (谏)	giving advice, persuasion
Shui/shuo (说)	persuasion/ explanation, idea, thought
Ming (名)	naming, symbol using, rationality, epistemology
Bian (辩)	distinction change, justice-eloquence, arguments, persuasion, debate, disputation discussion

So persuasion was known as *shui* (说), explanation *ming* (名), and argumentation *bian* (辩). Although there is overlap between these terms (and others), Lu argues that each word has a particular function in conceptualising and contextualising persuasive discourse. For example *shui* is associated with face-to-face persuasion and *ming* deals with the use of symbols in social and epistemological contexts. Lu suggests that the term *ming bian xue* (名辩学) is comparable to the Western study of rhetoric, with *ming* aiming to seek truth and justice and *bian* concerning the art of persuasion. This term also captures the contradiction inherent in the two key concepts of Western rhetoric, namely viz truth and/or persuasion.

A common misunderstanding is that Chinese rhetorical perspectives were monolithic. This was not the case. In ancient China, the Ming school whose best-known protagonist was perhaps Gong-sun Long (325-250 BCE), was concerned with probability, relativism and classification under the general umbrella of epistemology and social justice. Confucian concerns included issues of morality and the moral impact of speech and moral character of the speaker on ethical behaviour and social order. Mohism (480-250 BCE) was concerned with developing a rational system of argumentation (Angus Graham). The concerns of Daoism (cf. Zhuangzi 369-286 BCE) included "antirational and transcendental mode of philosophical and rhetorical enquiry" (Lu X., *"Ancient China"* 7). Legalism, founded by the philosopher Han Feizi (280-233 BCE), was concerned with the use of language and persuasion to strengthen centralised political power.

Rhetorical devices employed included metaphorical, anecdotal, analogical, paradoxical, chain reasoning, classification, and inference. In this context it is important to point out the fallacy believed and promulgated by many Western scholars of Chinese thought, of which Alfred Bloom's work provides perhaps the most striking example, that the structure of the Chinese language somehow impedes the Chinese from thinking and arguing in what Western scholars call a rational way. A major and long-standing controversy concerns the extent to which Chinese provides evidence for the strong version of the Sapir-Whorf hypothesis, namely that language determines thought. Many scholars have argued that it does, but we side more with Robert Wardy's view that "we must resist any initial inclination to discern limits to Chinese thought imposed by the Chinese language"(8) and provide evidence for this position throughout the book. This is not to say, of course, that language, thought and culture are not associated, only that one does not necessarily determine the other.

A second misunderstanding—something Lu terms a "myth"—is that speech in Ancient China was not appreciated. In fact, speech was highly valued and encouraged. Argumentation and debates were common among philosophers and disputers (*bian shi* 辩士 and *bing jia* 名家). Indeed Liu Yameng ("To Capture the Essence of Chinese Rhetoric") goes as far as to claim an oral primacy and oratorical basis to Chinese rhetoric. Perhaps this goes too far, but Confucius certainly taught his disciples to practice *xin yan* (信言, trustworthy speech). It was *qiao yan* (巧言, clever speech) that he disliked. Liu argues that Confucius' denunciation of clever speech shows that he was worried about certain people's abilities in argument. Such a person might well have been Mao Hiao-cheng, whom Confucius ordered executed during his brief spell as Minister of Justice because he could argue a right to be a wrong and a wrong to be a right. "What is deprecated by ancient Chinese philosophers is not speech in general but rather glib speakers or speakers with flowery and empty words" (Lu X. 31). This distaste is almost exactly mirrored by Aristotle and Plato's distaste for the Greek sophists.

As Anglo-American rhetoric owes much to its classical Greek and Latin forebears, we here briefly consider the different emphases placed on speaking and writing in Greek and Chinese rhetoric respectively. As is well known, Sicily was the birth place of classical Greek rhetoric. After the expulsion of the tyrants in 467 BCE, a number of civil law suits were brought by citizens. Many were eager to reclaim property that had been, as it were, "tyrannised" and a system for pleading these suits was developed by Corax, who wrote the first books on rhetoric, defining rhetoric as "the artificer of persuasion." Corax divided the plea, or speech, into either three parts, namely: the exordium; the arguments, both constructive and refutative; and the epilogue; or into five parts, namely: the exordium; the narrative; the arguments; the subsidiary arguments; and the epilogue. Although the speeches were written, they were written to be read aloud. The forensic nature of this rhetoric is of great importance as it presupposes two parties—the antagonist and the protagonist—who are trying to persuade a third party—usually some form of judge– of the justice of their particular case. Each case had its own facts and these facts could be shown or proved, although this is not to say this is what always happened. This forensic rhetoric was practiced under an adversarial legal system and practiced by people who were, to a large extent, political equals. This contrasts strongly with the Chinese legal system which was inquisitorial and hierarchical.

A further point of contrast between early Chinese and Greek rhetoric was that the ability to speak well and persuasively in public was essential to the ambitious Athenian of the fifth and fourth centuries BCE. People were expected to participate in politics.

In contrast, public speaking of this sort has had little place in Chinese political life. The conventional wisdom is of "agonistic Greeks and irenic Chinese" (Durrant 283). And while the force of Durrant's argument here is that the Chinese were able, on occasion, to be harshly critical, it is nevertheless true that criticism of their predecessors was a characteristic feature of Greek historiography, while Confucius is "repeatedly and respectfully cited to buttress the authority of the text" (284), in much the same way as Kirkpatrick was required to use quotations from Mao to buttress the authority of his thesis, referred to in the introduction. However, Durrant's argument is worth noting. Chinese can be antagonistic—and Durrant gives the examples of Yang Xiong 扬雄 (53-18 BCE), Wang Chong 王充 (27-110 CE) and Ban Gu 班固 (32-92 CE) as criticising the great historian Sima Qian (circa 145-90 BCE). Wang Chong, for example criticised him thus: "nevertheless he relied on what had already been completed and made a record of former events, and he did not produce anything from within himself [然而因成纪前, 无脑中之造]" (285). We return to Wang Chong in Chapter 2.

While Liu's ("To Capture the Essence of Chinese Rhetoric:") claims for an oral primacy and oratorical basis to Chinese rhetoric probably go too far, there have been periods in Chinese history when oral persuasion has been prevalent, most notably during the period of the Warring States (475-221 BCE) (Graham, *The Disputers of the Dao*). This was a time when central control collapsed and China comprised several competing fiefdoms when "kings and lords recruited learned individuals to form advisory boards" (You, "Building Empire" 368). These were the *bian shi* or *you shi* (游士), court counselors, and this is the period, when, in François Jullien's view, comparisons with Greece can be made. It was a time of "great collective and personal freedom" (124). But, again as Jullien points out, with the establishment of the unified empire in 221 BCE, the role of the *you shi* declined and the man of letters became "a cog in the machine" and "his independence of thought was subjected to the autocrats' often high-handed censorship."

The Confucian legacy was not sealed until several centuries after his death during the Western Han dynasty (206 BCE-9 CE) under Emperor Wu (r. 141-87 BCE). This was cemented by Emperor Wu's acceptance of the advice of one of his senior ministers, Dong Zhongshu, to establish an academy at which only Confucianism would be studied, other schools of thought being dismissed. This is of utmost importance, as this led to Confucianism becoming *the* state-sanctioned ideology. It became codified and from here stems its regulatory role. So, the Western Han "laid a cornerstone for the state-sanctioned argumentative tradition" (You, "Building Empire"). It might be more accurate, however, to say that there was now a state-sanctioned *canon*, rather than a state sanctioned *argumentative tradition*.

A famous debate, the Discourse on Salt and Iron (*yan tie lun*) took place during the Western Han. Court officials, many of whom were heavily influenced by legalism—to which we return later—argued with the Confucian literati over the imposition of taxes on salt and iron. The Confucian literati represented the landlord and merchant classes and they were successful in so far as the tax was lifted in various parts of the empire. The following excerpt exemplifies a typical "Confucian" argument and rhetorical structure. The use of analogy and historical precedent is evident.

> The Literati (The well-educated): Confucius observed that the ruler of a kingdom or the chief of a house is not concerned about his people being few, but about lack of equitable treatment; nor is he concerned about poverty, but over the presence of discontentment. **Thus** the Son of Heaven should not speak about much and little, the feudal lords should not talk about advantage and detriment, ministers about gain and loss, but they should cultivate benevolence and righteousness, to set an example to the people, and extend wide their virtuous conduct to gain the people's confidence. Then will nearby folk lovingly flock to them and distant peoples submit to their authority. **Therefore**, the master conqueror does not fight, the expert warrior needs no soldiers; the truly great commander requires not to set his troops in battle array. Cultivate virtue in

the temple and the hall, then you need only show a bold front to the enemy and your troops will return home in victory. The Prince who practices benevolent administration should be matchless in the world; for him what use is expenditure. (Gale 4–5, emphasis added)

Note how the rhetorical structure of the argument in this example of reasoning by historical precedent lends itself to what Kirkpatrick has called a "because-therefore" or "frame-main" sequence ("Information Sequencing in Modern Standard Chinese", "Are they really so Different?", "Traditional Chinese Text Structures"). It can be represented as (where "Ø because" indicates that there is no explicit "because" marker in the original Chinese):

Ø BECAUSE (Confucius-discontentment) — THUS (Son of Heaven-benevolence)

+

Ø BECAUSE (Son of Heaven benevolent) — THUS (people support)

+

THUS
(do not fight but cultivate virtue)

We return to the principles of rhetorical and argument sequence later, but this example serves to illustrate a standard form of rhetorical sequence in traditional Chinese, where the justification for an argument or position typically precedes it.

The Chinese respect for their predecessors and early texts and classics means that commentators over centuries have constantly referred to the same texts. We therefore provide some background to the classics and the times they are describing. The Zhou dynasty (1027-770 BCE) represented the Confucian ideal in that Confucius felt that the Zhou represented a time of harmony, where each person knew his place. King Wen was the founder, followed by his son King Wu. *De* (德, virtue) became the ultimate criterion for evaluating royal behaviour, while *li* (礼, rites) became important political and ideological means of control. The Zhou "is considered as a watershed for the production of written texts" (Lu X. *Ancient China* 56) We get the *Shi Jing* (The Book of Poetry), the *Shang Shu* (The Shang Histories, also known as the Book of Lord Shang, and which includes the Zhou History as well as that of the earlier Shang dynasty), the *Yi*

Jing (The Book of Changes, described as "the ultimate origin of writing and the fundamental treatment of the powers of visual signs" (Lewis 239). The *Zhou Li* (Rites of Zhou), which offers detailed rules and norms for speech and behaviour in social, official and family life, was also probably written at this time. As will be illustrated below, the writing of the *Zhou Li* could be very straightforward and earthy. Two kinds of speeches were recorded in the *Shang Shu*, the "shi" (誓), taking oath and the *gao* (诰), public advising. A *shi* was performed by a ruler before a war to encourage morale, and is a type of deliberative rhetoric. A *gao* was performed by the king at mass gatherings such as the celebration of a harvest and is a type of epideictic rhetoric, and which could also be offered by ministers to the king in order to inspire him to follow the examples of Wen and Wu, the wise, benevolent and virtuous founders of the dynasty.

In 770 BCE the Zhou were defeated by the so-called barbarians (i.e., those tribes not assimilated to Zhou culture) and we move to China's most chaotic and stimulating time with the rise of vassal states and competing schools of thought. The social and economic changes paved the way for social and cultural transformation. Changes began with the education system. Private institutions flourished and opened their doors to rich and poor alike. Rather than teaching by rote, "a master taught his disciples his own concepts about various subjects" (Lu X., *Ancient China* 63). Students could dispute with their masters and this critical thinking in education produced profound changes in cultural values, social stratification and interpersonal relations. A scholarly tradition or school was perpetuated across time through the production of texts, composed of bundles of bamboo or wooden strips. Authority was located in quotation and "since the Masters preserved or invented within the texts offered doctrines for creating and maintaining social order, the initial relation of the schools to the state was one of opposition" (Lewis 95).

It was believed that able and virtuous people should be employed ahead of relatives of the ruler. This is the beginning of meritocracy and the emergence of *shi* (士), the educated intellectual elite. Freedom of speech and argument became commonplace and persuasion and argumentation were popular rhetorical activities. The period was characterised by free expression, critical thinking and intellectual vigour. This is the time of the original "One Hundred Schools of Thought," and was the golden age for the production of written materials, as each school claimed a universal way. This is why Jullien identifies this period as the period with which comparison between China and Greece is possible. This led to the appearance of canons (*jing*), which were regularly paired with an explanation and a commentary (*zhuan*) which Lewis explains "articulated the significance of the master text." Lewis proceeds, "A permanent truth was attributed to the old texts with their archaic language, while the commentaries were used to successively apply this truth to changing social problems and evolving philosophical debates" (333). This time also saw the production of the historical texts such as the *Guo Yu* (Discourse of the States), and the *Zhan Guo Ce* (Intrigues of the Warring States). We also get the philosophical works such as the Confucian Analects, the *Dao De Jing* of Laozi, and books by Mencius, Mozi, Zhuangzi, Xunzi and Han Feizi. This is also the time of the *Zuo Zhuan* which uses historical chronicles to expound political theories and defines these theories through the dictates of ritual. It contains extensive narratives that demonstrate moral lessons and these narratives are interspersed with participants' speeches that discuss proper conduct. Judgements on individuals or events are supplied by a third person, usually Confucius.

The Book of Rites (*Li Ji*) describes the proper conduct—including ways of speaking—in maintaining the five key Confucian relationships. These relationships are those between: prince and minister; father and son; husband and wife; elder and younger; friends. All but the relationship between friends are hierarchical, with the second member of each pair being seen in some way as of inferior status to the first. The keeping of these relationships was considered essential for an orderly society and it is not hard to see how any use of rhetoric to destabilise the status quo was viewed negatively. This can be summed up in a quote from Confucius "Few who are filial and fraternal would want to offend their superiors; and when they do not like to offend their superiors, none would be fond of stirring up social order" (Wang G. 13). Indeed the Li Ji requires execution for those "who split words so as to break the force of the laws" and "who confound names so as to change what has been definitely settled" (*The Li Ki* 1). It is this type of attitude and its inevitable encouragement of indirect style (or complete silence) that has led Jullien to ask "In the name of what, therefore, can the Chinese man of letters break free from the forces of power, affirm his positions, and thus speak openly? This is a question that is still being asked in China, one that makes dissidence more difficult" (379). "With such obliquity, dissidence is impossible" (137). We return to this theme in Chapter 9.

An important figure in the history of rhetoric and persuasion who lived sometime during this period (481-221 BCE), and was thus more or less contemporaneous with Aristotle, was the philosopher Gui Guzi, whose name means The Ghost of the Valleys. As might be surmised, people who tried to persuade the emperor—the *bian shi* and the *you shi*, for example—had to be careful. As a philosopher of the Warring States period, Gui Guzi clearly understood the importance of the relative power of the speaker and listener in such persuasion. As we have seen, the unity enjoyed under Zhou federalism had collapsed, replaced by several competing fiefdoms. This period saw constant and chaotic political alignments and realignments as states ought to enhance their own positions while, increasingly, attempting to counteract the growing threat of the Qin, the state which eventually emerged triumphant in 221 BCE.

The travelling philosophers represented different schools. Gui Guzi is considered the founder of the Zong Heng (纵横) school. The attitude towards these philosophers has been ambivalent and recalls the common attitude to the sophists of Greece. For example, a well—known philosopher of the Zong Heng school, Hui Shi, was considered by his contemporaries to be only interested in confounding the arguments of others and not in projecting his own ideas. There are some remarkable similarities between some of Hui Shi's sayings and those of Zeno. Readers will be familiar with Zeno's paradox of the arrow which stated,

When the arrow is in a place exactly its own size it is at rest

In flight the arrow is always in a place exactly its own size

An arrow in flight is therefore at rest.

Hui Shi says "There is a time when a swiftly flying arrow is neither moving nor at rest" along with other contradictory aphorisms such as "The sun at noon is the sun declining" and "A creature born is a creature dying" (Forke 2). The ambivalence towards such philosophers was caused by an admiration for their persuasive skills coupled with a distrust of their motives. The Confucian philosopher, Xunzi described Gui Guzi's disciples as "ingratiating courtiers" who were "inadequate in uniting people domestically, inadequate in confronting enemies externally, unable to win the affinity of the people nor the trust of the nobles. But they were good at crafty persuasion and good at courting favour from the high ranks" (Tsao 19). The "courtiers" in question were Su Qin and Chang Yi and both appear in the *Zhan Guo Ce* (*The Intrigues of the States*), a volume which has been described by some scholars as a "manual of examples for rhetorical training" (Owen, *The End of the Chinese "Middle Ages"* 124). Rather than being faithful transcriptions of real debates, it comprises idealised accounts written after the events. James Crump even compares it with the Greek "suasoriae" by which students were given legends or historical facts as material on which to practice their debating skills.

To turn to Gui Guzi himself, it is far more likely that his eponymous book—a custom of the times—was compiled by his disciples rather than written by Gui Guzi himself. He was clearly influenced by *yin-yang* duality and considered that persuasion from below (yin) to above (yang) to be a disturbance of the natural order of things. Persuasion from below to above or from an inferior to a superior was *yin* and required special effort. Persuading from above to below, from Emperor to subject, required less effort. "Yang (persuading from above to below) encourages straightforward speaking. Yin (persuading from below to above) encourages speaking in forked tongue" (Tsao 103).

As examples of "straightforward" speaking, I provide two imperial edicts. These are characterised by the use of imperatives and modals of obligation. The first one clearly shows the emperor's irritation at philosophers such as Gui Guzi (see Kirkpatrick, "China's First Systematic Account").

> The edict appointing Long as official in charge of the use of words.
>
> Long! I am very fed up with the bad speech of expert speakers. They are people who confound good with evil and right with wrong and the rumours they spread frequently shock our people. I order you to take the position of official in charge of language. Whether representing the decrees I issue or reporting to me the ideas of officials and subjects, you must at all times ensure truth and accuracy.
>
> The edict appointing Feng Kangshu as Duke of Wei.
>
> The King said: Feng! You need to be careful! Don't do things that cause people to hold grudges, do not use incorrect methods or unfair laws in such a way that you conceal your honest heart. You should model yourself on the sensitive conduct of earlier sages to settle your thoughts. You should frequently ask yourself whether your words and deeds are appropriate, and establish far-reaching policies to govern the country. You need to promulgate magnanimous policies, to make the lives of the people peaceful and secure, and then they will not eliminate you because of your faults. The King said: Ai! I remind you, young Feng, the mandate of heaven is immutable and you need to observe it in earnest! Do not sever our ancestral sacrificial rites through your mistakes. To manage the people well, you must be clear about your role and responsibilities, listen to my advice and instructions, and follow the way the previous emperor pacified the people.

Examples of less straightforward "from below-to-above persuasion" are provided later.

The effect of the relative status and power of speaker and audience has been made, rather more recently, by Lasswell:

> When non-democratic attitudes prevail in a community, initiatives from below are phrased in somewhat laboured language. Elaborate words and gestures are used by a subordinate to show that he is not presuming to transgress the prerogatives of his superior. By contrast with the self-assurance of the superior, he represents himself as somewhat uncertain of judgement. (Laswell and Leites 30–1)

It can be argued that the relative status of participants has a fundamental effect on rhetorical style and persuasive strategy, no matter in which culture the interaction is taking place. And, when the emperor had ultimate power over the persuader, the persuader had to be resourceful. Gui Guzi understood that the persuader needed to know how he related to the audience. "Information of the audience and the situation is essential to persuasion" (Tsao 140). The ideal persuader requires several further key qualities: he is quick and perceptive; he is in control of himself and the situation; he is resourceful; he can assess people well; he can look after himself; and he can shepherd people. Gui Guzi also acknowledges the opportunistic and exploitative function of persuasion. "Speaking is like fishing. If the bait, language, is appropriate to the situation, then the human fish can be caught" (128). Silence and secrecy are considered valuable tactics. "If I keep silent so that he will open up, I may thus gain the advantage," and "When I want to persuade, I must conceal my calculation" (65).

The *Gui Guzi* resembles a tactical manual, listing a variety of means of bettering one's opponent. This, in turn, recalls Jullien's argument that Chinese rhetorical style is directly influenced by Chinese military strategy, a fundamental principle of which was to avoid direct confrontation. Indeed the art of war "taught how to triumph by avoiding battle altogether" (Jullien, *Detour and Access* 40). This principle of "avoidance" was later observed by Mao whose advice to "make noise in the east to attack in the west," Jullien describes as a summary of the whole of Chinese military strategy. Jullien goes on to argue that, in direct contrast, Greek military strategy sought face-to-face confrontation, an "agonistic" arrangement, as this was the most effective and efficient way of settling military (and thus civil) disputes.

This is an interesting and suggestive argument and the *Gui Guzi* provides further evidence for it. The *Gui Guzi* also encourages complexity. "The categories of speech are many. He who enjoys complicated language without getting confused, who soars high without getting lost...has learned the art of persuasion" (Tsao 93).

At the same time, there is no call for clarity or proof. There is no place for forensic rhetoric with its emphasis on proof and the search for facts. The political climate of China at the time ensured that pleasing the listener was the prerequisite of being a successful persuader. As the listener was often a ruler or prince with summative powers, then straightforward speaking was their prerogative. The hierarchical nature of society, involving as it did, having to persuade "upwards," required speaking in a forked tongue.

Perhaps the most famous essay on persuasion of the Warring States period was written by the legalist philosopher Han Feizi, who was born towards the end of the Warring States period in 280 BCE. His was a privileged background—he was a royal prince of the State of Han (at the time, one of the Warring States) and was a student of the Confucian philosopher, Xunzi. Despite his position, his many memorials were ignored. His book on political strategy, the *Han Feizi*, however, was read by the Prince of Qin over whom it exerted a significant influence. It is ironic, therefore, that Han Feizi died while on Han emissary business to the state of Qin, poisoned by the Qin ruler.

Burton Watson has described Han Feizi as the "perfector" of the legalist school (4). The major theme of his book was the preservation and strengthening of the state. The philosophy or ruling strategy it promulgated, legalism, differed markedly from Confucianism in almost all aspects. It had no faith in the Confucian notion that good conduct by the Emperor would result in good governance and a stable state. Thus it had no faith in the sages of earlier times. Far from being inherently innocent and malleable by good example, people were inherently evil and needed to be controlled by law. The state could only be stable if the central government was strong, if there was a strong centralised bureaucracy and the implementation of a harsh legal code. The Chinese scholar of the early twentieth century, Hu Shi (*The Development of the Logical Method* 175–83), has summed up the key points of the *Han Feizi*.

> In governing a state, the wise ruler does not depend on the people's becoming good for his sake, but on their necessity not to do evil.
>
> A wise man never expects to follow the ways of the ancients, nor does he set up any principle for all time.
>
> To be sure of anything without corroborating evidence is stupidity. To base one's argument on anything which one

cannot be sure is perjury. Therefore, those who openly base their argument on the authority of the sage-elders of antiquity, and who are dogmatically certain of the ages of Yao and Shun, are men either of stupidity or of wilful perjury.

It is worth noting how direct and *agonistic* the legalist style is, compared to the Confucian style. This shows that, while indirectness was normally adopted, this did not mean that directness never was. We shall return to this later when providing examples from Wang Chong's discourse and at various other points in the book. In his discussion of Arabic rhetoric, Hatim points out that "the motivated departure from linguistic norms" is a theme that has dominated Arab rhetorical thinking (25). This deliberate adoption of the unexpected is known in Arabic as "Iltiafāt," which Hatim describes as "the motivated switch from speaking in a more expected grammatical mode, to speaking in another, less expected mode" (25). The use of a direct rhetorical style by someone persuading from below to above can be seen as a type of "Iltiafāt."

Another way of considering this deliberate deviation from linguistic norms is to use the linguistic terms "unmarked" and "marked." Many rhetorical devices, expressions and even words can be classified as being unmarked or marked, depending on their use. For example, to ask, in English, "How old are you?" would be to use the unmarked form. But to ask, "How young are you?" would be to use the marked form. Many pairs of English adjectives operate in this way. "How tall/short are you?" would be another example. A second linguistic example is that the complex cause sequence which follows the subordinate to main sequence is unmarked in Chinese, while a complex cause which follows a main to subordinate sequence is marked. A simple example of this would be the following English sentence "You can't enter the building because there has been a fire," which follows an unmarked sequence in English. If translated retaining the main clause to subordinate clause sequence would be marked in Chinese.

As will become apparent, this is of particular interest for two reasons. First, the unmarked subordinate to main sequence allows for indirectness. Second the unmarked and marked orders in Chinese are reversed in English, where the main to subordinate sequence is the normal unmarked pattern.

Thus, in the Chinese context we can call indirectness the unmarked style, that is to say the style adopted in standard, normal circumstances, while the direct style is marked, that is to say it is used for special effect and/or in special circumstances.

To return to the text of the *Han Feizi*, Section 12 is called "On the Difficulties of Persuasion" (说难). By citing some excerpts, we hope the reader can gain a feel of the advice being given and will also, no doubt, be struck by the close similarities of the advice and strategies provided by both the *Hanfeizi* and the *Gui Guzi*. These translations are taken from Burton Watson.

> On the whole, the difficult thing about persuasion is to know the mind of the person one is trying to persuade and to be able to fit one's words to it.
>
> Undertakings succeed through secrecy but fail through being found out.
>
> The important thing in persuasion is to learn how to play up the aspects that the person you are talking to is proud of, and play down the aspect he is ashamed of.
>
> Men who wish to present their remonstrances and expound their ideas must not fail to ascertain their ruler's loves and hates before launching into their speeches … If you gain the ruler's love, your wisdom will be appreciated and you will enjoy favour as well. But, if he hates you, not only will your wisdom be rejected but you will be regarded as a criminal and thrust aside…. The beast called the dragon can be tamed and trained to the point where you may ride on its back. But on the underside of its throat it has scales a foot in diameter that curl back from the body, anyone who chances to brush against them is sure to die. The ruler of men too has his bristling scales. Only if a speaker can avoid brushing against them will he have any hope of success.

As with *The Gui Guzi*, there is no mention here of the justice of an argument or the necessity of proof. The main point, constantly reiterated, is not to displease the person one is attempting to persuade for fear of retribution, most commonly exile, but not infrequently execution, the fate suffered by Han Feizi himself, whose own directness may well have precipitated his downfall. Both works illustrate the intensely practical nature of rhetoric given the political conditions at the particular time. The need for extreme caution in such matters is described by Jenner, "The wise official did not take a strong position on matters that might bring a frown to the dragon countenance. That a few did is a mark of their personal courage" (41).

Legalism appeared to be vindicated as a more realistic and effective political system with the establishment of the Qin Dynasty, commonly regarded as the first State to unify China. It is perhaps worth noting however, that the term *Zhong Guo,* which is commonly translated as the Middle Kingdom and, in so doing, gives the idea of China in the Centre of the world, is more accurately translated as the "central states," meaning those states clustered around the yellow River in North China in contrast to the "barbarian" states to the North, West, and South (McDonald).

Legalism allowed no opportunity for arguing from below to above. While the strict and harsh laws applied to all citizens—and in this legalism claimed to be more egalitarian than Confucianism—the laws did not apply to the Emperor, whose task was not to obey the laws but to formulate them. The first emperor of China, Qin Shi Huang (r 221-210 BCE), exploited this to the hilt in establishing an empire in which all dissenting voices would be silenced. He ordered all books to be burned and several hundred scholars to be buried alive. His reign was mercifully short-lived.

The Han Dynasty (206 BCE-220 CE) replaced the Qin. Not surprisingly, the officials were still influenced by legalism and, again not surprisingly, these were opposed by the Confucian literati. The new empire encouraged debate and literati were invited to advise the emperor through court debates and "those whose arguments the emperor favoured would receive government posts" (You, "Building" 369). As we have seen, it was during one of these debates during the time of the Emperor Wu in 134 BCE that Dong Zhongshu successfully persuaded the Emperor to establish an academy that tolerated only Confucian schools of thought. This resulted in a Grand Academy with a state sanctioned Confucian canon. The canonical texts provided a route by which families entered into state service. This eventually led to the establishment of a civil service exam and, as we shall show in Chapter 3, the Song Dynasty inherited and then greatly expanded an exam system developed during the Sui-Tang dynasties. But the texts that constituted Chinese imperial culture were not fixed. The canon itself was expanded and read in different ways. As Lewis points out, "When the state defended itself through a group of texts, and justified itself through their teachings, then these writings could be invoked to criticise specific policies, or ultimately to condemn the state itself" (Lewis 362). The importance assigned to texts can hardly be overestimated. They created a model of society against which institutions were measured. Texts also created the basis of the educational program. To quote Lewis once more, "the Chinese empire became a realm built of texts" (362).

The importance and influence of these texts depended on the relative central authority of the empire at any one time and this also had a direct effect on the role and popularity of oral rhetoric. A centralised empire needs bureaucrats who can write documents. A centralised empire with a strong emperor is unlikely to create an environment conducive to public oratory. On the other hand, when the country comprises several competing smaller states, oral persuaders (the *youshi* and *bianshi*) become much in demand, as was the case during the Warring States period. In addition, China's imperial history has meant that China has traditionally favoured written rhetoric over oral, while the comparatively democratic institutions of Classical Greece gave rise to a rhetoric that was primarily oral, although it needs to be stressed that most speeches were first written to be read aloud later. The early Greek handbooks on rhetoric lack appeals to authority, as such use of authority was uncongenial to fifth century BCE democratic ideals (Kennedy). Similarly, pre-medieval rhetoric in Europe was primarily an art of persuasion, it was primarily used in civil life and it was primarily oral (Camargo). The relative emphasis placed on oral and written rhetoric at any time can partly be explained by the nature of the political institutions in power at that time. This phenomenon is by no means uniquely Chinese. For example, the rise of city states in Italy by the end of the twelfth century saw the rise once again of spoken rhetoric as people needed to address assemblies.

In this chapter we have provided a brief introduction to the major rhetorical schools and styles of Ancient China. We have shown that the Chinese rhetorical tradition is not monolithic, but characterised by different and competing schools, although the Confucian school became dominant after it won imperial favour during the Han dynasty. As we shall show, however, the rhetorical tradition remained diverse. We have also shown that rhetorical styles are dynamic and heavily influenced by the relative status of writer/speaker and reader/listener. In Chapter 2 we turn to a survey of literary styles.

We conclude this chapter by summing up the main points:

(i) Western rhetoric has its origins in the rhetoric of the law courts. While open to abuse, this presupposes a goal of discovering the facts or justice of a case, and is dependent upon proof. The protagonists in these debates were often equals, whose task was to persuade a third party.

(ii) There was no such forensic rhetoric in China. The official law always operated in a vertical direction from the state upon the individual rather than on a horizontal plane between equal individuals. This meant that there was little adversarial debate between equals.

(iii) The conditions surrounding the development of Western rhetoric encouraged direct, confrontational and agonistic exchanges, although that is not to say that arguing by analogy and other more oblique and indirect methods were not adopted when times justified this.

(iv) The conditions surrounding the development of Chinese rhetoric encouraged those persuading up to couch their arguments in indirect ways—of speaking in "forked tongue"—for fear of offending the listeners. This is not to say that direct methods of argument were not adopted when times justified this or when the author was prepared to take a calculated risk.

(v) To use a linguistic distinction, in classical Greece, direct methods of argument were unmarked, while indirect methods were marked. In Classical China, the opposite was true: indirect methods or argument were unmarked, while direct methods of argument were marked.

(vi) The relative power of the emperor had a direct effect on rhetorical style, whether this was in China, early Greece and Rome, or Europe.

(vii) Conditions in Classical China and respect for authority and hierarchy led to a preference for written rhetoric and "an empire built of texts."

(viii) The focus of rhetoric shifts between oral and written expression in both the "Western" and Chinese traditions.

2 THE LITERARY BACKGROUND AND RHETORICAL STYLES

In moving to consider the literary background and rhetorical styles we shall consider texts that can conceivably be classified as being primarily concerned with literary and rhetorical style, or at least have some important things to say about it, even if it is not their primary focus. This chapter also recounts the debate between the competing styles of *guwen* (classical prose) and *pianwen* (flowery prose) and concludes with texts that exemplify typical methods of reasoning.

An early work that was influential to the development of rhetorical and literary style was Dong Zhongshu's *Chun Qiu Fan Lu* (春秋繁露), known in English as *Rich Dew of the Spring and Autumn Classic*. As noted in Chapter 1, Dong, who died in 104 CE, was an advisor to the Emperor Wu and who managed to persuade the Emperor to establish an academy at which Confucian thought be taught at the expense of all other schools of thought. Although his book deals with the theory of government, it is, however, important to style, as it elevated Confucius to the status of a sage. This in turn ensured that Confucian style would become the orthodox style. As has been illustrated earlier, the orthodox Confucian style can be classified as being both plain and clear. Pu Kai and Wei Kun quote a number of Confucian remarks on the use of language, which can be summarised in the phrase "explaining things plainly and simply is good enough" (111–24). It is important to stress, however, that Confucius did not write explicitly about language and rhetoric. Rather, there are references to these topics which are scattered throughout the Analects, which, it needs to be remembered, were written down by his disciples after his death. Despite these caveats, when later scholars call for a return to a Confucian style, they are almost always calling for a return to plain speaking.

The later years of the Han dynasty saw the publication of several works of significance to literary style. These included The Disquisitions (*Lun Heng*) of Wang Chong (27-100 CE). Wang Chong's criticism of the historian, Sima Qian, as being unable to produce anything original was cited in Chapter 1.

Although primarily a book about political theory, this is an important book with regard to style because Wang Chong attacked the then current fashion of slavishly imitating the ancients. At the same time, he severely criticises his contemporaries for ignoring their own times.

> The story tellers like to extol the past and disparage the present time. They make much of what they see with their own eyes. The disputants will discourse in what is long ago and literati write on what is far away. The curious things near at hand, the speakers do not mention, and the extraordinary events of our own time are not committed to writing. (Kinney)

Wang Chong is significant as his own style is characterised by a penchant for direct or deductive reasoning and, as such, represents an interesting counter example to the usual indirectness of "oblique" style commonly reported by others, including Jullien (*Detour and Access*) and Kirkpatrick ("Traditional Chinese Text Structures"). However, it is perhaps instructive to note that Jullien makes only a single passing reference to Wang Chong throughout *Detour and Access* and that is in the conclusion where he reiterates that the implicit, oblique and indirect—the Chinese notion of *hanxu* (含蓄)—is of fundamental importance in Chinese culture. Here he cites Wang Chong as a writer of "clarity of discourse" but he then adds that Wang Chong's "prose is unpopular" (374). While his prose may well have been unpopular with those whom he attacked, his style and bravery was much admired. The example below is our translation of the summary of one of Wang Chong's essays, *Ding Gui* or "Conclusions about Ghosts." The summary is provided in Wu Yingtian (165).[2]

> General Statement: (*zonglun*)
>
> ghosts and spirits are the illusions of sick minds.
>
> Individual Arguments (*fenlun*)
>
> 1 sick people are terrified of death and so they see ghosts.
>
> 2 sick people seeing ghosts is just like Bo Le looking over a horse or Pao Ding (a chef) looking over a cow.[3]
>
> 3 when a sick man is in pain, he sees or thinks ghosts are hitting him.

4 sick people seeing ghosts are but dreaming.

This is a deductive arrangement of ideas, in that the main point is made first and then justified with a series of arguments which follow. As such, it is therefore a "marked" sequence in Chinese rhetorical terms. In his discussion of the sequence of this argument, Wu brings in political criteria. He points out that Wang Chong was writing at a time Wu calls a "feudal theocracy" (*fengjian shenquan*) (165). To propose, therefore, a theory that ghosts and spirits were merely the products of sick minds would have been extremely controversial. Wu then argues that the use of this deductive reasoning suited the polemical nature of Wang Chong's argument. It is direct and establishes the author's point of view at the beginning. So we must ask why Wang Chong chose to use this style, as he would have known that a more indirect oblique style would have been the norm. It might have been wiser for Wang Chong to have followed Gui Guzi's advice to speak with "forked tongue."

Not surprisingly, Wang Chong was renowned for his revolutionary and outspoken ideas. Feng Youlan, the famous Chinese philosopher, called him "the great atheist and materialist philosopher" (238), which, in the context of Chinese communist society, are terms of great approbation. By using a marked sequence represented by deductive and direct reasoning, Wang Chong is deliberately being provocative and outspoken.

We have argued, however, that the use of indirect language is the default or "unmarked" style in much Chinese rhetoric and persuasion. There are many ways of describing this indirectness. Gui Guzi recommended speaking in "forked tongue." Chinese terms include the notion mentioned earlier of *hanxu* (含蓄), which has the sense of implicitness and concealment. Li Xilan has suggested that, when the weak are dealing with the strong, they should use indirect and diplomatic language. "Use indirect and tactful (*weiwan* 委婉) language to broach the crucial point and thus preserve yourself and obtain a diplomatic victory" (14–24). The following letter, written some one hundred and fifty years after Wang Chong's death is a prime example of the use of such language.

The author, Li Mi (225-290 CE) is writing to the Jin emperor Sima Yan. In this letter Li Mi turns down an appointment at court that the emperor has offered him on the grounds that he has to look after his ailing grandmother. However, as the Jin emperor has just defeated Li Mi's native state of Shu, he has other reasons for not wanting to become a servant of the "enemy." It hardly needs to be said that such a letter would need extremely tactful language in order to avoid offending the emperor. It will also be noted that the main point—the request themselves or the *petitio*—come at the end of the letter after an extended background or *narratio*. I have italicised the requests. The translation is by David Knechtges (75–7).

> Li Mi: Memorial Expressing My Feelings
>
> Your servant Mi states: Because of a parlous fate, I early encountered grief and misfortune. When I was an infant of only six months my loving father passed away. When I was four my mother's brother forced my mother to remarry against her will. Grandmother Liu took pity on this weak orphan and personally cared for me. When young, I was often sick, and at nine I could not walk. Solitary and alone I suffered until I reached adulthood. I not only had no uncles, I also had no brothers. Our family was in decline, our blessings were few, and thus only late in life have I had offspring. Outside the household, I have no close relatives whom I can mourn; inside, I have not even a boy servant to watch the gate. All alone I stand, my body and shadow console each other. Grandmother Liu long has been ill and is constantly bedridden. I serve her medicinal brews, and I have never abandoned her or left her side.
>
> When I came into the service of this Sage Dynasty, I bathed in your pure transforming influence. First Governor Kui sponsored me as Filial and Pure. Later Inspector Rong recommended me as a Flourishing Talent. But because there was no one to care for grandmother, I declined and did not take up the appointment. An edict was especially issued appointing me Palace gentleman. Not long thereafter I received imperial favour and was newly appointed Aide to the Crown Prince. I humbly believe that for a man as lowly and insignificant as I to be deemed worthy of serving in the Eastern Palace is an honour I could never repay you for, even with my life. I informed you of all the circumstances in a memorial, and I again declined and did not go to my post. Your edict was insistent and stern, accusing me of being dilatory and disrespectful. The commandery and prefectural authorities tried to pressure me and urged me to take the road up to the capital. The local officials approached my door with the speed of shooting stars and fiery sparks. I wanted to comply

with your edict and dash off to my post, but Grandmother Liu's illness daily became more grave. I wished temporarily to follow my personal desires, but my plea was not granted. Whether to serve or retire truly was a great dilemma!

I humbly believe that this Sage Dynasty governs the empire by means of filial piety, and all among the aged and elderly still receive compassion and care. How much more needful am I whose solitary suffering has been especially severe! Moreover, when young I served the false dynasty, and I have moved through the various gentleman posts. I originally planned to become illustrious as an official, but I never cared about my reputation and character. Now I am a humble captive of an alien state. I am utterly insignificant and unimportant, but I have received more promotions than I deserve, and your gracious charge is both liberal and generous. How would I dare demur, with the hope of receiving something better? However, I believe that Grandmother Liu, like the sun going down, is breathing her last breaths. Her life has reached a precarious, delicate stage, and one cannot predict in the morning what will happen in the evening. Without grandmother I would not be alive today. Without me grandmother will not be able to live out her remaining years. Grandmother and grandson have depended upon one another for life. Thus, simply because of my own small, selfish desires I cannot abandon or leave her. I am now in my forty-fourth year, and Grandmother Liu is now ninety-six. Thus, I have a long time in which to fulfil my duty to Your Majesty and only a short time in which to repay Grandmother Liu for raising me. *With all my filial devotion, I beg to be allowed to care for her to her final days.* My suffering and misery are not only clearly known by the men of Shu and the governors of the two provinces, they have been perceived by August Heaven and Sovereign Earth. I hope Your Majesty will take pity on my naive sincerity and will grant my humble wish, so that Grandmother Liu will have the good fortune to preserve the remaining years of her life. While I am alive, I shall offer my life in your service. When dead, 1shall I shall "knot a clump of grass" for you.[4] With unbearable apprehension, like a loyal dog or horse, I respectfully present this memorial to inform you of my feelings.

We have chosen to include this long memorial, not only because it represents a nice example of "bottom-up" persuasion, but also because it is a request with an unmarked "frame-main" schema. This is remarkably similar to a "Ciceronian" schema, which we shall consider in Chapter 3. Li Mi's request starts with an introduction to himself and his situation. He then describes his association with the present "Sage Dynasty" and these two sections of his letter provide the *captatio benovolentiae* (or the facework). Towards the end of the third paragraph, he gives a series of reasons why it is important for him to stay and look after his grandmother. These reasons are also acting as reasons for the request, or *narratio*. The requests, the *petitio*, are made at the end of the letter.

This then is a further example of the common-sense strategy of using an indirect approach to persuasion when there is an unequal balance of power between persuader and listener. Kao has called this the art of "criticism by indirection" (121).

This art becomes important in circumstances where persuasion is "bottom-up" and is manifested in the persuasions of the political counselors as they advise or criticise their rulers' policies throughout Chinese dynastic history.

However, not all requests of this type necessarily followed this arrangement. Here is Bao Shuya of Qi also politely declining the position of prime minister.

> I am a commonplace minister of the king. The King is benevolent and kind towards me and ensures I suffer from neither cold nor hunger. This is the King's benevolent gift to me. *If you definitely want me to govern the country, I'm afraid that that is something I may be unable to do.* If we are talking about governing the country, then Guan Zhong is probably the man with the talent for the job. I measure up badly against him in five areas: his policies are magnanimous and have the advantage of pacifying and stabilising the people and I am not as good as he is here; in governing and not violating basic principles, I am not as good as he is; in establishing sincere relationships with the people, I am not as good as he is; in establishing the correct standards of etiquette and ensuring that the models are followed everywhere, I am not as good as he is; and in standing outside the city gate, holding the drumsticks and the battle drum to inspire great bravery in the people, I am not as good as he is.[5]

While this request starts with a *capitatio benevolentiae*, the *petitio* (italicised) comes immediately after it and is followed by what might be called the *narratio*, where the author offers justifications for his request. Just then as the component parts of the medieval European letters were not absolutely fixed in terms of their order, so is the arrangement flexible in Chinese texts.

As we have argued, the hierarchical nature of Chinese society meant that persuaders normally needed to employ methods of indirect criticism. Kroll (125–7) has pointed out that many of the rhetorical devices employed in chain reasoning and reasoning by analogy were ideal for indirect criticism. For example, the devices of joining objects of the same kind (*lien lei*) and comparing things create possibilities for the indirect communication of ideas.

An important work on rhetoric and literary criticism in the immediate post Han period is a descriptive poem on literature, the *Wen Fu* (文赋, On Literature), written by Lu Ji (261-303 CE). This has been called by one Chinese scholar "a radiant triumph in early Chinese literary criticism" (Wang D. 50). The work is important as Lu Ji developed an analysis of genres that identified ten genres: the lyric; the exhibitory essay; monumental inscriptions; the elegy; the mnemonic; the epigram; the eulogy; the expository; the memorial and finally the argument. (Cao Pi's third-century "Discourse of Wen" had identified four pairs of genres: the memorial and deliberation; the letter and the treatise; the lyric poem and rhapsody; and the inscription and the dirge.) Lu Ji has this to say about the process of composition:

> A composition comes into being as the incarnation of many living gestures. It is the embodiment of endless change. To attain meaning, it depends on the grasp of the subtle, while such words are employed as best serves beauty's sake. (*The Literary Mind and the Carving of Dragons* xxviii)

However, it is the *Wen Xin Diao Long*, (*The Literary Mind and the Carving of Dragons*), written by Liu Xie (465-520 CE) which is considered by many to be China's earliest account of rhetoric, although it is probably more correct to call it a book of literary criticism. Liu Xie is certainly unusual in being known first and foremost as a critic. Not all scholars are convinced by Liu's scholarship. S. K. Wong (121), while enthusing over the language and organisation of the book, says "we had better not think him original, or suppose he exerted any influence on Chinese literature before the Qing period" (121). Cai Zongqi describes him "as a scholar of no great distinction in his own day" (1).

By Liu Xie's time, the plain and simple Confucian style had given way to a florid and verbose literary style called *pianwen* (骈文), often translated as "parallel prose" and which is described and illustrated further below. An early meaning of *pian* (骈) is of a carriage being drawn by six horses and it thus provides an image of ornateness. Liu, who traces all literary genres back to the Confucian Classics, argues that the writer who used the Classics as models would develop a style free from verbosity. The following excerpts from the *Wen Xin Diao Long* come from Vincent Shih's translation.

> The five classics are masters moulding human nature and spirit and the great treasure house of literature, unfathomable and illustrious, the source of all literary forms. (21)

> The obligation Liu Xie feels to praise the Classics and Confucius reflects the importance the Chinese ascribe to traditional models.

> *Jiao*, or to teach, literally means *xiao*, or to imitate. Words once spoken form models for people to imitate… therefore the words of kings and lords have come to be grouped under the general term of *jiao* or teaching. (114)

Liu, however, is not prescriptive. His advice to the author on composition and organisation stresses flexibility and sensitivity to context. For example:

> The division into paragraphs and the construction of sentences conform to different tempos at different times. For these differences there is no fixed rule, and one must adapt… to varying circumstances. (186)

Paradoxically, then, although it appears that Liu was clearly proposing a return to Confucian style, he also believed that literary style should change with the times and that, to endure, literature needed to be adaptable. These two apparently contradictory strands are encapsulated by Shih: "We must conclude that his conservatism is a matter of habit, while his progressive ideas arise from convictions" (xliv).

This tension is reflected in Liu Xie's style itself. "In comparison to contemporary masters of parallel prose, Liu Xie's chapters have an unmistakable awkwardness," and this is because "there are two writers competing for control of the text" (Owen, "Liu Xie" 191).

The balance between respect of the classics and their use as literary models, and the needs of the writer to be flexible and adaptable to the needs of the time and the genre is one that has occupied the minds of Chinese scholars since time immemorial. This tension is nicely expressed in the verse that concludes the chapter in the *Wen Xin Diao Long* on literary development, and highlights how the needs of a particular time condition the preferred rhetorical style:

> Against the background of the ten dynasties, literary trends have changed nine times.
>
> Once initiated at the central pivot, the process of transformation circles endlessly.
>
> Literary subject matter and the form in which it is treated are conditioned by the needs of the times,
>
> But whether a certain subject matter or a certain form is emphasised or overlooked depends on the choice made by the writers.
>
> Antiquity, however remote, can be made to display itself before us like a human face. (*The Literary Mind and the Carving of Dragons* 224)

Liu Xie was writing when the parallel prose style, *pianwen*, was at its most popular. The style was itself a reaction to the plain and simple Confucian style (Hightower). *Pianwen* is characterised by the use of four and six word parallel phrases, with four words in the first phrase, six words in the second and so on. This syllabic correspondence can be heightened by the use of similar or deliberately contrasting tone patterns across the phrases. *Pianwen* continued to be popular—even dominant—until the Song dynasty (960-1278 CE), when the *guwen* (古文) (see below) movement succeeded in replacing parallel prose with a more conservative style. We consider developments in the Song in the next chapter when we introduce the Song dynasty scholar, Chen Kui's, *Rules of Writing*.

In the same way that *pianwen* developed as a reaction against the earlier Confucian style, so the *guwen*, or "ancient prose" movement, was a reaction against the parallel prose style of *pianwen*. Han Yu (768-824 CE), a Confucian conservative of the Tang dynasty, was the major force behind the *guwen* movement, although there had been earlier proponents. Luo Genze has argued that the *guwen* movement began when Su Chuo (498-546) rejected *pianwen* and drafted the edict entitled "The Great Announcement." But it is Han Yu who is most closely associated with the movement and who promoted the simple straightforward style of pre-Han models of expository prose (hence the name *guwen* or ancient prose). In Han Yu's day, *guwen* meant "literature of antiquity" or "ancient style prose" (Bol 24). One of Han Yu's own essays, "The origin of Dao," explains his own firm conservative commitment to upholding the ways of the past:

> What Dao is this Dao? The answer is, this Dao what I call Dao and not an inquiry into what Lao Tzu and the Buddha meant by Dao. This is what Yao transmitted to Shun, Shun transmitted to Yu, Yu transmitted to T'ang, T'ang transmitted to King Wen, King Wu and the Duke of Chou, King Wen, King Wu and the Duke of Chou transmitted to Confucius and Confucius transmitted to Meng K'o (Mencius). When Meng K'o died there was no one to transmit it to.... Now the ways of the barbarians have been elevated above the teachings of the ancient kings. How far are we from degenerating into barbarians ourselves? (Chen Shou-yi 289).

Han Yu's promotion of *guwen* had considerable influence upon the exam system for the selection of civil service candidates. During the eighth century, the style required of candidates for the civil service exams was the popular *pianwen* style and the major canon which candidates had to know was the *Wen Xuan* or "Selection of Literary Writings" which had been compiled by Xiao Tong sometime between 501-503 CE.

The level to which the influence of Confucianism had declined and foreign influences—most importantly Buddhism—had been established during the time of the Six Dynasties (220-589 CE), (and so called because this period saw the successive establishment and collapse of six short-lived dynasties) was that the *Wen Xuan* included none of the Classics. Literature was seen as a civilising influence and was able to transform men into civilised beings. The *pianwen* age of the Six Dynasties saw the "increasing belletricisation of Chinese literary criticism and theory that paralleled the Buddhicisation of Chinese society" (Mair 81). Civil service exam candidates were judged, not on their knowledge of Confucian Classics, but on their ability to manipulate the complex forms of *pianwen*. Han Yu and people of like mind considered such people as being unqualified for employment in the civil service. Ignoring the sages and favouring embellishment meant that "the literary brush became ever more lush and the government ever more chaotic" (Bol 91). The *pianwen* style attracted ridicule from its opponents, characterised by one scholar as being "a boat of magnolia wood propelled by ostrich feather oars" (Chen P. 6). Yet Han Yu's promotion of *guwen* met with harsh opposition, not least because *guwen* required more time and erudition to master. With the comparative success of Han Yu and the *guwen* movement, however, it now became possible for candidates to write about the Confucian classics in *guwen* style in the exams, although it was not until the later years of the Song dynasty that the *guwen* movement reached its height and Han Yu's goals were realised. Ouyang Xiu (1007-1072) took up the *guwen* cause and made it the accepted examination style. Not surprisingly he favoured content at the expense of form. His own style has been described as follows:

> The works of Ouyang Xiu are lucid and fluent; his style is easy and unaffected. In his prose writings, he showed his mastery by a continuous flow of thought and argumentation, with a significant content couched in clear and simple language. (Chai 46)

Bol has argued that *guwen* was primarily a search for the *values* associated with the style, rather than a wholehearted endorsement of the style itself. Ouyang Xiu himself announced that he did not agree that *guwen* writing was necessarily right and *pianwen* or ornate writing wrong, although, by the time he became Superintendent of Examinations in 1057, he said he favoured passing those who had comprehended the methods of the Classics and wrote in *guwen*. But the debate was more about values and content rather than style. *Dao* (the way) and *wen* (writing) are, along with *li* (ritual) three key terms in Chinese rhetoric (You, *Writing in the Devil's Tongue* 10). Another way of looking at this debate has been to compare the respective roles of *dao* (道), which we might translate in this context as "meaning" or "content," and *wen* (文) which we might translate as "language," "literature" or even "form." The *pianwen* movement was associated with the development of an ornate *wen*. The *guwen* movement was associated with *dao* or meaning. In the early Tang, intellectuals had the freedom to move among the three competing ideologies of Confucianism, Daoism and Buddhism. This encouraged a freedom of style and the use of ornate writing or *pianwen*. Intellectuals were probably not narrow dogmatists. Rote repetition of authoritative interpretation was still part of the tradition but it was not as highly valued as producing a new interpretation (Owen, *The End of the Chinese "Middle Ages"*). But, as we shall see in the next chapter, by the time of Chen Kui (1128-1203), the Neo-Confucian movement of the Song had become ascendant and the Confucian classics were back as the key objects of study and the *guwen* style was the style in which to write about them. Scholars now had to aim at giving contemporary form to the original models. People needed instruction in ways of doing this. As we shall show

Chapter 2

in Chapter 3, this was an important motivation for Chen Kui to write his *Wen Ze* (文则) or *Rules of Writing*.

In the final section of this chapter, we exemplify typical Confucian methods of argumentation, illustrating these with a variety of texts.

Confucian thinkers usually employed one of three types of argumentation, "the rhetorical chain argument, argument by appeal to antiquity and argument by analogy" (Wyatt 46). Garrett (128) distinguishes two types of chain-reasoning common in Chinese argument, one which relates propositions and one which relates terms within propositions. Below is an example of the first type, interpropositional chain-reasoning.

> If the people are farmers then they are naturally simple. If they are naturally simple then they are easy to use. If they are easy to use then the borders of the state will be secure and the position of the chief will be honoured.
>
> If the people set aside the base (farming) and serve the peripheral then they will be fond of being intelligent. If they are fond of being intelligent then they will be deceptive most of the time. If they are deceptive most of the time then they will cleverly twist the models and commands and take right as wrong and wrong as right.

As an example of the second type of chain-reasoning, the one that relates terms within propositions, Garrett gives:

> Before the time of Ch'ih Yu [a mythical rebel] the people did definitely whittle pieces of wood to do battle with, and those who won became the leaders. The leaders still were not sufficient to put the people in order, so (*gu*) they set up rulers. Again, the rulers were not sufficient to put them in order, so (*gu*) they set up the emperor. The setting up of the emperor comes from the rulers, the setting up of the rulers comes from the leaders, and the setting up of the leaders comes from the conflict. (130)

We could set up a rhetorical structure of this passage that would follow the "because-therefore" and "frame-main" patterns, examples of which we have already illustrated and which we shall develop in more detail in later chapters.

Ø BECAUSE (leaders not sufficient)—THEREFORE (set up rulers)

+

Ø BECAUSE (rulers not sufficient) — THEREFORE (set up emperor)

+

Ø THEREFORE
(emperor comes from rulers, etc.)

This type of chain-reasoning displays a preference for "because-therefore" and "frame-main" sequences. The following example of chain reasoning displays a similar preference for "frame-main" reasoning. This is translated by Graham (*Yin Yang and the Nature of Correlative Thinking*) and is taken from the *Huai Nanzi*.[6]

> The Way of Heaven one calls round, the Way of Earth one calls square. It is primary to the square to retreat to the dark, primary to the round to illuminate. To illuminate is to expel *ch'i*, for which reason fire and sun cast the image outside. To retreat to the dark is to hold *ch'i* in, for which reason water and moon draw the image inside. What expels *ch'i* does *to*, what holds *ch'i* in is transformed *by*. **Therefore** the Yang does *to*, the Yin is transformed *by*. (31)

Reasoning by analogy is also common. Smith suggests that this Chinese preference for argument by analogy can partly be explained by the structure of the language itself, its stylistic requirements and "the penchant for relational thinking" (Smith 92).

In a discussion on ethical argumentation in the works of the Confucian philosopher Xunzi (298-238 BCE), Cua argues that the methods of explanation (*shuo*) and justification (*bian*) involve the comparison of kinds of things and analogical projection. A.S. Cua defines analogical projection as reasoning that:

> involves a number of complex considerations that lead to a terminus... the different considerations are not necessarily connected with one another, forming, as it were, a chain of premises leading to a single outcome. Thus, the knowledge of the application of the standards of the past, information concerning the present circumstance, appreciation of the problem at stake, and the variety of archetypes that aid in

Chapter 2

selecting the baseline for analogy between past and present circumstance, all together converge on a terminus that constitutes the judgement, which represents the solution to the problem at hand. "(*Ethical Argumentation* 93)

In support, Cua cites Richards where Richards argues that the notion of reasoning in Mencius is not an inference from explicit premises to a definite conclusion according to specific rules, but the placing of a number of observations in an intelligible order. Crump calls this type of reasoning the progressive analogy, and suggests that the information sequence is from subordinate to main as the progression is from the:

far away and inconsequential toward the important and near at hand, until, at the end, the persuader applies the whole set of analogies, which then has the force of a sorites or chain-syllogism, to the case at hand. (Crump 50)

Argument by historical example(s) is also very common. This use of argument by historical examples as opposed to deductive argument is well summed up in the following way. "Philosophy meant a kind of wisdom that is necessary for the conduct of life, particularly the conduct of government" and "it sought to exercise persuasive power on princes, and ... resorted, not to deductive reasoning, but to the exploitation of historical examples" (Cua, *Ethical Uses* 133).

An excellent example of this argument by analogy and historical precedence was the excerpt from *The Discourses of Salt and Iron* analysed in Chapter 1 as following the "because-therefore:" and "frame-main" rhetorical sequence. Here we provide a second example and this is taken from Sun Tzu's, *The Art of War*, which was written sometime between 480 and 221 BCE.[7]

Do not move unless it is advantageous.

Do not execute unless it is effective.

Do not challenge unless it is critical.

An intense View is not a reason to launch an opposition.

An angry leader is not a reason to initiate a challenge.

If engagement brings advantage, move.

If not, stop.

Intensity can cycle back to fondness.

Anger can cycle back to satisfaction.

But an extinct organisation cannot cycle back to survival.

And those who are destroyed cannot cycle back to life.

Thus, (*gu*) a brilliant Ruler is prudent.

A Good leader is on guard.

Such (*ci*) is the Tao of a Stable Organisation and a Complete Force.

There are several points of interest here. The first is that the English translation of the first three lines of this extract follows a main clause-subordinate clause sequence. In the original Chinese, however, the sequence is subordinate clause-main clause which indicates that the unmarked clause orders in MSC and English differ, a point made earlier and to which we return later. The second is that the argument here follows the familiar rhetorical structure of "because-therefore" and "frame-main" sequencing, with the reasons explaining why prudence and being on guard are qualities of a leader preceding the statements to that effect. The third is the use of a final summary statement which is introduced by *ci* (thus). The function of *ci* here is similar to the function of the contemporary conjunction *suoyi* (therefore) in signaling a final summary statement, which we analyse in Chapter 7. The final line could be translated, "Thus the state is kept secure and the army preserved."

These examples show that argument by analogy and by historical example naturally follow the rhetorical "frame-main" structure. We now describe and illustrate a particularly well-known Chinese text structure and one which is often used for indirection of one sort or another.

THE QI-CHENG-ZHUAN-HE (起 承 转 合) STRUCTURE.

A text type which was frequently used to convey indirect criticism was the four-part *qi-cheng-zhuan-he* pattern. However, the *qi-cheng-zhuan-he* structure has altered in both form and function over several hundred years.

The *Dictionary of Chinese Rhetoric (DCR)* defines this rhetorical structure as follows:

> A common logical belle-lettres (诗文) structure and sequence but also the epitome of a common structural pattern for a variety of texts, both ancient and modern. *Qi* is the opening or beginning, *cheng* continues or joins the opening to the next stage. *Zhuan* is the transition or turning point, used either to develop or expound the argument, *he* is the summary or conclusion. (Zhang 314)

As an early example of this form, the *DCR* cites one of Li Po's[8] most famous poems:

"At the front of my bed moonlight shines	(*qi*)
I think there is frost on the ground	(*cheng*)
Raising my head, I look at the moon	(*zhuan*)
Lowering my head, I think of home."	(*he*)

It is significant that the DCR should give a Tang Dynasty (618-907) poem as an early example of this structure. Chen Wangdao (233), possibly the most famous and influential Chinese rhetorician of the twentieth century, quotes Fan Heng (1272-1330) on the stylistic requirements of this structure, but no explicit reference to poetry is mentioned:

> "*Qi* needs to be level and straight
>
> *Cheng* needs to be the shape of a mortar
>
> *Zhuan* needs change
>
> *He* needs to be like some deep pond or overflowing river (or needs to leave the reader pondering over the meaning)".

Wu Yingtian (204), on the other hand, takes the view that the origins of the *qi-cheng-zhuan-he* lie in the poems of the Tang Dynasty, and is able to trace the development of the structure from poetry to prose. He argues that, by the end of the Yuan Dynasty (1368), the *qi-cheng-zhuan-he* had been adopted as a structure for prose writing. Wu goes on to argue that this is the forerunner of the contemporary four-part prose structure of *kaiduan* (beginning 开端), *fazhan* (development 发展), *gaochao* (climax 高潮) and *jieju* (conclusion 结局). In this, Wu is in disagreement with those contemporary Chinese linguists who claim that the modern four-part structure came into Chinese via translations in the 1950s of *Russian* literary theory. Wu is thus being "patriotic" in claiming the contemporary four-part structure, which is primarily used for narrative texts, is home-grown produce and not some foreign import. Wu attempts to prove this by analysing this contemporary four-part structure against a narrative text written in 100 BCE. He is unsuccessful, however, in this, as the third part of the contemporary narrative structure (the climax or *gaochao*) is not equivalent with the transition stage (*zhuan*) of the traditional structure. We shall not argue this rather arcane case further here. What is beyond dispute is that the *qi-cheng-zhuan-he* became commonly used as rhetorical structure to express indirect criticism.

Di Chen provides an excellent example of this with an indirect political polemic which adopts this rhetorical structure (Di). The piece, a famous one, was written by Gong Zizhen in 1839 when he was in his forties. He had just returned south after being dismissed from his post. We indicate each of the respective four parts of the structure so that the structural pattern may become clearer.

> A Sanitarium for Sick Plum Trees
>
> (*Qi*)
>
> Longpan Mountain in Jiangning, Dengwei Mountain in Suzhou and the Western banks of West Lake in Hangzhou all have an abundance of plum trees.
>
> (*Cheng*)
>
> It is said: the beauty of the branches of a plum tree lie in their crooked shape, there being no charm in ramrod straightness; their beauty lies in their jagged angles, as being upright and straight is not pleasing to the eye; their beauty lies in their sparseness, as dense abundance has no definition. This has long been so. Scholars and artists believe this in their hearts but do not openly shout aloud these criteria for the judgement of plum trees, nor can they tell those cultivators of the plum tree that, by hacking them into shape, by viciously cutting

back their abundant foliage and by lopping off branches, they can turn prematurely dead or diseased plum trees into a profitable enterprise. The tortured crookedness and bare sparseness of the plum branches is not caused by those who, as soon as they sense profit, can use their skill to obtain it. But, someone has explained in clear terms this unsocial desire of the scholars and artists to the sellers of plum trees. These, then, to obtain a higher price for their trees, cut off the straight branches and tend the crooked ones, cut back dense foliage and destroy delicate buds and uproot and kill off any plum trees that grow straight. And so the plum trees of Jiangsu and Zhejiang have all become ill and deformed. What a serious disaster have these scholars and artists brought about!

(*Zhuan*)

I bought three hundred pots with plum trees in them and they were all sick; not a single pot contained a completely healthy plant. I grieved for them and wept for three days and then vowed that, to cure them, I should indulge them and let them grow freely. I destroyed the pots, planted all the plum trees in the ground and cut free their encompassing and binding twine. I still need five years to restore the plum trees to their original state. I have never been a scholar or an artist and am happy to have scorn heaped upon me, but I want to build a sanitarium for sick plums where I can place these plum trees.

(*He*)

Ai! How I wish I had the free time and the idle land so that I could gather in the sick plum trees of Jiangning, Hangzhou and Suzhou, and within my lifetime, cure them!

Following Di Chen's analysis, the first paragraph is the *qi* of the text. The second paragraph describes the underhand schemes of the scholars and artists and recounts how they have oppressed the growth of the plum trees. This is, of course, an analogy, with the scholars and artists representing the reactionary feudal classes. It lays bare the crimes of the Qing dynasty rulers in destroying men of talent. This is the *cheng* and it continues and explains the topic, elaborating the opening sentence. The third paragraph recounts how the author opposes all this and this is the *zhuan*. This represents a change, a change from one view of the situation to another. The fourth paragraph describes the author's desire to cure the sick plum trees. This is the *he*, the conclusion of the piece. It demonstrates the author's resolve to fight to change society. The whole piece demonstrates the use of analogy as a weapon of indirect criticism being directed against tyrannical and corrupt dynastic government.

The *qi-cheng-zhuan-he* structure was often used as a form in which to express unofficial criticism from below to above. In this it differs from the *ba gu wen* (八股文) or eight-legged essay, perhaps the most famous Chinese rhetorical structure with regard to written texts. The *ba gu wen* is the topic of Chapter 4.

SUMMARY

In this chapter we have reviewed the literary background and the development of Chinese rhetoric and writing, giving illustrations from a variety of texts. We explained how Confucian texts became officially sanctioned as the state canon and provided a rhetorical analysis of texts which show a Chinese preference for because-therefore or frame-main reasoning. However, we have also shown that the deductive style was also known to and used by Chinese writers. In Chapter 3, we describe the book *Wen Ze* (Rules of Writing), which has been described as China's first systematic account of rhetoric and writing and compare the advice provided there with advice given in medieval European treatises which were written at around the same time.

3 THE RULES OF WRITING[9] IN MEDIEVAL CHINA AND EUROPE

The Rules of Writing (*Wen Ze*, 文则) has been called the first systematic account of Chinese rhetoric (Yancheng Liu).[10] Its author, Chen Kui (陈骙) (1128-1203), was born at the beginning of the Southern Song dynasty (1127-1279). He lived at a time of great change, being born one year after the beginning of the Southern Song period. The Northern Song emperors had ruled from 960, but had been forced to flee south in 1127 in face of invasion from the north.

Chen Kui was a member of the intellectual elite and passed the extremely prestigious and competitive metropolitan exam to become a *jinshi* (进士) at the comparatively early age of 24. This was no mean feat. John Chaffee has eloquently recorded the trials and tribulations of being a scholar in Song China. During the Song dynasty, the number of people taking the series of exams that culminated in the *jinshi* exam increased dramatically. There were two major reasons for this. First, the Song emperors desired to create a meritocracy by increasing the number of able men in the civil service. Exams replaced privilege as the main gateway into the civil service. Second, the advent of printing opened up education to more people: "The spread of printing transformed Chinese book culture" (Cherniack 5). *The Rules of Writing* may thus well have been stimulated to provide a writing and rhetorical guide for the many thousands of men who were now preparing for one of the imperial civil service exams.

Chen Kui himself held a number of senior official positions. In 1190, during the reign of the Emperor Guang Zong, he was appointed secretary of the Imperial Library and was the author of *The Record of the Library of the Southern Song*.

Here, we first briefly summarise how Chinese scholars have evaluated *The Rules of Writing* and then focus on three topics that we hope will be of particular relevance to those interested in rhetoric and the teaching of writing: the first topic concerns Chen Kui's advice on the use of simple and contemporary language; the second concerns his advice on the sequence of argument when writing discursive texts; and the third concerns the correct use of citations.

THE RULES OF WRITING

The Rules of Writing (hereafter *ROW*) is primarily concerned with the study of "essays" (*wenzhang*文章), which, in another context, Bol has translated as "literary composition" (16). The *ROW* is concerned with literary composition of a particular type—the writing of compositions suitable for the examination system as it was during the Southern Song. These compositions were based on the *guwen* (古文) style of the classics and which presented the messages of the classics in contemporary language. The type of composition that Chen Kui is concerned with is *lun* (论), discourse or discussion. In summary the *ROW* is concerned with the composition of *lun* for use in the Song civil service exams.

The *ROW* is accepted by contemporary Chinese scholars as **the** study of Chinese classical rhetoric. Indeed it has been described as the benchmark for the study of Chinese rhetoric as a whole (e.g., Wang; Zhou Z.).[11] Chen Kui's major aim in writing the *ROW* was to identify and summarise the rules of writing literary composition, using classical texts as his source material. The *ROW* thus discusses and exemplifies principles of composition and rhetoric, including aspects of genres, styles and methods of composition at the levels of word, sentence and text (Liu Yancheng). The book comprises five main topics: genre, "negative" rhetoric, "positive" rhetoric, syntax and style.[12]

Chen Kui's research method is also praised. Tan discusses this in detail and classifies Chen's use of the comparative method into seven categories. We list them in the order Tan does (Tan Quanji):

1. comparing the beginnings and endings of texts;
2. comparing different genres;
3. comparing one book with another;
4. comparing works written at the same time;
5. comparing contemporary texts with classical texts;
6. comparing different ways of expressing the same or similar meanings; and
7. comparing the use of the same method to convey different meanings.

Tan also praises Chen for his use of what he calls the inductive method, *guinafa* (归纳法) and gives as an example Chen's classification of metaphor into ten categories based on countless examples. As a further example of Chen's use of induction, Tan gives his elucidation of the rhetorical pattern of balanced parallelism based on the study of forty-four separate words, each supported by numerous examples.

The *ROW* is made up of ten chapters which themselves each comprise a number of sections, ranging from one (Chapter 10) to ten (Chapter 5). As Chapter 10 is actually the longest chapter, it follows that the number of sections per chapter has little to do with the overall length of each chapter. There are sixty-three sections in all. The numerical references used below refer to the chapter of the *ROW* and section within it. So (1/3) refers to Chapter 1, Section 3.[13] In the selections below, we have chosen parts of the book which are of particular relevance to rhetoric and persuasion.

ADVICE ON LANGUAGE USE

The first topic we shall consider is Chen Kui's advice on language use. As a fervent advocate of the *guwen* style, Chen Kui identifies the general overriding principle that language should be simple, clear, succinct and contemporary. "To be good, things need to be simple and easy; to be appropriate, language needs to be simple and clear" (1/4).

Good texts need to be succinct and concise. However, being succinct, texts must also be complete and logical. If the reader feels that a text has gaps and omissions, then it cannot be considered succinct, but rather one that has been constructed carelessly. Chen Kui praises the brevity and clarity of the example below from the Spring and Autumn Annals and criticises the Gong Yong commentary of the same event. The criticised Gong Yong version reads: "*Hearing the sound of falling meteorites, as soon as I realised these were stones that were falling, I examined them carefully and found that they were five meteorites.*"

The praised version in the Spring and Autumn annals reads: "'*Five meteorites fell on Song territory.*' Chen Kui exalts, 'This is a succinctness that is hard to achieve'" (1/4).

It is interesting to compare Chen Kui's treatment with the ways other scholars have analysed this passage. For example, Jullien (*Detour and Access* 105–6) cites the same excerpts in his discussion on the *Wen Xin Diao Long* as an example of how a commentator "scrutinises every notation, for nothing in the mention of an event is seen as either fortuitous or innocuous."

> Why does it say "fell" before "stones"? The falling of stones repeats the way it is heard: one hears the noise of something falling, and in looking at the thing that has fallen, one sees that it is stones; in looking at them closer, one can count that there are five.

Rather than the commentator scrutinising every notation, however, we suggest that the *Wen Xin Diao Long* commentary stresses the logical, chronological and natural order of the events. This notion of "logical" order is an accepted principle of sequencing in Chinese and we discuss this in more detail in Chapters 6 and 7. Here, however, Chen Kui's focus is on the importance of clarity and succinctness. He further illustrates this in the example below, in which he compares the relative economy in the use of characters in three different texts all expressing the same idea.

> Xie Ye (洩冶) is recorded as saying: "The guidance and help a ruler gives to his subjects is like wind blowing among grass; when the wind blows from the east, the grass bends to the west, and when the wind blows from the west, the grass bends to the east; when the wind blows the grass bends."
>
> This excerpt needs thirty-two characters to make its meaning clear.
>
> *The Analects say: "The behaviour of people of position can be compared to the wind, while the behaviour of normal people can be compared to the grass; when the wind blows through the grass, the grass bends accordingly."*
>
> This uses half the number of characters that Xie Ye used, but its meaning is clear.
>
> *The Shang Histories say: "Your behaviour can be compared to the wind, and the behaviour of the people can be compared to the grass".*
>
> This uses nine fewer characters than The Analects but its meaning remains very clear (1/4).

Chen Kui also calls for writing that is both natural and coherent. "If a musical performance is not harmonious, then music is unpleasant; if a text is not coherent, then it cannot be read... classical texts were natural and coherent and were without adornment and embellishment" (1/3).

To help ensure this, writers should use the language of the people and the time. "The use of language that was the common speech of one period will be found abstruse and difficult by people of later periods" (1/8).

He continues:

> Although classical texts used classical language, classical language cannot be fully understood by later generations, unless there are explanatory notes. Reading classical books without notes is like scaling a tricky peak, after each step you need to take several deep breaths. If, after arduous study, one picks up some classical language and uses it to record contemporary events, one can be compared with maidservants who tried to act like their mistresses, but whose attitudes and postures were very unnatural and did not look right. (1/8)

As an example of the use of the language of the time, Chen Kui cites excerpts from The Book of Rites. As he points out, this often used plain and simple language. It is also completely straightforward and to the point. There is no indirection or obliquity here. For example:

> "Use your hand to cover your mouth when speaking to avoid breathing over people";

> "When dining as a guest in someone's house don't toss your leftover bones to the dog, so showing that you do not give a fig for the things of your host";

> "Even when eating the leftover sauce from the vegetables still use chopsticks";

> "When men and women meet they should observe the proprieties";

> "If you have an itch do not scratch it in front of your relatives".

Chen Kui explains:

> Although the meaning of these extracts is complex and is concerned with preventing people violating the rites, there is

very little literary embellishment. The language used is plain and simple. Writers who study historical literary forms and who adopt classical language to write texts frequently produce muddled gibberish. (5/1)

Chen Kui concludes this section with a striking metaphor. The old saying says:

"Dimples on the face are very attractive, but on the forehead, they are very ugly." This saying is absolutely right. Ever since the Jin Dynasty (265-420 CEAD), there have been far too many people who have longed to imitate the classics when they pick up their pens to write. (5/10)

Chen's main concern here is with the language of the classics and its influence on contemporary (Song) writing. He realised that, as language changed with the times, writers should not slavishly mimic classical texts. They should not use classical language to write about contemporary events. He pointed out that the language used in the classics was, at the time, contemporary language, and was language that could be easily understood by the people. Simply put, he opposed the misuse of classical language and promoted the use of common and contemporary language. He cites many examples from different texts to show how the simply expressed text is more effective than the more complex or embellished one. He championed the use of the vernacular and spoken language.

These principles are stressed throughout the *ROW*. He fully understood the phenomena of language change and language variety. "The language used in the *Pan Geng* section of *The Shang Histories* was contemporary and vernacular. It was the common language of the people and language, therefore, that everyone could understand" (5/2).

He also advocates the use of regional varieties and low-brow genres. He quotes, with approval, this builder's ballad:

"Within the city's Southern gate, the people's skin is white,

Urging us to work hard

Within the city, the people's skin is black,

Consoling us" (9/5).[14]

Coupled with these principles of language use is Chen Kui's belief that form should serve meaning. As discussed above, throughout the Chinese rhetorical and literary tradition there has been a constant debate about the relative importance of *dao* (道) (meaning) and *wen* (文), language and/or literature, or form. This is obviously closely linked with the debate over the relative merits of the flowery literary form known as *pianwen* (骈文) and the simpler classical form known as *guwen* (古文). In the *ROW*, *dao* (content) is primary and *wen* (form) is subordinate to *dao*. Words must serve meaning. This notion held true, whether Chen Kui was discussing the use of words, syntax and sentence construction, or rhetoric itself.

THE ARRANGEMENT OF IDEAS

A second topic that Chen Kui discusses in the *ROW* that is of direct relevance to rhetoric concerns the sequence or arrangement of argument. There are, says Chen Kui, three ways in which texts can enumerate the conduct and deeds of people:

> They can first state the summary or overall point, and then list the individual details. For example, when judging Zi Chan, Confucius said: *"Zi Chan had four aspects of behaviour fitting for the way of a ruler: his own moral conduct was dignified and respectful; he waited upon the ruler in a dignified way; he nurtured the people kindly; and he made sure that the people followed the truth"* (4/4).

> The second method of sequencing information is to list individual details first and then summarise and explain. For example, when enumerating the charges against Gong Sun Hei of Zheng, Zi Chan said:

> "Your turbulent heart cannot be satisfied, and the State cannot condone this. Usurping power and attacking Bo You, this is your first charge; coveting your brother's wife and resorting to violence, this is your second charge; setting up local factions on the pretext of being ruler, this is your third charge. With these three charges, how can your behaviour be condoned?" (4/4).

The third way is to provide the overall or main point at the beginning, then list the individual details and then conclude with the overall point again. For example, Confucius said:

> *"Zang Wenzhong did three cruel-hearted and stupid things: he gave a low official position to Hui 'beneath the willow;' he set up a toll-gate and collected taxes; and he allowed his concubines to sell their woven mats on the open market. These were the three cruel-hearted things. Zang exceeded the bounds of his duty. He kept a giant turtle; he failed to stop Xia Fuji when Xia violated the rituals of sacrifice; and he ordered the entire country to make sacrifices to some seabird. These were the three stupid things."* (4/4)

In the next section of the same chapter (4/5) Chen Kui continues this theme of sequencing by saying that when writing about events, one can first introduce the argument or judgement and then write about the events, or one can write about the events and then make some judgement about them. As an example of first introducing the argument, Chen Kui cites the excerpt in the *Zuo Zhuan* where it records Jin Linggong's imposition of tax revenues, using money obtained through usury to paint and decorate the palace walls. "It firmly states at the beginning: *'Jin Linggong had no principles and did not have the moral conduct of ruler."* (4/5).

An example of drawing a conclusion after describing the events also comes from the *Zuo Zhuan*.

> First, the noble deeds of Duke Wen are recorded, including how he trained the people and then put this training to use. The passage concludes: *"one battle caused the Jin State to become a hegemony, this was the result of Wen's training!"* (4/5)

The striking aspect of this advice about sequencing is that it is not dissimilar to the advice given by "Anglo" teachers of rhetoric today. In providing three ways of arranging argument, Chen gives cause to doubt that the commonly expressed view that the rhetorical structure of Chinese argument and writing is somehow uniquely Chinese. In fact, the three methods of sequencing information identified by Chen Kui will appear familiar to many. The first was to summarise the main point(s) and then provide the details, and this looks very much like a deductive pattern; the second was to provide the details first and then summarise, and this looks very much like an inductive pattern; and the third was to use a three-part structure whereby the main points were stated at the beginning and recapped at the end, with the details being provided in the middle. This looks very much like the three-part structure of introduction-body-conclusion. This is of particular interest as it would appear that Chen Kui is promoting a "marked" "main-frame" rhetorical structure, rather than the unmarked "frame-main" sequence which might be expected and which we have ourselves argued to be the preferred default rhetorical structure. The advice to adopt this main-frame sequence is, however, linked to the type of text *The Rules of Writing* is aimed at producing. It needs to be remembered that Chen Kui was adamant that a return to the plain and simple *guwen* style was needed, and that this style should not encumber itself with obscure classical language, but be written in a way which would be clear to contemporaries. We should also remember that the Song empire of the time was keen to establish a meritocracy and therefore to employ only deserving people in the civil service. This was a relatively open time in which people felt they could express their ideas "up" without too much fear of retribution if they displeased the emperor. Nevertheless, Chen Kui himself appears to have overstepped the mark on a number of occasions in his own memorials to the emperor, of which he penned thirty or so. On one occasion, for example, he wrote to criticise the extravagance of the imperial court, and for this he was demoted and sent to cool his heels for a time in an official position in the provinces (*Nan Song Guan Lu* 465).

There is evidence that Chen Kui's influence was felt throughout later periods of Chinese history and can be traced through later handbooks. For example, his influence upon Gui Youguang's (1506-1571) *Guide to Composition Writing* (文章指南) is clear. Gui's handbook advises the writer that three arrangements for an essay are possible.

> Present the main idea at the beginning, then break the idea into several points/aspects devoting one paragraph to the elaboration of each; discuss the component points first one by one, then present the main idea in the end; or, best of all, on the basis of the first layout, add a summary of the main idea at the end. (Liu Yameng, "Three Issues" 327)

A much more recent text which shows apparent influence from Chen Kui—although we have been unable to identify a direct link—is the twentieth-century reformer Hu Shi's promotion of the vernacular as the medium of educated discourse. Hu Shi formulated eight famous rules for writers, which bear a striking similarity to Chen Kui's advice:

(i) Language must have content.

(ii) Do not (slavishly) imitate classical writers.
(iii) Make sure you pay attention to grammar and structure.
(iv) Do not complain if you are not ill—in other words, don't overdo the emotion.
(v) Cut out the use of hackneyed clichés.
(vi) Don't cite or rely on the classics.
(vii) Don't use parallelism.
(viii) Embrace popular and vernacular language.(Hu S., "Literary Innovation" 5–16)

It is commonly assumed that Hu Shi was influenced by his time in the United States—he studied at Cornell and did his PhD at Columbia where he studied under John Dewey, with whom he maintained a lifelong professional relationship—and that it was his experience in the United States that led him to promote the use of the vernacular and *bai hua* Chinese in place of the traditional literary *wenyan* style. But we argue that he was also influenced by the Chinese rhetorical tradition, including by scholars such as Chen Kui.

To move to the third topic of Chen Kui's ROW to be considered here, his advice on the use of citation is also relevant to rhetoric and writing, as citation gives authority or support for an argument or claim. He starts by pointing out that *The Book of Poetry*, *The Shang Histories*, and the many books that explain the classics and histories all contain many citations. There were definite rules for citing and, generally speaking, there were two methods: "The first was to use citation as evidence about an event or action that had taken place, or to exemplify appropriate behaviour; the second was to use citation to prove one's argument" (3/2).

At the same time, copying without acknowledgment, plagiarism, was not condoned (5/5).

Chen Kui illustrates ways of using citation to provide evidence that an event has taken place and gives examples. One such reads.

> *The Zuo Zhuan records: "The Book of Poetry says: 'A person who sought for himself worry and sadness,' this was really talking about Zi Zang!"* (3/2).

Among the many examples provided by Chen Kui of using citation to explain or promote actions and behaviour are these two.

> *The Zuo Zhuan records: "The Book of Poetry says: 'Where does one go to pick wormwood? By the banks of a pond or on a small sand*

bar. Where can you use it? At the funeral ceremony of a duke.' Tai Mu Gong did this" (3/2).

"Work hard and do not let up at dawn or dusk to pay respect to someone. Meng Ming did this" (3/2).

Chen Kui also gave three ways of using citation to prove one's argument. It could be done by citing widely from the Classics, or by presenting one's argument and then using citations to support it, or by analysing the cited excerpts and showing that they supported one's argument. As an example of citing from the Classics, Chen Kui provides this excerpt:

Shang Tang says: "If one day you can get rid of the old customs and renew yourself, with this new foundation, by renewing daily and constantly, you can arrive at a brand new realm." Kang Gao says: "Education stimulates the masses, makes them get rid of old customs, and become new people." The Book of Poetry says: "Although Zhou was an ancient state (by the time of King Wen), it received the mandate of heaven in a further renewal of virtue, and replaced Shang. Therefore we say that a ruler, in order to build a good state, must try all methods and must explore all paths" (3/2).

Finally, the method of analysing cited text to support one's argument is illustrated with this passage from *The Zuo Zhuan*:

The Zuo Zhuan says: "Appoint people you can use, and respect men worthy of respect." This extract is discussing the Duke of Jin's rewarding of those who render outstanding service. It also says: "Although the last ruler of the Shang dynasty had millions of subjects, dissension and discord was in them all; The Zhou dynasty had ten great officials who helped in ruling and they were all united and in accord." "The point of this passage is that virtue can serve the people. If the emperor has virtue, the masses must come together and turn to him" (3/2).

Chen Kui's discussion of the use of citation suggests that the claim that Chinese do not acknowledge sources as frequently or as comprehensively as Western scholars (Bloch and Chi) does not have a historical origin. Chen Kui shows that citation was an important part of scholarly writing at the time and gives a detailed explanation of the ways in which this could be done and for what purposes. He also explicitly states that copying another person's work without acknowledgement cannot be condoned. We should make it clear that we are not claiming that this means that Chinese scholars used citation in the same way as Western scholars do today. On the contrary, certain styles of Classical Chinese writing required the listing, one after the other, of many citations from the Classics, with the author providing little of his own voice, or, at least, providing his voice in characters of smaller size than those of the citations themselves (Moloughney 23). Chen Kui's comments do show however, that Chinese scholarship has been familiar with the practice of citation for centuries and that plagiarism is understood and condemned. Moloughney provides further evidence of this when he translates a witty aphorism of Zhang Xuecheng, a Chinese scholar of the late eighteenth century: "The plagiarist fears only that people would know of his source; the creative user that they would be ignorant of it" (136). It is also worth noting that the importance we currently attach to citation and acknowledgement has at least as much to do with copyright law as with a genuinely altruistic wish to acknowledge the work of others (Scollon). Writers in medieval Europe were notorious for not acknowledging the work of others. For example, St. Jerome "borrowed" complete excerpts from Quintilian (Lanham 83).

There is much more to the *ROW* than we can summarise here. Chen Kui made an extraordinary contribution to the study of Chinese rhetoric. In addition to his advice on clarity, the arrangement of ideas and the importance and use of citation, he categorised metaphor for the first time, and many of his categories are still used today. He showed how a whole range of function words were used. He illustrated the rhetorical effect of tropes such as inversion, repetition and balance. He discussed the relative merits of sentence length. He identified and discussed a number of genres and took genre theory forward. Yet, it was also the manner in which he did this that made him stand out as an original thinker and groundbreaking rhetorician. For the first time, rules of writing and principles of rhetoric were identified from a close study of real texts. Chen Kui compared texts and deduced rules from a close study of numerous examples. The ROW is peppered with examples that illustrate the points Chen Kui is making. In this way, he provides hard linguistic and rhetorical evidence for all of his claims. Finally, this is all presented in a non-prescriptive way, in that the final determiner of use has to be the context and the rhetorical effect the writer wishes to make.

In the next section of this chapter we compare and contrast the ROW and a selection of the *Ars Dictaminis* of Medieval Europe, as these were written at around the same time.

ARS DICTAMINIS

The *ars dictaminis* became popular in Europe from the eleventh century and flourished in the twelfth and thirteenth centuries. The major treatises concerning the *ars dictaminis* are thus more or less contemporary with Chen Kui's "Rules of Writing." While the *ars dictaminis* was the art of letter writing, it is important to note that letter writing covered a very wide field and was the most common written genre at the time, and also that *ars dictaminis* could also refer to prose writing in general and had clear ties to classical rhetoric (Camargo). For example, the first major treatise on the *ars dictaminis*, *Flores Rhetorici*, written by Alberic of Monte Cassino and published in 1087, was based on Ciceronian precepts. We discuss the social and political conditions that gave rise to the need for this new medieval genre of *ars dictaminis*, and consider examples from treatises on *ars dictaminis* and draw attention to similarities and differences between the situation in Europe at this time and China, and also between the advice given in the ROW and that given in the treatises on the *ars dictaminis*, based, as they were, on the Roman tradition. As we assume readers will be familiar with the key tenets of classical rhetoric, we shall limit reference to these to where they are directly relevant or comparable, with a particular focus on the Latin tradition as developed by Cicero and Quintilian.

The Greek rhetoricians such as Aristotle, Isocrates and Plato had little influence on medieval rhetoric, while Roman rhetoric did. Indeed, Aristotle's *Rhetoric* only became available in the twelfth century once it was translated into Latin. The Middle Ages were not the direct successors of Greek but of Latin antiquity, and there was virtually no knowledge of Greek in the early Middle Ages. But we must remember that something of the Greek tradition survived in the Roman one. As James Murphy has pointed out (*A Short History*), Roman educators took the loose ideas of the Greeks and moulded them into a coherent system. And, as the Roman education system as developed by Quintilian had the specific purposes of turning out eloquent speakers and political leaders, rhetoric was a fundamental component of each person's education. Quintilian's system was long lasting, surviving for centuries and into the Renaissance.

A major objective of the educational process devised by Quintilian was to enable students to create their own texts. It was designed to produce what Quintilian called *facilitas*, defined as the ability to produce appropriate language on any subject in any situation. It was a painstaking process. It comprised several stages and these are described in Quintilian's work, the *Institutio Oratio*. The importance attached to rhetoric is clear, as it takes up eight of its twelve books. The division of rhetoric into these component parts is derived from Cicero's

De Inventione, published a century earlier in around 90 BCE, where he had also divided rhetoric into invention, arrangement, style, memory and delivery, based on concepts first stated by Isocrates (Murphy, *Three Medieval Rhetorical Arts*). Invention is the devising of material that will make the case convincing. Arrangement concerns the ordering of the material. Style is the adaptation of words and sentences that are suitable and appropriate for the material and the case. Memory requires remembering the material, the arrangement of it and the style of it. Delivery is the graceful regulation of voice, facial expression and gesture. In the event, however, Cicero only ever wrote about the first. A book published a few years after Cicero's *De Inventione*, the *Rhetorica ad Herennium*, did develop all five divisions and Quintilian also derived much of his work from this.

The techniques associated with imitation did not simply mean the rote memorisation and copying of texts. They included: reading a model text aloud; a very detailed, word by word and line by line, analysis of the text; memorisation of models; paraphrase of models; transliteration of the models, whereby students had to rewrite the model text as a different genre, perhaps turning a piece of prose into a poem; the recitation of the student's paraphrase or transliteration in front of the class; and finally, the correction of the paraphrase or transliteration. This system of teaching rhetoric was longer lasting than might be supposed. The author remembers going through these exercises while a schoolboy struggling with Latin and Greek.

To show something of how students worked in a twelfth-century classroom, Carol Lanham provides an extensive passage that describes how a famous teacher, Bernard of Chartres, taught grammar. We quote from it extensively, as it has echoes of the *Rules of Writing*.

This method was followed by Bernard of Chartres. By citations from the authors he showed what was simple and regular; he brought into relief the grammatical figures, the rhetorical colours, the artifices of sophistry, and pointed out how the text in hand bore upon other studies.... For those boys who had to write exercises in prose or verse, he selected the poets and orators, and showed how they could be imitated in the linking of words and the elegant ending of passages. If anyone sewed another's cloth into his garment, he was reproved for the theft, but usually was not punished. Yet Bernard pointed out to awkward borrowers that whoever imitated the ancients should himself become worthy of imitation by posterity. He impressed upon his pupils the virtue of economy and the values of things and words: he explained where a meagerness and tenuity of diction was fitting, and where copiousness or even excess should be allowed, and the advantage of due measure everywhere. He admonished them to go through the histories and poems with diligence, and daily to fix passages in their memory. He advised them, in reading, to avoid the superfluous, and confine themselves to the works of distinguished authors (94).

By the fourth century, the formal study of prose had increased, as the needs of the time were changing. The practice of addressing a public audience had disappeared. The Roman Empire did not produce conditions conducive to public oratory. Nor, of course, did the Chinese empire. An increasingly bureaucratic imperial government started to favour "technical legal skills, streamlined procedural exactitude and written documents over extended oral presentation" (104). Rhetoric started to become specialised, and written rhetoric took precedence. Out of this developed the *ars dictaminis*, as social, political and religious pressures for change created a huge bureaucratic demand for letter writing of various types. By the twelfth century, Europe had changed dramatically. The increase in economic trade and the rise of towns and cathedral schools, all coupled with the needs of an expanding bureaucracy gave rise to the *ars dictaminis*. The eleventh and twelfth centuries saw a dramatic increase in letter writing. Problems within the church produced a widespread reform movement and people started to write polemical tracts. These tracts were in the form of letters. The *ars dictaminis* taught the rules of letter writing and other prose, and, with related subjects, became the core of medieval rhetoric.

THE ARS DICTAMINIS—THE MANUALS

Over three hundred treatises on the *ars dictaminis* survive. Treatises on *dictamen* concentrated on genres and placed emphasis on the overall structure of the document and the arrangement of its component parts. Like Chen Kui, they championed brevity and simplicity. The manuals devote the majority of their space to the salutation. Correct forms of address were determined by the relative status of writer and receiver and the importance of *captatio benevolentiae*, the securing of goodwill, was emphasised, thus further indicating their Ciceronian heritage. As Cicero had pointed out, the exordium or opening of a speech should make the listener well-disposed, attentive and receptive. Examples and models usually concluded the manuals.

As mentioned above, the first major treatise was Alberic's *Flores Rhetorici* and this was published sometime between 1075 and 1090. Alberic was, to quote Lanham "a pivotal figure." He places letter writing in the context of rhetoric as a whole. His book starts with a discussion on the parts of speech, and then gives five model salutations and three model letters. The main part of the book, however, is actually devoted to figures of speech. Here, we quote in part the excerpt concerning the salutation.

> The first consideration should be the nature of the sender and that of the person to whom the letter is sent if he is of high rank, it should be written in an elevated style; if humble, in the simple style.... You will represent a prelate in one way, a subordinate in another. (Lanham)

Two treatises which bracket, in chronological terms, the ROW, and that have been translated or made available by contemporary scholars are: the anonymous *Principles of Letter Writing* (*Rationes Dictandi*), written in 1135 and translated by Murphy (*Three Medieval Rhetorical Arts*); and the *Summa Dictaminis* by Guido Faba, written between 1228-9 and discussed by Faulhaber. Murphy considers the *Principles of Letter Writing* a standard treatise on the subject. And Faba has been described as probably the most outstanding dictator in the history of the genre. (Dictator here means letter writer.) Here we briefly summarise the key points of both treatises, starting with the *Principles of Letter Writing*.

THE PRINCIPLES OF LETTER WRITING

The Principles of Letter Writing (hereafter *Principles*) was written in response to great demand. The opening lines read, "We are urged by the persistent requests of teachers to draw together in a brief space some certain points about the principles of letter writing"(Murphy, *Three Medieval Rhetorical Arts* 5)". *Principles* became the standard and set out the five parts for a letter. This again showed Ciceronian influence. The *dictamen* divided the Ciceronian exordium into two parts, giving a separate part to the *captatio benevolentiae* where, as we have seen, the writer sought to place the reader in a receptive frame of mind. Then came the *narratio*, or background and this was followed by the *petitio*. The *petitio* replaced Cicero's stages of presentation and rebuttal of evidence and was concerned with the real business of the letter, which might have been a request or the urging of some form of action. The *conclusio* ended the letter. This is the normal sequence and schema of a letter, and, as we shall show later, is very similar to the schema of certain types of contemporary Chinese request letters. The author of the *Principles* points out, however, that the stages of this schema were neither obligatory nor fixed in this particular sequence. The author then gives examples of where parts can be omitted, altered in their sequence or even intermixed. "And thus in all similar letters the intermixture can go on quite correctly as desired. Or, after all elements of the Narration have been set forth, all the elements of the Petition can then be paced in unbroken succession, however it pleases the discretion of the letter writer" (24).

Having defined a letter and set out the five parts, the author then discusses the salutation. The importance given to the salutation can be seen here, as, together with the seeking of good will, it takes up about half of the book. The author first defines the salutation as an expression conveying a "friendly sentiment not inconsistent with the social rank of the persons involved." The consideration of the respective social rank and status of writer and recipient was of the utmost importance. "Of course, among all people some are outstanding; others are inferior, and still others are just in between. Now people are said to be "outstanding" to whom no superiors are found, like the Pope or the Emperor. Therefore, when a letter-writer (dictator) undertakes to write, and the difference between the ranks of the persons involved is known, he must take into account... whether equal is writing to equal, inferior to superior, or superior to inferior" (7–10). Contemporary Chinese documents also reflect the importance of this tri-partite distinction, as special names are given to documents depending on whether they are written among equals (*pingxing gongwen*), by inferiors to superiors (*shangxing gongwen*) or superiors to inferiors (*xiaxing gongwen*) (Dai 7ff).

The author then turns to the securing of goodwill, the *captatio benivolentiae*, which as he points out is, in the main, secured in the course of the salutation itself and key strategies include humbling oneself and praising the recipient.

The author then provides a mere three paragraphs on the Narration and seven on the Petition. The Narration should be brief and clear and The Petition is where "we endeavour to call for something"(Murphy, "Rhetoric, Western European" 18). The author then lists nine forms of these, from supplicatory, through menacing to direct. Finally, the Conclusion, where it is customary "to point out the usefulness or disadvantage possessed by the subjects treated in this letter." He gives two examples: "If you do this you will have the entirety of our fullest affection," and "If you fail to do this you will without doubt lose our friendship" (19).

THE SUMMA DICTAMINIS

Guido Faba, the author of the *Summa Dictaminis* (hereafter *SD*), wrote eight major works, all of them dealing with the *ars dictaminis*. He was from Bologna, which had become virtually synonymous with the *ars dictaminis* and this, together with the quality of his own writing, made him the most influential and imitated "dictator" in the later Middle Ages (Faulhaber). The SD is more practical handbook than theoretical treatise and sits alongside his *Dictamina Rhetorica*, written a year or two earlier, in which he gives a total of 220 real letters of various types, including letters from a wife to her husband pleading for his return home and his letter of refusal, and a bishop writing to the Pope for the absolution of an excommunicative. The following description of the SD is a summary of Faulhaber.

Unlike the *Principles of Letter Writing* the SD deals with faults that writers commit when writing *dictamen*. He lists four main ones: first, when one part of the letter does not follow logically on from another; second, when the writing becomes irrelevant; third, when the letter is too short for its purpose to be understood; and fourth, when the writer adopts different styles in the same letter. Faults associated with the particular sections of the letter include not being able to secure goodwill in the opening or writing too general and bland an opening. Recalling Chen Kui, the *narratio* must not be verbose or obscure, but "brief, lucid and plausible" (97). In the petition, the writer must only ask for that which is useful, necessary and honest. The salutation must take into account the person of the sender, the subject of the letter, and, particularly the social status of the recipient. "If one equal writes to another, it is more polite to put the recipient's name first; if an inferior writes to a superior, or a superior to an inferior, the superior's name goes first" (95). In addition to securing goodwill, the exordium was also used to lead into the specific facts of the *narratio*, often by quoting some proverb or biblical citation and, as with the Chinese, this was often some appeal to authority or precedent. "The letter thus becomes a sort of enthymemic argument from authority, with the *exordium* serving as the major premise, the *narratio* as the minor premise, and the *petitio* as the conclusion" (97).

The relative status of the writer and the recipient also influenced the choice of style. Faba also gives other guidance about style, which appears to come somewhere between *guwen* and *pianwen* in its allowance of some form for form's sake. For example, rhymed prose is condemned, but final syllable rhyme is allowed, provided that the penultimate syllables differ. The repetition of the same vowel or consonant at the end of one word and the beginning of the next is also to be avoided, as is alliteration. Metaphors should not be used unless they are very common. Nevertheless, rhetorical tropes are admitted to "empurple" the letter. The proverbs of the wise should also be used to add strength to the letter, and in a further echo of Chen Kui, "ornament yields to authority" (103).

The SD concludes with a list of rhetorical tropes, a list of citations from the Bible that might be suitable for use in the exordium and a series of grammar exercises based on the parts of speech.

These treatises of *ars dictaminis* were successful because they were written in response to a real demand. They were indispensable for those who worked in the bureaucracies of either the church or state, as they had to know how to draw up formal documents. As writing manuals for the bureaucracy they paralleled the *Rules of Writing* and we draw further comparisons between these in the next section.

THE ROW AND ARS DICAMINIS

The *ROW* and the treatises of the *ars dictaminis* (AD) were written when their respective societies were undergoing great change. Both Song Dynasty China and twelfth-century Europe saw significant increases in prosperity. In turn, the various bureaucracies grew and there was thus an urgent demand for people who could write official and commercial documents. Education expanded dramatically and the AD was written to help students master the art of writing for their respective bureaucracies. It is our contention that the ROW was written to meet a similar need in China.

The principles of writing contained in both sets of texts are similar in some cases. The ROW stresses the importance of clarity, simplicity, succinctness and the use of contemporary understandable language. The AD treatises also underline the importance of brevity and simplicity. The narration or background section must be short (Lanham 115), and the petition only ask for that which is useful, necessary and honest (Faulhaber 98).

The AD treatises specify the set pattern, or schema for these letters, although, as we have seen, this order of the component parts is not fixed. There is less advice in the treatises on the way to sequence an argument per se. However, Faba has suggested that the normal sequence of *exordium, narration, petitio* can be seen as an enthymemic argument, with the *exordium* serving as the major premise, the *narratio* as the minor premise and the *petitio* as conclusion. Geoffrey of Vinsauf, writing at almost the same time as Chen Kui, points out that this order follows the sequence of placing the more general before the specific. This order, from general to specific, is also recommended by Gervase of Melkley, an Oxford grammar master writing at the beginning of the thirteenth century (Camargo). In the ROW, Chen Kui gives three possibilities for the sequence of an argument, of which two, the first and the third, encourage the sequence of general to specific. As was illustrated earlier, Chen Kui's three models are: from main topic to supporting details; from supporting details to main topic; or a three part arrangement of main topic-supporting details-restatement of topic. We have earlier argued that Chen Kui's promotion of this "main-frame" pattern suggests that the time at which he was writing was more open to ideas than was normal and that writers had less fear of retribution than normal. This is just one of many instances, therefore, where politics and power relations influence rhetorical style in China, just as it did in Europe. The default and unmarked "frame-main" sequence comes into its own when the hierarchies are clearly established and the power of the superior instills fear in the person writing and persuading "up."

The authors also stress the importance of context and content for the choice of style. Meaning takes precedence over form. By the same token, rules are for guidance and should not be followed slavishly. There are also similarities in the appeal to or use of authority. Faba's *Summa Dictaminis* provides a list of one hundred and four biblical citations that may be useful for supporting the letter writer's petition, for inclusion in the exordium section of the letter. There are, of course, significant differences in the use of authority as justification. Chen Kui's examples are all from the Chinese Classics. Faba's are all from the Bible. Murphy has argued that the eagerness to use the past for the needs of the present is a fundamental aspect of the Middle Ages (Murphy, "Rhetoric, Western European"). He cites Cicero's influence in the development of the new genre of the *ars dictaminis* in support of this. There are also differences in the ways the Medieval Chinese and Europeans used the past for the needs of the present. In the context of Medieval Europe, Cicero was used as a rhetorical model for a way of speaking and writing, but not as an ideological model. In contrast, the ROW provides both rhetorical and ideological models. The ideologies, the *dao*, of the Chinese Classics were used to inform the present and their message needed to be phrased in a rhetorical style based on *guwen*, but in language which could be readily understood by contemporary audiences. The AD treatises are about ways of using traditional genres for a relatively new purpose.

Comparisons in the use of rhetorical tropes can also be drawn. A sample of thirteenth-century European student work recorded by Woods mirrors the use of repetition of specific words for stylistic effect, in much the same ways as advised by Chen Kui. Although this example does not come directly from an *ars dictaminis* treatise as such, it shows what students were being taught to practise in schools in thirteenth-century Europe. Two examples show the repetition of the words, "how" in the first, and "why" and "this" in the second.

> How stupid, how insane, how wicked it is to vex the Gods,
>
> Why do you do this? Why do you affect this? Why do you believe that you can profit in this? (Woods 135).

Compare this with these extracts from the Analects, cited in The ROW 4/3. "Confucius also says, How wise and worthy is Yan Hui! He only has a bamboo basket for food and a gourd ladle for water. How wise and worthy is Yan Hui!"

Another example from the Analects of the rhetorical use of repetition is when Confucius praises Da Yu: "Confucius says, I have no complaint to make against Da Yu: his own table is simple, but the sacrificial offerings he prepares are abundant and he demonstrates sincere respect towards the gods. I have no complaint to make against Da Yu."

Attention to complex stress patterns and rhymes is found in both Chen Kui and the AD treatises. One possible reason for this attention to stress and rhyme may be the lack of punctuation in traditional Chinese and Greek and Latin. This certainly explains the great attention to individual letters and syllables in Quintilian's education system. For Quintilian, there was no short cut with syllables; they had to be learned thoroughly. The way Latin was read explains this. Before Jerome introduced the arrangement of text by sense units in the fourth century CE, the reader had to deconstruct the text. It is not until the ninth century that word separation and punctuation in manuscripts became widespread. Stress patterns and rhymes were thus vital clues in helping the reader deconstruct the text. In a comment that could apply as well to Classical Chinese, Lanham points out, "The lack of a fixed word order and the absence of word separation and punctuation in written texts made reading a matter of decoding, even for the experienced reader" (96).

We shall conclude this chapter on medieval China and Europe with an example from contemporary China (see also Kirkpatrick, "The Arrangement of Letters"). We have chosen to end this chapter in this way, as the arrangement in the exemplar Chinese letter of request bears a striking similarity to a Ciceronian or medieval European arrangement.

The example comes from a study conducted on letters of request written by Chinese living in the Mainland to the China Service of Radio Australia, based in Melbourne (Kirkpatrick, "Information Sequencing"). The China Service of Radio Australia broadcasts into China in Chinese and it naturally employs many native Chinese speaking staff. These letters were thus written by Chinese to Chinese. They were letters of request, but, as is clear from the example below, the requests were not onerous. However, the Chinese letter writers, almost all of whom were in their late teens or early twenties, would have considered that they were, in Gui Guzi's terms, writing from below to above.

The great majority of these letters of request followed the same rhetorical structure and, as shall be illustrated below, this structure shows a quite remarkable similarity to the arrangement proposed by Cicero and then taught in the *ars dictaminis* manuals. The letter below was the one chosen by native speakers of Chinese as being the most appropriate model of the genre and this explains why it has been selected as a representative example here. We assign Ciceronian terms to the respective parts of the letter, and also include in parentheses, the names Kirkpatrick gave to the parts of the schema in the 1991 analysis. It is worth underlining that this example was originally written by Chinese in Chinese and for Chinese in 1990, some nine hundred years after the treatise on letter writing, written for Medieval Europeans writing in Latin (Kirkpatrick "Arrangement" 256).

Salutatio (Salutation)

Respected Radio Australia producers.

Capatatio benovolentiae (Facework)

I have been a loyal listener to Radio Australia's English teaching programmes and to "Songs You Like" for several years. I consider both programmes to be extremely well produced.

Narratio / Background (Reasons for Requests)

Let me describe myself a little: I am a middle school student, I am eighteen and my home is in—, a small border city. The cultural life really isn't too bad. Because I like studying English, I therefore follow those programmes closely. But because the Central Broadcasting Station's English programmes are rather abstruse, they are not really suitable for me and therefore I get all my practice in listening comprehension and dialogue from Radio Australia's English programmes. This practice has been of great benefit. As I progress, step by step through the course, I am keenly aware that not having the teaching materials presents several difficulties.

Petitio (Requests)

Because of this, I have taken time to write this letter to you, in the hope that I can obtain a set of Radio Australia's English programme's teaching materials. Please let me know the cost of the materials.

In addition, I hope to obtain a radio Australia calendar. Wishing Radio Australia's Mandarin programmes even more interest.

(Sign Off)

(Listener's name and date)

As intimated above, what is particularly interesting here is that this Ciceronian / AD arrangement could not have been explicitly taught to these Chinese letter writers. Instead this style appears to develop naturally in contexts where hierarchy is important and the relative status of writer and reader has to be taken into account. As we shall show in the next chapters, this indirect "frame-main" style, in which the main point (i.e. the request itself) comes at the end of the letter and is prefaced by the reasons for it and some form of *captatio benevolentiae*, is the preferred or unmarked style in much Chinese rhetoric, involving as it does, speaking from below to above.

In the next chapter, we turn to a description and a discussion of perhaps the most iconic of all Chinese text structures, the *baguwen,* or the civil service exam essay.

4 THE BA GU WEN （八股文）

This chapter provides a brief history of the Chinese civil service exam and then describes and critically discusses the most (in)famous essay structure associated with the exam, the *baguwen*. It concludes with an example and analysis of a contemporary *baguwen*. Despite its re-emergence in a modern form, we argue that this is unlikely to herald the re-emergence of *baguwen* as a popular Chinese text structure. While this chapter focuses on the civil service exam and the *baguwen* itself, the next chapter, Chapter 5, provides a historical account of the famous *shuyuan* or academies where students would be taught to compose *baguwen*, among other academic skills. Chapters 4 and 5 are therefore complementary.

The *baguwen* is defined in the DCR as being a regulated exam style of the Ming (1368-1644) and Qing dynasties (1644-1911). While this is true, it hides what the *baguwen* came to represent in post-imperial China. The views of the following three scholars, expressed over a time period of some sixty years, can be taken as generally representative:

> Because the function of the *baguwen* was to attain emolument and had ossified forms and rules, they therefore always comprised fawning and empty flattery. (Zhu Zicui 395)

> There is no question that the 8-legged essay holds no place whatsoever in China's intellectual history except as a glaring example of demerit. (Chen Shou-yi 509)

> The term *baguwen* has long been a byword for petrification in the world of letters: it stands nowadays for empty formalism, saying nothing at great length and with tiresome posturing. (Pollard 167)

There is some evidence, however, that attitudes towards this rhetorical form may be changing. After briefly reviewing the history and form of the *baguwen*, we shall argue, using contemporary Chinese sources in support of our argument, that there is a call for the *baguwen* to be re-evaluated and to be classified as an important Chinese rhetorical style. The significance for Chinese of this shift in attitude for Chinese rhetoric will also be considered.

THE HISTORICAL BACKGROUND

The history of the *baguwen* is inextricably linked to the history of the Chinese imperial civil service exams, so we shall start by providing a brief history of the exam system, known in Chinese as the *keju* system. It was founded during the Sui Dynasty (581-618) (Chaffee 15). The Sui dynasty survived less than forty years and was followed by the Tang (618-907), one of the golden ages of Chinese history. The Tang examination system comprised six different degrees, three specialist and three general. Law, calligraphy and mathematics were the three specialist degrees. The *jinshi* (进士) was the most important of the general degrees. The exams were held, annually, in the capital. However, the number of civil servants who entered the service via the exam route during the Tang Dynasty was very low, between 6-16%. The vast majority of civil servants were drawn from the families of people who were already holding office. This is not to say that there was no interest in scholarship or in becoming an official. In fact, there was intense competition to become a civil servant and scholarship was highly prized. There were four categories of scholarly writing. These were: canonical scholarship; state ritual scholarship; scholarship associated with the compilation of dynastic histories; and the publication of bibliographical catalogues and literary anthologies (McMullen).

Skill in the composition of both prose and verse was highly prized and needed to cover a range of some fifteen or so genres and meant "demonstrating command of a tacitly acknowledged memorisation corpus of canons, histories and belles-lettres, facility and even speed in composition. It required an aesthetic sense and an ability to innovate, within certain limits, which themselves changed over the dynasty" (McMullen 203). These composition skills became very important in the examination process and this led, by the end of the seventh century, to the pre-eminence of the *jinshi* exam as this was the examination which tested composition skills. Study of the memorisation corpus and practise practice in fashionable verse and prose styles became obligatory. McMullen also shows that, compared with the Neo-Confucian attitude of the later Song Dynasty, the dynasty during which the *baguwen* became an established part of the exam system, there was a relatively open attitude to dissent. Permitting Confucian scholars to argue among themselves was seen as a way of ensuring their loyalty and support. The dynasty adopted a pluralistic approach—this, after all, was a time when Buddhism was embraced—and when the dynasty endorsed a particular interpretation of a canonical tradition, it did not become exclusively wedded to it.

By the time of the Song Dynasty (960-1279), it was possible to receive a doctorate in letters (the *jinshi*), law, history, ritual or classical study. The chief emphasis was placed on "the study of the older writings as a guide to present conduct" (Kracke 62); Kracke's study shows us that the doctorate of letters exam was different from the other exams, and knowledge and reasoning were tested in a different way. The candidate was required, for example, to demonstrate his knowledge of the Analects by completing from memory ten test passages to which he was given a few words as a clue.

Two major changes in the exam system can be traced to the Song. First, the advent of printing and the desire of the Song Dynasty emperors to attract men of talent to the civil service led to an exponential increase in education and a resultant increase in the number of men taking the exams. This led to the rise of a new intellectual class in China, which Miyazaki has likened to the rise of the bourgeoisie in Europe. As indicated earlier, it was the emergence of this new intellectual class and their need to pass the civil service exams which created the market for Chen Kui's *Rules of Writing*. The introduction of the *baguwen* itself into the exam system can indeed be traced to the Song reformer, Wang Anshi (1021-1086), although it was not until the following Ming Dynasty that the rules for the composition of the *baguwen* were explicitly laid down.

The second major change in the exam system resulted from the shift from the pluralism of the Tang to a neo-Confucian orthodoxy based on the works of Cheng Yi (1033-1107) and Zhu Xi (1130-1200). This was reflected in the need for exam applicants to write their essays in accordance with this new orthodoxy. As this more or less coincided with the introduction of the *baguwen* as an exam essay form, the form soon became associated with Cheng-Zhu orthodoxy. The later Ming (1368-1644) and Qing (1644-1905) preserved this orthodoxy (Woodside and Elman) and thus the *baguwen* form became inseparably linked to neo-Confucian orthodoxy. Writing *baguwen* meant writing the orthodox line that had been determined from above. It is this association between form and content and between form and unquestioning acceptance of authority that led the scholars to the views quoted above. A second quote from Zhu underlines this, "Actually, the *bagu*, as everyone knows, was a senseless thing, but the ruling classes used it to encage the intellectuals…talent selection became talent obliteration" (406).

Qi (1) sums these views up:

> The *baguwen* has been called stale and rotten, cliché-ridden, rigid and well past its use by date. It is despised and rejected and those who are against it have given it the epitaph of being the essence of all evil.

Dissatisfaction with the *baguwen* was also occasionally expressed during imperials times. For example, at the beginning of Kang Xi's reign (r 1661-1722), the empire was ruled by the Oboi regents who issued an order rescinding the need for all exam essays to follow the *baguwen* form (Elman 119). However, the order was so unpopular with the Chinese scholars who had invested their entire careers in mastering the form, that the order was revoked a few years later. Elman also reports that, as Emperor, Kang Xi oversaw further efforts at reform, but none were long-lasting. And Kang Xi's grandson, the Emperor Qian Long, who reigned from 1736-1796, is on record as complaining that he could not understand many of the *baguwen* essays written in the exams.

Nevertheless, despite some changes—for example the length of the *baguwen* essay gradually increased from 550 characters to 700—it remained an integral part of the examination system until the system was abolished in 1905. In other words, the *baguwen* was part of the imperial Chinese exam system for some 1,000 years.

The form of the baguwen

Several scholars have argued that the *baguwen* is some form of amalgam of the *qi-cheng-zhuan-he* structure and both the *pianwen* and *guwen* style. Wu Yingtian has said that the *baguwen* usurped the *qi-cheng-zhuan-he* structure (217ff. Tang Tao has labeled the *baguwen* the "bloodchild" of *pianwen* and *guwen* and quotes Zhou Zuoren, the brother of China's greatest contemporary writer, Lu Xun, as describing it as the "crystalisation" of Chinese literature (28). This indicates that not all scholars view the form completely negatively. The form itself is, if nothing else, complex, as the following description and example will demonstrate.

Zhu Binjie identifies three key features of the *baguwen* (472ff.). The first two concern content: they had to be based on the Confucian canon and they had to take the neo Confucian "*Cheng-Zhu*" school as orthodox. The third feature was that they had to follow a regulated format. Zhu provides alternative names for some sections of this format, and we give these in brackets after the English translation.

1. *Poti* (破题) (Opening the topic). Here two sentences were required to introduce the topic.

2. *Chengti* (承题) (Carrying the topic forward). This section provided further information about the topic and could contain 3 or 4, or 4 or 5 sentences.
3. *Qi Jiang* (起讲) (Elaborating). A more profound discussion about the topic was provided here. The length of this section might vary considerably, from "a few sentences" to "more than ten."
4. *Ruti* (入题) (Revealing the topic) (*Lingti* 领题, *Tiju* 题举, or *Rushou* 入手). This section used either 1 or 2, or 4 or 5 sentences and its function was to clarify ideas of an essay topic that was of some length. For example, an essay topic could be a substantial extract from one of the Confucian classics. Thus, this section was optional. In the example *baguwen* provided below, this section actually occurs after section five, the first of the parallel legs.

These first four sections, along with the conclusion, were written in a relatively free prose style. After these opening four sections, there followed the parallel legs from which the eight-legged essay derives its name. Unlike the first four sections and the concluding section, each of these sections required at least two sentences and they had to provide stylistic balance. The required style has been described "as one falls another one rises" (Tang 27). It should be noted, however, that the form varied. First, as noted above, the *Ruti* section was optional. Second, while four sections of parallel legs are described here, the final parallel leg, the *Shugu*, was also optional. This meant, of course, that an essay that omitted the final *Shugu* might have only six legs. The third point of note, however, is that each parallel "leg" might have more than two legs. Some *baguwen* had as many as twenty legs. The four customary parallel legs were:

5. *Qigu* (起股) (Opening legs) (*Qibi* 起比, *Tibi* 题比, *Qiangu* 前股 *Tigu* 题股).
6. *Zhonggu* (中股) (Middle Legs) (*Zhongbi* 中比).
7. *Hougu* (后股) (Latter legs) (*Houbi* 后比).
8. *Shugu* (束股) (Concluding legs) (*Shubi* 束比).

After these parallel legs, the baguwen ended with a final section, the conclusion.

9. *Dajie* (大结) (*Luoxia* 落下).

Chapter 4

The Baguwen: A Traditional Example

As an example of a traditional *baguwen,* we provide one translated by Andrew Lo in an edition of the Chinese translation magazine *Renditions* ("Four Examination Essays" *Renditions* 33 & 34 169–72). We have included comments in italics in brackets. This essay was written by Tang Shunzi and helped him win first place in the examination of 1529. Lo uses some of the alternate terms for some of the sections but we have retained the terms proposed above by Zhu, for ease of reference.

> The topic of the essay was:
>
> "*Zi Mo* (子莫) holds on to the middle…Holding on to the middle is closer to being right, but to do this without the proper measure is not different from holding to one extreme."
>
> *(The topic is an extract from a quotation by the Confucian scholar, Mencius.)*
>
> *Poti* (Opening the topic)
>
> Mencius' contemporary Zi Mo wanted to rectify the deviation of heterodox teachings, but did not realise that he himself fell into deviation.
>
> *(This and the chengti section following provide a brief introduction to the main ideas. As Lo points out, names should only be referred to obliquely in this section, but could be referred to directly in later sections. The Chinese has the equivalent of "his" for Mencius' and simply "his contemporary" for Zi Mo.)*
>
> *Chengti* (Carrying the topic forward)
>
> The fact is, the middle is defined as "not deviant," and the correct application of the middle is the proper measure. Zi Mo wanted to rectify the deviant ways of Yang Zi (楊子) and Mo Zi (墨子), but did not know the proper measure, so this was but another deviation. This was the standard Mencius used to repudiate his error and to establish our way.

Qijiang (Elaborating)

To elaborate, for our Way is the principle one, but the manifestations are many; egoism and indiscriminate love certainly deviate from the Way. And our way uses the one principle to join together the many, but those who hold on to egoism or indiscriminate love are certainly holding on to an extreme which leads nowhere. Thus there was Zi Mo who understood the errors of Yang Zi and Mo Zi, and thereupon mediated between the two in order to grasp the middle course.

(As Lo points out, the author brings in "Confucian authority" here to support his argument. In the parallel legs below, the argument develops incrementally.)

Qigu (Beginning legs)

Zi Mo would probably say, I cannot bear to be like Yang Zi, who cut off all ties with others in a niggardly fashion; I simply stop short of loving indiscriminately.

I have not time to be like Mo Zi who joyfully sacrifices himself for others: I simply stop short of being an egoist.

Because one rejects egoism, one may be thought to be escaping from the error of Yang Zi and heading towards benevolence.

Because one rejects indiscriminate love, one may be thought to be escaping for the error of Mo Zi and heading towards righteousness.

(There are two sets of parallel legs here and we have made a line space between each parallel leg in each section. As pointed out above, however, in this particular baguwen, the ruti section follows the beginning legs.)

Ruti (Revealing the topic)

Zi Mo seems to be close to the Way, but he does not understand the following: the proper measure is defined as following the

Way at the right time; the middle is defined as others with the proper measure; and the position between Yang Zi and Mo Zi is not the place to seek the middle.

Zhonggu (Middle legs)

If one just knows that one should not sever ties with others but does not know how to weigh others to give evenly, then there is no danger of becoming an egoist, but on the other hand those who follow the Way and strive to perfect themselves will also be seen as approaching egoism and consequently one will not dare act in like manner.

If one understands that one should not sacrifice oneself for others but cannot give to others on an individual basis, then there is no danger of loving indiscriminately, but on the other hand those who follow the Way and strive to perfect the whole Empire will also be seen as approaching indiscriminate love and consequently one will not be willing to act in like manner.

Hougu (Latter legs)

One may say that I plan to escape from Yang Zi. However, Yang Zi saw himself and not others, while Zi Mo saw a fixed position not an open passage. In essence, all these are but parochial teachings. Really, can those who know how to adapt to myriad changes be like this?

One may say that I plan to escape from Mo Zi. However, Mo Zi saw others and not himself, while Zi Mo saw tracks and not transformations. In essence all these are but one-sided delusions. Really, can those who respond to eternal inconstancy be like this?

Shugu (Concluding legs)

The point is, egoism is one extreme, and indiscriminate love is another extreme. That is why it is easy to understand that Yang Zi and Mo Zi each held on to an extreme.

The middle is not an extreme: but if one holds on to the middle without applying the proper measure, then this is also an extreme. That is why it is difficult to understand that Zi Mo was holding on to an extreme.

Dajie (Conclusion)

If Mencius had not demonstrated this with his eloquence, then most people would have thought that Zi Mo was able to be one with the Way.

Contemporary critique

A number of Chinese scholars who see nothing but bad in the *baguwen* were cited earlier, along with some who have classified it more positively. It is, perhaps, not altogether surprising that many scholars view it negatively, given that the *baguwen* has become so closely associated with the dying end of a corrupt imperial system that it has sometimes been seen as one of the causes of the corruption and failure rather than a symptom of it. The rigidly prescribed structure exemplified above also tended to rigidly prescribe the views of the writers. This was also the case in other types of essays that students were required to write, the policy essay (*ce*) and the discourse essay (*lun*). "The examinees' opinions were often trampled in the policy essay" (You, "Building Empire" 25). Cahill has written that "since its late nineteenth century demise no Chinese or Taiwanese writers appear to have regarded the *baguwen* as worthy of resuscitation......." (235). While this is certainly true in a general sense, a number of Chinese scholars, albeit a minority, are beginning to call for a reassessment of the *baguwen*. Qi argues that the *baguwen* is merely a form of writing and therefore cannot intrinsically be either evil or good. He is scathing about critics of the *baguwen* who do not know that it is the name of a genre, much less being able to provide a rational explanation for why it is bad.

In the same book, Jin Kemu stresses that the *baguwen* existed for several hundred years and that it was a special textual style composed by China's literate elite and one that has had a profound influence upon Chinese cultural history. He is saddened that so few people have seen a *baguwen* or even heard of it. It deserves, in his view, scientific study. A major problem in this is that so few people have a thorough understanding of the *baguwen* and how to write it.

An earlier voice for a reassessment of the *baguwen* is provided by Tang Tao (28) whom we quoted above as classifying the *baguwen* as the "bloodchild" of *pianwen* and *guwen* styles. He argues that, while, in general it was used by people to seek position, power, fame and fortune, it should not be viewed with distaste on these grounds. It represented a mix of Chinese prose styles and parallelism and reflected Chinese written culture.

The most complete study and spirited defence of the *baguwen* is provided by Tian Qilin. Illustrating his argument with scores of examples of *baguwen* from different periods, Tian points out that the imperial exam system and the *baguwen* were uniquely Chinese and have had a profound influence on Chinese culture. Despite being consigned by most to the "dustbin of history," the *baguwen* is, in Tian's view, an immensely complex cultural and literary phenomenon that needs to be studied. As he points out, a huge number of politicians, philosophers, scientists and outstanding scholars all went through it. Tian concludes that the *baguwen's* place in history is indisputable. While there are those who see it as rotten and to blame for China's humiliation at the hands of the West and call it a "heap of cultural rubbish" (1221), he classifies it as a representative of China's unique cultural heritage. Tian's book is an attempt to preserve and pass on knowledge about the *baguwen* for future generations.

In summary, a number of scholars are now beginning to argue that the *baguwen* deserves serious study. It is a literary form which is part of the Chinese rhetorical treasury and thus needs to be understood. The form is not to blame for the use to which it was put by earlier authorities and there is an urgent need to educate Chinese about it before it becomes completely forgotten.

The question that now arises is whether this reassessment of the *baguwen* is seeing a re-emergence of its use. In response to the claims of some Western scholars that they could identify the influence of the *baguwen* in the English essays of their Chinese university students, Kirkpatrick has elsewhere argued that it is unlikely that the *baguwen* exerts an influence on the contemporary writing in Chinese of Mainland Chinese writers, both because of its association with the imperial past and also because it is a form that requires time and skill to master ("Traditional Chinese Text Structures"). We make no such claim about Taiwan, where it is quite plausible that the tradition has been maintained. But, in a review of contemporary Mainland Chinese composition textbooks, Kirkpatrick was unable to find even a reference to the *baguwen* let alone advice on how to write one ("Chinese Rhetoric by the Book"). However, You argues that the series of *English* composition textbooks for university students written by Cai Jigang in the late nineties and early two thousands encourage a *baguwen*-type style in that the writers are given no freedom to express their own opinions and are required to follow a given five-paragraph pattern and to express ideas that conform to the accepted ideology ("Conflation of Rhetorical Traditions"). However, You is here talking about English composition rather than Chinese composition, and the form of the five-paragraph pattern is quite different from the form of the traditional *baguwen*, although the heuristic aim of the essays might be similar. In fact, as You points out, the form of the five-paragraph pattern required in English composition in China has strong similarities with the standard American pattern (You *Devil's Tongue* 52). We return to this in Chapter 10 when we discuss current Chinese composition textbooks.

A CONTEMPORARY EXAMPLE OF A BAGUWEN

After several years of fruitless searching for contemporary *baguwen* essays in Mainland Chinese publications, to come across an article written in the form of a *baguwen* was a happy surprise. This article was written by Zhou Youguang in a 2004 issue of the Chinese journal *Xiuci Xuexi*, The Study of Rhetoric. Zhou Youguang, needs some introduction, not least because of his rich past and scholarly eminence.

Zhou Youguang was born in 1906 and, at the time of writing, was still living in Beijing. While he had an extremely distinguished academic career, he also worked overseas and in other occupations. For example, he spent time in New York as an employee for the New China Bank. He returned to China in 1949 to become Professor of Economics at the prestigious Fudan University in Shanghai. He was a member of the language reform committee whose major task was to seek ways of increasing the literacy rate of the Chinese people through reform of the written language. To this end, the Committee introduced a raft of simplified Chinese characters and introduced the Roman *pinyin* script. In 1958 he gave courses in language reform at both Beijing University and The People's University in Beijing. As well as his work on the language reform committee, Zhou is the author of some twenty books on Chinese language and culture including *The New Language of the New Age*. In 2010, he published a new book, *Collecting Shells*, which "expresses the bitterness and anger of thousands of intellectuals of his generation who felt that the Communist Revolution betrayed them and wasted their talents and patriotism" (O'Neill). But as he says "I am 105. I will die tomorrow, so I can say the wrong things" (O'Neill).[15]

In the 2004 article, Zhou uses the traditional form of the *baguwen* to criticise the then President of China, Jiang Zemin. Zhou first provides the briefest of histories of the *baguwen*, saying its "fountainhead" was at the time of Northern *Song* and that its zenith occurred during the *Yuan*, *Ming* and *Qing* dynasties. He gives 1906, his date of birth, as the date of the *baguwen's* death. In the article he explains that he was encouraged to write the article because many of his friends had recently been approaching him asking him to tell them what a *baguwen* was. Zhou provides an example of a traditional *baguwen*, but then provides one he has written himself in Modern Standard Chinese. We translate this modern *baguwen* below and provide notes in the brackets. We have not attempted to place the legs in parallel as with the traditional example above, primarily because the author does not write the legs in such an explicitly parallel style, although he does use a great deal of repetition. We have retained the author's original paragraphing. Thus sections 6 and 7, the middle and latter later legs, both contain three paragraphs in the original. We provide comments in italics and brackets.

The "essay topic": "Moving with the times" "与时俱进"

(This is a saying of Jiang Zemin's, a past President of China, and would be immediately recognisable as such by all educated readers.)

1 *Poti* (Opening the topic)

Of the four words (of the title), "time" and "moving" are linked. "Time" refers to both the present and the past; "moving" refers to development and change.

2 *Chengti* (Carrying the topic forward)

To which era does the twenty-first century belong? It belongs to the era of globalisation. How can we obtain progress? Progress is no more than the regulated development of globalisation. "Time" does not remain stuck in some historical rut; "moving," and the blossoming of change (allows us) to enter the ranks of advanced nations and to put in place advanced economic and political systems.

3 *Qijiang* (Elaborating)

Every country is developing, how could China be any different? The economy progresses through industrialisation to the information age; the political system progresses through autocracy to democracy; culture progresses through the use of knowledge to confine, to the use of knowledge to liberate. This is the pulse of globalisation.

(The elaboration of the topic is startling here, given Zhou's background and previous positions. He is clearly presenting his own voice here and arguing for a more democratic system.)

4 *Ruti* (Revealing the topic)

The information revolution is the determining characteristic of globalisation. Information technology has developed at a phenomenal rate. Televisions, computers, mobile phones along with an endless stream of specialist IT products have become leading resources. Thus labour has moved from industry and agriculture to sales and service, labour-intensive industries have become knowledge-intensive industries, and white collar workers now exceed blue collar workers. Knowledge has become the leading capital.

In America, farmers account for slightly more than 1% of the population and workers for something more than 10%. The agricultural and working class represents the smallest proportion of the population. Had I not seen with my own eyes the "farmer-less farms" and the "worker-free factories" of America and Japan, I would be continuing to promote the slogans "all land to the peasants" and "workers of the world unite."

(The slogans quoted in the final sentence of this section would be immediately familiar as Communist slogans of the Revolution. Zhou is clearly using these ironically.)

5 *Qigu* (Beginning legs)

There's nothing mysterious about the information age. Speaking, writing, using the phone and using computers are all part of the information age. Being able to travel across China speaking *putonghua* without needing interpreters is part of the information age.

Inputting *pinyin* into a computer and its automatic conversion into Chinese characters are part of the information age. The internet and electronic mail are part of the information age.

Links between a computer and a mobile phone, the sending and transmitting of text, of speech, of figures and of images are part of the information age. The national and international exchange of learning is part of the information age. The information age is standing right next to you. The information age gives you breaking news and new knowledge.

(The author achieves a sort of parallelism here by the frequent repetition of the phrase "part of the information age." However, these legs are not written in a parallel style comparable to the traditional baguwen.)

6 *Zhonggu* (Middle legs)

Today each country continues and advances its traditional culture on the one hand, while, on the other, adopts and creates a contemporary international culture. We can call this the age of twin cultures. This age of twin cultures promotes the development of culture but also stimulates cultural clash and, in the clash between the advanced and the backward and in the contradiction between the traditional and the new, lies the ship's wheel guiding the history of "moving with the times."

The pursuit of advanced productive forces requires moving from imitation to creative invention. An environment that will allow creativity to develop in freedom is a prerequisite. The pursuit of an advanced culture requires breaking free from the fetters of thought. An advanced culture is the flower that springs forth from the soil of freedom.

The use of broadcasting, television, computers and other tools of the information age needs to be fully exploited and not limited. If the information age leads to the restriction of information, how can this lead to the liberation of the self?

The easier times are the easier it is for unrest to occur in society. When chickens and dogs hear each other but never come into contact they can live at peace with each other. But put 18 crabs in a bamboo crate, and how can one not claw the other? How can a woman who drapes herself head to food foot in a black robe saunter hand in hand down *Wang Fu Jin* with another who sports a bikini and has her belly button exposed? Cultural clash is actually the clash between the gap between cultures.

(Wang Fu Jin is Beijing's main shopping street.)

7 *Hougu* (Latter Later legs)

"Moving with the times" is not an automatic choice, but an objective law; it's not unique or special, but general. You can deviate from this only for a short period, you can't do so over a long period. Society's progress is orderly but falling behind or excelling is by chance. Orderly progress is the norm.

Society's development is characterised by four leaps: the first is the leap from backward society to slave; the second is from slave to feudal; the third is from feudal to capitalist; the fourth is from capitalist to post-capitalist.

"Moving with the times" alerts people not to make historical mistakes: ruthless autocracy; wantonly engaging in military aggression; the defeat of Nazism; the disintegration of the Soviet Union. The twenty-first century cannot revisit the Breshnev's "society of developed socialism," because it was all propaganda and none of it was real.

8 *Shugu* (Concluding legs)

Truth also changes over time, it is not immutable. "Practice is the sole criterion for the test of truth."* Truth is not afraid of criticism; criticism is the nurturer of truth. Whatever fears criticism is not truth. What fears truth are religions or dogmas that are out of step with the times. The superstitious age is going to become a thing of the past,** the age of following blindly is going to become a thing of the past,** Today is the age of independent thought, the age of following that which is good, the age of the unconstrained in which we spare no effort in pursuit of "moving with the times."

---

*   *This is the slogan of the Chinese Communist Party.*
** *These terms will bring to mind Falun Gong and the Cultural Revolution respectively.*

What is of greatest interest in this contemporary *baguwen* is the content. Far from mouthing the orthodox line, Zhou is explicitly criticising the Chinese government for dragging its heels over the necessary reforms. For example, in Section 3, he talks about the need to move towards democracy from autocracy and about the liberating role that knowledge must play. In Section 4, he mocks Communist Party slogans, and, in the final section, the very motto of the Communist Party itself. In other words, the author is using a rhetorical structure traditionally associated with imperial control to criticise authority. In this way, Zhou turns the traditional function of the *baguwen* on its head. The possibility of this "byword for petrification in the world of letters" becoming a rhetorical style for the expression of dissident voices is intriguing to say the least.

While this modern example of the *baguwen* is written within the framework of a traditional *baguwen*, it does not employ the two different styles required in the traditional *baguwen*, and there is little attempt to balance sentences in the legs of the contemporary version. A major reason for this, of course, is that modern Chinese does not lend itself to this type of parallel writing to anything like the extent the more succinct *wen yan* or classical writing did. Readers may feel they are reading an essay that has been divided up into *baguwen* sections rather than a real *baguwen*. Perhaps the linguistic features of Modern Standard Chinese mean that true *baguwen* are a thing of the past and that contemporary *baguwen*, if they reappear, will capture only an overall argument structure rather than a strict linguistic style. And the overall argument structure is hardly unique. The *baguwen* adopted the traditional four-part poetic structure of *qi-cheng-zhuan-he*, and this structure is certainly not quintessentially Chinese. As Kent Guy has argued, the *baguwen* form "imposed on authors a logical structure of argumentation not unlike that imposed in, say, American collegiate debate format" (170). While this may be true in one sense, the complexity of the traditional *baguwen* form sets it apart and, as suggested above, the linguistic changes that Chinese has seen, mean that *baguwen* of the traditional type and complexity are unlikely to re-occur. However, it may be that the current interest and pride in traditional Chinese culture evidenced most clearly in the resurgence of interest in Confucianism will lead to a resurgence of interest in the *baguwen*. If it does reappear, it will be as a more flexible form than that decreed by the imperial exam system, but one that follows a four-part logical structure that derives its shape from the *qi-cheng-zhuan-he* model.

It is important here to reiterate the importance of *baguwen* as a historical literary genre. It represented an imposed rhetorical pattern through which exam candidates were required to express ideologically orthodox views. As earlier noted, Zhu identified being based on the Confucian canon and taking the Neo-Confucian school as orthodox as two of three criteria of a *baguwen*

(Zhu B. 472ff). The question thus arises as to whether the form used to express unorthodox views can be considered a true *baguwen*.

As suggested above, it will be intriguing to see whether a simplified *form* of the *baguwen* is developing a role as a vehicle for the dissenting voice and that the form, traditionally associated as being an imperial fetter, becomes associated instead with a genre used to criticise the government or the orthodox position. Shu Wu has argued that it can never be forgotten that the *baguwen* was a style of China's "slave literature" (82). There is no reason, however, why a form traditionally associated with imperial control cannot adopt new functions. It remains to be seen, however, whether Zhou Youguang's text represents the start of a new use of the *baguwen* as a form of dissent literature, or whether it will remain a unique example of this. We suspect, however, that Zhou's essay will remain a one-off rather than lead to a renaissance of the traditional *baguwen*.

In Chapter 5, we turn to a discussion of the academies (*shuyuan*) where *baguwen* would have been taught as the main rhetorical style.

5 *SHUYUAN* AND CHINESE WRITING TRAINING AND PRACTICE

Chinese writing has a long tradition, dating back to writing training and practice in traditional Chinese schools, the *Shuyuan*. In this chapter, we shall provide an overview of the *Shuyuan*, including its history, structure, curriculum, book collection, and academic activities. This overview may help readers understand what ancient Chinese students, writers, and scholars read and wrote, and the implications of this for contemporary Chinese writing.

Originating in the Tang Dynasty (618-907), the *Shuyuan* flourished during the Song (960-1279), Yuan (1271-1368), and Ming (1368-1644) Dynasties, lasting until the end of the Qing Dynasty (1644-1912). They are commonly known in English as academies or private establishments for classical learning. Over 7,000 *Shuyuan* or academies are recorded as existing throughout the history of China. The four best known, the so-called Great Academies, were the Yuelu Academy, the White Deer Grotto Academy, the Yingtian Academy, and the Songyang Academy. These all existed during the Northern Song period (960-1127).

According to Yang and Peng, "A Chinese *Shuyuan* was essentially a comprehensive, multi-faceted cultural and educational institution, and it served multiple functions, as a school, a library, a research centre or institute, and others including religious and spiritual functions" (1). There are thus many different aspects of the *Shuyuan*, including school education, book collection and printing, academic research, the study of the religious and the philosophical systems of Confucianism, Buddhism, and Daoism, architecture, archive-management, and cultural communication. This chapter focuses on the *Shuyuan's* curricula, book collection, and academic research and study activities in relation to Chinese reading and writing.

The *Shuyuan* played a key role in the Chinese history of education. The historical facts and records that are presented in this chapter show that the most significant developments in ancient Chinese education, i.e., teaching and learning, knowledge creation and transmission, and academic exchange and activities during the Song, Yuan, Ming, and Qing dynasties, have been closely related to the evolution and development of the *Shuyuan*.

THE ADMINISTRATIVE STRUCTURE OF THE SHUYUAN

The administrative structure of the *Shuyuan* reflects the structure of contemporary Chinese universities. However, the *Shuyuan* structure was of a much smaller scale, which, to a large extent, helped make the influence of the *Shanzhang* (a person similar to the contemporary chair professor, president, or vice chancellor of a university) over the *Shuyuan* activities and academic development much more tangible. The following is a description of the *Shuyuan* structure, based on Yang and Peng (5–15).

Shanzhang 山长[16] (a position equivalent to combining a modern chair professor, and college president) headed a *Shuyuan*. The *Shanzhang* normally had a certain social, political and academic status over the region or the nation. A *Shuyuan's* educational and administrative systems centred around a *Shanzhang*. Under the leadership of the *Shanzhang*, there was a deputy *Shanzhang* who took care of teaching, administrative and management duties on a daily basis. Other *Shuyuan* employees included teaching assistants, lecturers, managers (government representatives, who audited and monitored the *Shuyuan*), finance and estate officers, student affairs officers, assistant president (who assisted the *Shanzhang* with bureaucratic chores such as file-keeping and addressing enquiries), class monitors, logistics officers, receptionists (taken up by students in turns), subject monitors or representatives, administrative officers, and student representatives. In addition, there were also cooks, door keepers or cleaners, hall men, hall administrative staff, patrol staff, pavilion and stone carving managers, librarians, and security guards (night shift only, and who were also responsible for sounding the time).

This administrative structure of *Shuyuan* has some semblance to that of contemporary universities. However, contemporary universities have distinct faculties, departments and research centres, and these cover a wide range of disciplines from sciences, (e.g., physics, chemistry, biology and geology), social sciences (e.g., sociology, economics, politics, cultural and media studies, and psychology), arts and humanities (e.g., language studies, fine art, and religious studies), and applied disciplines (e.g., business and management, philosophy, health, and engineering). While *Shuyuan* had a comprehensive structure, their disciplinary focus was more integrated than the fine disciplinary divisions we find in contemporary universities. In addition, *Shuyuan* focused on the training of literacy skills, e.g., reading and writing, so that the students could prepare for the imperial examinations to become government officials of various categories, including ministers of major national departments, provincial governors, education commissioners, district magistrates, and other high-power positions. Contemporary universities, on the other hand, have far wider scope, teaching and training their students to become qualified professionals in virtually all fields in society. The following discussion on the curricula of the *Shuyuan* shows how the literacy skills of the students were systematically taught and trained in ancient Chinese *Shuyuan*.

THE CURRICULUM OF SHUYUAN HAD A FOCUS ON READING AND WRITING

The teaching and curriculum in *Shuyuan* usually enjoyed more freedom than in government institutions. Nevertheless, it also followed a certain model or pattern. The curriculum of *Shuyuan* evolved steadily alongside social, political, economic and academic developments. In the Song, Yuan, Ming and Qing Dynasties, the curricula of various *Shuyuan* were relatively rich and extensive. In general, they centred around the studies of the *Jing* (the Classics, e.g., the Five Classics and the Four Books) and the *Shi* (histories, e.g., The Book of Historical Records). (Yang and Peng 15)

The major curriculum component for the *Shuyuan* in the Song dynasty was the "Five Classics". It was not until the later Southern Song dynasty that the "Four Books" (with Zhu Xi's connotations and commentaries) took the place of the "Five Classics". Ever since then, the "Four Books" became the required texts for various *Shuyuan* and schools, and they were regarded as "standard keys or answers" to the Chinese Imperial Examinations, the historical civil service examination system of China (Yang and Peng 15). The Five Classics and the Four Books include the *Yi Jing* (the Book of Change), the *Shu Jing* (the Book of History), the *Shi Jing* (the Book of Songs), the *Li* (the Book of Rites), the *Chun Qiu* (Spring and Autumn Annals), the *Lun Yu* (the Analects), *Mengzi* (Mencius), the *Da Xue* (the Great Learning), and the *Zhong Yong* (the Doctrine of the Mean).

The historical civil service examination system of China, known as the *Keju* system, is commonly regarded as originating in the year 606 and officially ending in 1905, with a total span of 1,298 years. Through the *Keju* exams, Chinese emperors identified

Chapter 5

> individuals who would either immediately or eventually serve as grand councillors, ministers of major national departments, provincial governors, education commissioners, district magistrates, and in other high-powered positions. These positions bestowed financial rewards, prestige, power, fame, and many advantages to the official's entire extended family, including all descendants. Additionally, within hierarchical Confucian society, overall class, power, status, and prestige were generally reflected by such official positions won through success in these exams. (Suen and Yu 48)

Given the importance of the civil service examinations in China, the *Shuyuan*'s curriculum played a key role in developing the reading and writing skills of *Shuyuan* students. Apart from the "Five Classics" and the "Four Books" being the required texts or courses, there were also elective texts or courses, including "The Thirteen Classics with Commentaries", "The Records of the Grand Historian", "The Book of Han", "The Book of Later Han", and "The Records of Three Kingdoms". The students were expected to select one of these elective texts and then study it thoroughly. The learning styles, according to historical records, included reading the sentences aloud, adding annotations and commentaries, copying key selected texts, and elaborating on texts. The students were provided with a diary so that they could record what they did according to the pre-determined schedule. These learning styles show that, in Imperial China, much emphasis was laid on the relationship between reading (including reading the texts aloud), memorisation of classic texts, and writing. In other words, writing was heavily dependent on what the students read, how much they could memorise of what they had read, and how much of what they had read they could understand and elaborate on.

Since reading was so important in the *Shuyuan* curriculum, a detailed description of the readings is essential in helping readers understand how the *Shuyuan* curriculum was structured. The teaching and learning content of *Shuyuan* centred around the *Jing* (classics) and *Shi* (histories). There were eight major subjects in the curriculum, namely:

> (i) The *Jing* classics: In the Song dynasty, this included nine classics, e.g., "Mao's Poetry" (Mao Shi), "Documents of the Elder" (Shang Shu), "the Books of Rites" (Zhou li, and Li ji), "the Book of Changes" (Zhou yi), "the Spring and Autumn Annals" (Chun qiu zuo shi zhuan), "the Analects" (Lun Yu), "Mencius" (Meng Zi), and "the

Book of Filial Piety" (Xiao jing). The total number of words in the nine classics is approximately 480,090.

(ii) The *Shi* histories: In the Qing dynasty, the study of history comprised four topics, namely biographies, chronicles, historiographies, and studies of decrees and regulations.

(iii) Classical Chinese literary studies, e.g., the study of selected works of a particular school of scholarship. For example, during the Qing dynasty, there was a school of writing, named "Tongcheng school", in which Yao Nai—whom we shall meet again in Chapter 8—was an influential figure. He had been a *Shanzhang* (Head of *Shuyuan*) for over 40 years, and many writers had been students at his *Shuyuan*.

(iv) Poetry: *Shuyuan* promoted poetry reading and writing. The Imperial Examination also included poetry writing. Most *Shuyuan Shanzhang* and their students were poets. The commonly adopted poetry books in *Shuyuan* included "The Complete Tang Poems" (*Quan Tang Shi*), "The Selected Poems of the Song Dynasty" (*Song Shi Chao*), "The Selected Poems of the Yuan Dynasty" (*Yuan Shi Xuan*) (in three volumes), and "The Total Collection of Ming Dynasty Poetry" (*Ming Shi Zong*).

(v) The study of written Chinese characters, their etymology and phonology: In teaching this subject, the *Shuyuan* would use "*Erya*" and "*Shuo Wen Jie Zi*" as key textbooks. The *Erya* is a dictionary or glossary. It contains definitions of abstract words and concrete words such as items of flora and fauna, including grasses, trees, insects and reptiles, fish, birds, wild animals, and domestic animals. The *Shuo Wen Jie Zi* is a comprehensive Chinese character dictionary from the Han Dynasty with detailed analyses of the structure of the Chinese characters.

(vi) Mathematics, Arithmetic: the key text for this subject in the *Shuyuan* was "The Nine Chapters on the Mathematical Art" (*Jiu Zhang Suan Shu*).

(vii) *Bagu* eight-legged essays and *Shitie* poems: Since the Southern Song and Early Yuan dynasties, the *Shuyuan* had evolved towards official or government institutions in terms of providing preparation courses for imperial examinations. In the Qing dynasty, there was a shift towards an "examination-oriented" curriculum centring around the *bagu* essays. Bagu essays were primarily based on Zhu Xi's Collected Notes on the Four Books. Zhu Xi was regarded as the leader of the neo-Confucian school. Scholars in those days complained about the "shift" of the teaching focus in the *Shuyuan*, and some *Shuyuan Shanzhang* even regarded the *bagu* as "an enemy" (吾道之敌). However, since the civil service imperial examinations required it, they had to read and write these Neo-Confucian texts. Some *Shuyuan* took the reading of these "contemporary texts" as compulsory. The *Shuyuan* promoted the reading of around 100 Qing contemporary texts and some 20-30 Ming texts to help students learn how to write *bagu* essays appropriately.

(viii) Natural science and technology: although the *Shuyuan* curriculum was heavily oriented towards the Classics and the Histories, there were also courses in natural sciences and in mathematics, physics, chemistry, astronomy, geography, biology (including medical science and agriculture). Nevertheless, the knowledge of these disciplines was taught primarily through the learning of Confucian classics, not as independent disciplines. For example, the "*Shi Jing*" (*the Book of Songs*) provides knowledge of biology, phenology, meteorology, and agricultural science. (Yang and Peng 16–21)

THE TEACHING OF READING AND WRITING IN THE SHUYUAN

The *Shuyuan* advocated learner autonomy or self-study. Lectures were only given by *Shanzhang* to the students two to three times per month. The remaining time would be for the students to engage themselves in self-study. The learning activities of the *Shuyuan* students comprised attending lectures and self-study.

One of the roles that *Shuyuan* would play was to monitor the students' learning activities and progress. Unlike contemporary university students, who have more flexibility and freedom in determining their individual learning activities, the *Shuyuan* students had to record what they read on a daily basis into their learning schedule books. These schedule books were then carefully examined by the *Shanzhang* on a regular basis.

The teaching of reading and writing in the *Shuyuan* was arranged in such a way that progressive training was implemented in three major stages, equivalent to the contemporary primary, secondary, tertiary and postgraduate education (Yang and Peng 22). During the first stage, students between the ages of 8-15 would spend seven to eight years learning eleven course books. These included the *Xiaoxue* (books on Chinese characters, etymology and phonology), the *Daxue* (classics and biographies), the *Lun Yu* (*The Analects of Confucius*), and *Mengzi* (*The Book of Mencius*). They also included the Five Books and the *Spring and Autumn Annals*. It should be noted that students at this stage were exposed to the reading of the Classics, regardless of how much of them they could understand. They would be required to read the texts aloud, copy the texts, and memorise the texts. There was not much creative writing involved at this stage, with "writing" often being interpreted as copying Chinese characters or texts.

During the second stage, students between fifteen and twenty-two years of age would spend three to four years reading course books, such as *Questions on the Great Learning, Collected Notes on the Analects, Collected Notes on Mencius, Questions on the Doctrine of the Mean*, and the Five Classics. There were also the original classical texts that they had read during stage one, but with connotations and commentaries. Their learning styles were not very different from those for stage one, but they were required and expected to understand the major texts they were reading. They would still copy and read aloud as their major learning activities. They would then spend another two to three years (equivalent to contemporary tertiary education) focusing on the *Tong Jian* (Documents of Ancient Books), the *Han Wen* (texts and grammar), the *Chu Ci* (*The Songs of Chu*), and the *Tong Dian* (The *Universal Encyclopedia of Statecraft*).

During this second stage, the students were not only expected to comprehend the texts that they had read during stage one, but also to start writing texts based closely on what they had read and comprehended. Reading and writing at this stage were integrated. The training of writing skills was particularly evident in the reading of texts and grammar sections. This training comprised analysing and understanding the discourse patterns and rules and the lexical and sentence grammar in the texts that students read. Intensive reading, instead of extensive reading, was emphasised at this stage, where the students were required to focus on reading one or two texts, by reading them over one hundred times. This differs from the reading requirements for contemporary school and university students in that disciplinary and cross-disciplinary extensive reading is now emphasised and encouraged. One of the advantages of this type of intensive reading for the *Shuyuan* students, however, is that they could not only understand the content of what they were repeatedly reading, but also figure out and internalise the outline structures and the rhetorical devices through which meanings and intended meanings had been encoded by well-known and well-established authors. This process would lay a good and solid foundation for the *Shuyuan* students in terms of their writing output. Quality writing in *Shuyuan* focused both on structure and content. One of the desirable outcomes of the *Shuyuan* intensive reading was that the students could take the classic texts as models, and write similar well-constructed and content-rich texts with appropriately chosen or imitated rhetorical devices. *Shuyuan* students were well motivated because this intensive reading approach could lead to, in their own belief, achieving first-class learning, writing first-class essays, and becoming the educated elite, which would, in turn, lead them to promising and prestigious careers. The *Shuyuan* education had a good reputation for quality. It focused on both the process and the product in Chinese literacy development. While students at the first two stages of *Shuyuan* education were well trained in terms of accumulating subject knowledge for writing, they also acquired skills during the process of reading and writing process in order to focus explicitly on the writing product in the final stage of their education. This model of process- versus product -oriented Chinese writing also applies to contemporary teaching of Chinese writing, where primary and secondary school education are process-oriented while post-secondary and particularly post-graduate studies focus on writing output of the students. Students in post-graduate studies primarily learn to write, and write to learn.

Stage three was the stage where students were engaged in more advanced studies. This was also the final stage of their *Shuyuan* studies in the sense that the students rigorously prepared for the imperial civil service examinations. By this time, the *Shuyuan* students would normally be between twenty-two and twenty-five years old. The exclusive focus of this stage was on writing (learning to write), practicing contemporary writing, and practicing *bagu* writing, with the ultimate aim of achieving a first-class result in the imperial civil service examinations. All *Shuyuan* at the provincial and municipal levels became examination oriented, particularly during this third stage.

Although this third stage focused on writing, reading still occupied the majority of the students' learning time. The usual time allocation and study pattern was that the students would read for nine days, followed by a day of writing in whatever genre they were practicing. The rationale behind this was that, by the time of the writing day, the students had already studied and internalised the writing style and the content. The reading days were seen as writing preparation time. On the writing day, when the topic was released, the students were thus usually well-prepared and confident enough to set up their theses or themes and develop the rhetorical structure, while recalling what they had read over the previous nine days. They were able to come up with a draft very quickly and to revise and fine-tune their essays. The power of brush strokes could become sharp and unstoppable, as the Chinese would say. In terms of the content, the theses and themes were expected to lead the whole text or discourse in its opening and conclusion through twists and turns. To adopt the metaphor of writing as a "battlefield", the theses or themes were like a commander with a bugle horn. Sentences were like generals, words and characters were like soldiers. The previous readings and writing material were like weapons. The "soldiers" would centre around or follow the generals. As far as the magic key to success in writing is concerned, Su Shi, one of the eight prose masters of the Tang and Song Dynasties, suggested that "The theme is what the writing is all about. Other aspects of writing have all been scattered through the *Jing* classics, the *Shi* histories, the works of the philosophers, and collections of essays. It is only when the theme is settled, can other things then be taken up or considered" (Cheng D. 487). What leads to poor writing is that, by the time of writing, the discourse, theme and the structure are still unsettled. Then no matter how much effort and heart one puts into the writing, it will not be done appropriately.

This third *Shuyuan* stage was important in that it integrated the writing skills with all the previous training of reading and preliminary writing (merely in the form of copying characters and texts). According to Cheng Duanli of the Yuan Dynasty, if all the three stages were completed successfully, by the time a student reached twenty-two to twenty-three, or twenty-four to twenty-five, he should be able to have read enough to write good essays. Even if a student missed some time, or did not follow the exact sequence, he could still make it up before reaching thirty by spending two to three more years on additional reading and writing. "Writing an essay is like planting and harvesting. Haste makes waste, and the cart cannot be put before the horse" (Cheng D. 488).

THE EXAMINATION-ORIENTED ASSESSMENT OF THE SHUYUAN

In later years, the examination courses of the *Shuyuan* laid exclusive emphasis on writing *bagu* essays (eight-legged essays) and *shitie* poems (standard exam poems). These were an indispensable part of the *Shuyuan* curriculum, particularly during the Qing Dynasty. However, in the earlier Song dynasty, the *Shuyuan* put an emphasis on the writing of prose masters or *Shanzhang*, and down-played the role of being examination preparation courses. The *Shuyuan* students studied, what were for them, contemporary essays on their own rather than reading the Classics and Histories in their preparation for the imperial civil service examinations. However, by the time of the Northern Song Dynasty in the thirteenth century, examination courses had become an essential component of the *Shuyuan* curriculum.

Examination courses became even more dominant in the Ming and Qing dynasties (Yang and Peng 25). Examinations fell into two types: those held by the government; and those held by the local government officials. In addition, there were also examinations within the *Shuyuan* and which were administered by the *Shanzhang*. The frequency of examinations varied from *Shuyuan* to *Shuyuan*, ranging from one to six examinations per month.

The major content of the *Shuyuan* examinations included one *baguwen* based on Four Books, and one *shitie* poem (standard exam poem). The examination courses were primarily to prepare students for the Imperial Examination (or Civil Service Examination). There were also awards for top achievers.

As *shitie* poems and *baguwen* essays comprised the major content of the imperial civil examinations, it is important for the readers to have some background knowledge of these unique genres of writing. We have discussed and illustrated *baguwen* essays in the previous chapter, so we briefly describe the *shitie* poem in this section. The *shitie* poem was a format for testing poetry writing in the imperial civil service examinations during the Ming and Qing dynasties, basically from the mid-seventeenth century until the turn of the twentieth century. In addition to the encoded and implied meanings in the poetry, the very specific requirements for rhyming, symmetry, tonal balance and couplet styles also make these *shitie* poems difficult to write or compose. In this, they resemble the medieval *cursus*. The form originated in the Tang dynasty. Like the *baguwen*, the format of *shitie* poem changed over time. In the Tang and Song Dynasties, it comprised four or six couplets, while in the Qing Dynasty, it became eight couplets to complement the eight-legged style. Each couplet contained two five-character verses, and the verses had to be rhymed in various ways. There were many other specific requirements for composing *Shitie* poems. For example, certain rhymes such as a repetition rhyme and a synonym rhyme had to be avoided. The titles of *Shitie* poems were usually taken from a verse in a classical poem, or from a proverb. Those who took the civil service examinations had to be very knowledgeable about these verses and proverbs so that they could elaborate on them, and follow the explicit regulations for *shitie* poem writing. This made the intensive and extensive reading in the earlier stages of *Shuyuan* education described earlier so essential.

THE SHUYUAN'S COLLECTION OF BOOKS

One of the major functions of the *Shuyuan* was to collect and print books. The *Shuyuan's* collection of books fell into three categories, namely "books for the public", "books for teaching and learning", and "academic books". The "books for the public" offered an extensive range, covering *Jing* (Confucian classics), *Shi* (historical records), *Zi* (philosophical writings), and *Ji* (belles-lettres). The "books for teaching and learning" included textbooks and other curriculum teaching materials and references, and they were mostly related to specific courses within the curriculum. The "academic books" included research findings of *Shuyuan* staff and students. The latter two categories were unique to *Shuyuan*, and they were accorded high value.

The "books for the public" were classified into four sections, namely the Classics, the Histories, Philosophy and Belles-lettres pieces. Even though some will by now be familiar to readers, here we give a full list of titles under the Classics and Histories categories to show how diverse these were. Section 1 included "Jing (Classics)", and comprised the *Yi Jing* (*The Book of Change*), the *Shu Jing* (*The Book of History*), the *Shi Jing* (*The Book of Songs*), the Li Ji (*The Book of Rites*), the *Yue* (*The Book of Music*), the *Chun Qiu* (The *Spring and Autumn Annals*), the *Xiao Jing* (*The Classic of Filial Piety*), the *Si Shu* (*Four Books*), i.e., the *Lun Yu* (*The Analects*), the *Mengzi* (*The Book of Mencius*), the *Da Xue* (*The Great Learning*), the *Zhong Yong* (*The Doctrine of the Mean*), the *Xiao Xue* (*The Lesser Learning*); and a number of dictionaries such as the *Erya*.

Section 2 included Shi (Histories), comprising the *Zheng Shi* (*Standard Dynastic Histories*), the *Bian Nian* (*Annals or Chronicles*), the *Ji Shi Ben Mo* (*Historical Events in their Entirety*), the *Bie Shi* (*Alternative Histories*), the *Za Shi* (*Miscellaneous Histories*), the *Zhao Ling Zou Yi* (*Edicts and Memorials*), *Zhuanji* (*Biographies*), *Shi Chao* (*Historical excerpts*), *Zaiji* (*Regional Histories*), *Shi Ling* (*Seasonal Ordinances*), *Di Li* (*The Geographical Gazetteer*), *Zhi Guan* (*Offices: official ranks and titles*), *Zheng Shu* (*Political Treaties and Ordinances*), *Mu Lu* (*Bibliographies*) and *Shi Ping* (*Historical Critiques*).

Section 3 focused on the major philosophers including the Confucians, the Buddhists, the Taoists and a number of other sects and texts, including books on agriculture, medicine and magic and divination.

Section 4 comprised *Ji* (*Belles-lettres*) which is where the *Wenxin Diaolong* was found as were other books of literary criticism and general collections of prose and poetry.

The "books for teaching and learning", included annotations and commentaries of the classics and histories by influential scholars and the final category of "academic books", included academic works by various *Shuyuan* staff and students as well as famous scholars, including Zhou Zunyi, Cheng Hao, Cheng Yi, Zhang Zai, and Zhu Xi. This category also includes works by *Shuyuan Shanzhang*, and *Shuyuan* masters, and also collections of well-written pieces by *Shuyuan* students.

THE ACADEMIC RESEARCH OF SHUYUAN

As far as the academic research atmosphere was concerned, *Shuyuan* placed a significant emphasis on self-study and academic interaction among the staff, as well as between staff and students. *Shuyuan* masters would generally aim to inspire learning, rather than "duck-feed" (spoon-feed) their students. For example, they would give one example for students to grapple with and understand so that they could then come up with three comparable examples themselves. Such an atmosphere created a positive influence for the development of creative and critical thinking skills in students' writing.

There were three types of academic activities in *Shuyuan*: the normal day to day teaching activities within the *Shuyuan* (e.g., the various courses); academic exchanges between *Shuyuan*; and activities that were open to the general public. In the Southern Song dynasty, academic exchange activities were extremely popular. One example was the famous Neo-Confucian scholar, Zhu Xi, becoming involved in in-depth discussions with Zhang Shi, another famous Song dynasty scholar. Records show that the two masters argued for three days and nights over the meaning of "Doctrine of the Mean".

In some ways, the influence of the *Shuyuan* can be seen in contemporary Chinese universities. For example, the types of interaction between students and staff, academic exchange activities, and community service, in particular providing books and seminars for the general public reflect *Shuyuan* practice. Contemporary Chinese university students and staff interact in many ways, not only through lectures, tutorials and seminars, but they also engage in face-to-face and online communication. They advocate learning and teaching autonomy. They do not, of course, write poetry or *baguwen* as *Shuyuan* students did, but they read and write academically within their disciplines and follow explicit and implicit discipline-specific academic writing rules and conventions.

Contemporary Chinese university students and staff also engage in academic exchange activities. They participate in exchange programs and attend local, regional and international conferences through which academic ideas are disseminated, exchanged and debated. Contemporary students and staff also realise the importance of serving the community and try to apply what they have learned and researched within the ivory tower to real and relevant issues of concern to the community. In this way, universities aim to make students professionals who are able to serve the society in much the same way as the *Shuyuan* aimed to produce literate and educated people who could take up various important social roles in traditional Chinese society.

THE TRANSFORMATION OF SHUYUAN IN THE TWENTIETH CENTURY

After a history of more than a millennium, the *Shuyuan* were abolished towards the end of the Qing Dynasty at the time of major social and political change, which we consider in detail in Chapter 8. Western influence and China's desire for modern knowledge and science undermined the role of the *Shuyuan* and created an urgent need for modern schools and universities. Chen Pingyuan (63-4) lists the following reasons to account for the demise of the *Shuyuan* in the twentieth-century China:

1. The irresistible Western learning (to be discussed in Chapter 8). Chinese in the twentieth century were desperate to learn about science, democracy and law. The establishment and dissemination of such disciplinary knowledge required a new educational system, which differed significantly from the traditional *Shuyuan*.

2. The propensity for "practical science". The Chinese education in the twentieth century wanted science rather than humanities. As we have seen, the major curricula of the traditional *Shuyuan* were not science- oriented.

3. Traditional *Shuyuan* lacked efficiency because of its high cost in terms of human resources. Western "class" teaching provided strong economic advantages.

Chen (63-4) also points out, however, that the traditional *Shuyuan* has contributed to the current universities in many ways. For example, the tradition of holistic and whole-person education has been inherited from the *Shuyuan*.

In this chapter, we have reviewed the history of Chinese *Shuyuan* particularly in their relation to Chinese academic reading and writing. Chinese has a long tradition of reading classics, the histories and other iconic texts in order to prepare students to write. This tradition helps explain why modern Chinese students may have a propensity to quote the classics without explicit referencing, as this shows their competence, their extensive reading, and their remarkable ability to memorise. This chapter also shows that Chinese have traditionally paid great attention to the symbiotic relationship between reading and writing, especially in terms of what, how and when to read for subsequent writing activities. In addition, while the examination-oriented *bagu* essays and *shitie* poems are heavily dependent upon form, Chinese scholars, such as Chen Kui and Su Shi stressed that the meaning or theme was important. So meaning was often the primary concern, despite the apparent rigidity of the forms. The chapter concluded with reasons for the demise of *Shuyuan* and the rise of modern schools and universities, while indicating certain *Shuyuan* influences that can still be seen in contemporary Chinese universities.

In the next chapters, we move from the historical background and propose a number of fundamental principles of rhetorical arrangement and sequencing in Chinese.

6 PRINCIPLES OF SEQUENCING AND RHETORICAL ORGANISATION: WORDS, SENTENCES AND COMPLEX CLAUSES

In this chapter we review and describe principles of rhetorical organisation in Chinese. We start at the level of phrase and sentence, moving to the ordering of complex clauses. Chapter 7 continues the discussion and considers these principles of rhetorical organisation operating at the level of discourse. During the discussion we touch on the role that Western influence played on the sequencing in Chinese. Chapter 8 will discuss this in more detail, and provide the historical context which saw the rise of Western influence.

PRINCIPLES OF RHETORICAL ORGANISATION

To date we have provided a review of historical aspects of Chinese rhetoric and persuasion, along with a number of examples and illustrations. We have argued that people engaged in bottom-up rhetoric and persuasion in a hierarchical society naturally adopted a rhetorical arrangement that followed a "because-therefore" or "frame-main" sequence, although we also stress that this was by no means exclusively so. This is the unmarked rhetorical sequence. Here we consider the principles of rhetorical organisation primarily from a linguistic standpoint, and will argue that the principles that operate at the level of the sentence also operate at the higher levels of discourse and text. In doing this, we hope to show that the preferred and unmarked rhetorical patterns exemplified earlier are themselves shaped by these principles of sequencing. Implicit in all this will be the extent to which language is shaped by social and political realities. Later we shall consider how rhetorical organisation in Chinese has been influenced by Western contact.

THE SENTENCE: TOPIC-COMMENT AND/ OR MODIFIER-MODIFIED.

A fundamental principle of organisation in Chinese is contained in the topic-comment construction, although, subject-predicate sentences are also common. Here we argue that the topic-comment structure is also linked to the modifier-modified sequence commonly seen in Chinese.

Some sixty years ago, Hockett suggested that topic and comment constructions generally characterise the immediate constituents (ICs) of these constructions. "The speaker announces a topic and then says something about it" (201). In discussing Chinese, however, Hockett points out that many Chinese comments themselves consist of both a topic and a comment. In this way, a Chinese sentence can be built up of predications within predications. Hockett's example of this is:

1. *Wo jintian cheng-li you shi*

   I today town-in have thing

   I have business in town today.

As Hockett points out, the topic *wo* can be deleted leaving the sentence *Jintian chengli you shi* where, in Hockett's view, *jintian* now becomes the topic. Similarly, the sentence can be further reduced to *chengli you shi* where *chengli*, (in town), becomes the topic. Even *you shi*, (have business), which has no topic, can stand as a complete sentence.

Li and Thompson classify Chinese as a topic prominent language, that is, a language in which the basic structure of sentences favours a description in which the grammatical relation topic-comment plays a major role. In defining topic, Li and Thompson say that the topic of a sentence "is what the sentence is about" and that "it always comes first in a sentence and it always refers to something about which the speaker assumes the person listening to the utterance has some knowledge" (15).

They therefore use both syntactic and semantic criteria in their definition of topic. As an example of a topic-comment sentence, they give:

2. *Zhe-ke shu yezi hen da*

   This-(Cl-classifier) tree leaf very big

   This tree, (its) leaves are very big

Topic is here distinguished from subject by stressing that "this tree" is the topic and has no direct semantic relation with the verb. *Yezi*, however, is the subject as it is they that are very big.

TOPICS AS SENTENCE FRAMES

Although Li and Thompson say that topics are typically noun or verb phrases, they later argue (95) that sentence initial time and locative phrases should also be seen as topics. For example:

   3. (a)   *nei nian ta hen jinzhang*

      that year he (was) very anxious

   3. (b)   *xinfeng-li zhuang bujin zhexie zhaopian*

      Envelope-in N enter these photos

      These photos won't fit into this envelope.

Li and Thompson classify these time and locative phrases ("that year" and "in the envelope" respectively) as topics because they set the frame, they are definite, and they may be followed by a pause particle. Earlier, however, topic has been defined as "what the sentence is about" and that it "names what the sentence is all about." Here, in contrast, topics "set the frame within which the sentence is presented." This would appear to be defining topic in two different ways.

Chafe has noted that certain topics in Chinese do not precisely fit the characteristics that a topic is "what the sentence is about." In his view, topics in topic prominent languages provide the "frame within which the sentence holds" and that they set "a spatial, temporal or individual framework within which the main predication holds" (50). Again topic is apparently being defined in more than one way. The Korean scholar, Her, proposes that topic should not be defined semantically but should "strictly refer to a syntactic notion" and that the topic of a sentence, being always preverbal and before the subject, usually encodes the semantic/discoursal frame (4–5). Her then argues that the semantic relation between subject (topic) and predicate (comment) in Chinese is that of frame and comment. In other words, Chafe's definition of topic quoted above, now becomes, in Her's analysis, a definition of frame, with the term topic being reserved for its grammatical function. This, however, still leaves the problem of the definition of these frames, which are encoded by topics. Frame is now semantically defined as topic was defined. Again we have two distinct and different definitions for what is purported to be the same concept. The problems associated with the semantic definition of topic now surface for the semantic definition of frame.

The problem of topic definition gets even more complex. Zhao (Yuen Ren Chao) categorises all temporal, locative, and concessive, causal and conditional clauses as topics (120). Among his reasons for classifying all these clauses as subjects are that they can have a pause after them and before the principal clause; and that they occur at the beginning of sentences unless they are an afterthought. As will be shown later, however, these clauses may occur after their principal clauses for a number of reasons, of which being an afterthought is only one, so they are not as restricted to sentence initial position as suggested by Zhao. Indeed, as we shall illustrate later, Western influence is one of the major reasons for the common presence of these clauses appearing after the main clauses in contemporary Chinese. Zhao's acknowledgement that these adverbial clauses are not the principal clauses in these sentences suggests, however, their role is more a modifying one for the principal clause rather than being topics. Thus, for our purposes, we will adopt this notion and classify these adverbial clauses as performing a modifying function, and not classify them as topics.

The distinction between topics being what the sentence is about and adverbial clauses setting the frame for the sentence will be made clearer by considering the examples below.

4. *Zhangsan wo yijing jianguo le*

    Zhangsan I already see-EXP-A

    Zhangsan, I've already seen him

5. *Zhe ke shu yezi hen da*

    This-Cl tree leaf very big

This tree, (its) leaves are very big.

The topic in both these sentences can be identified without controversy. In (4) the topic is *Zhangsan* and in (5) the topic is "this tree." It makes sense to say that these topics are what their respective sentences are about.

Two further points are of interest here. The first is that both these sentences have subjects as well as topics and that these are also easy to identify. In (4) the subject is "I" and in (5) it is the "leaves." The second point is that both subjects have a semantic relationship with the verbs and with the topics of these sentences. But their semantic relationship with their topics is different. The relationship between "I" and "Zhangsan" is one between actor and patient, and Zhangsan looks like an example of what Foley and Van Valin call the "preposed topic construction (PTC) of topicalisation" (30). In the other example of a PTC, the relationship between "tree" and "leaf," however, is not one of actor to patient but of whole to part, where the leaf is part of the larger whole. As we shall show below, the sequence of whole-part or big-small is another principle of rhetorical organisation in Chinese.

Now let us consider (6), which is a cause-effect complex sentence (*pianzheng fuju*).

6. *yinwei feng tai da, suoyi bisai gaiqi-le*

   because wind too big, therefore competition change time-A

   Because the wind was too strong, the competition was postponed.

This sentence is not about the strength of the wind, in the same way that (4) was about Zhangsan or (5) was about the tree. Despite its place at the beginning of the sentence and despite Zhao's assertion that causal clauses are all topics, we argue here that, by semantic criteria, this initial adverbial clause cannot be the topic. The topic in this sentence, with topic being defined as what the sentence is about, is the competition. We suggest, therefore, that (6) is not a topic-comment sentence like (4) and (5). It is, rather, a sentence whose principal clause is preceded by a clause that sets the framework for it and it follows a modifier-modified sequence. The sentence structure of this sentence is not topic-comment, therefore, but modifier-modified or subordinate-main, as indeed is acknowledged by the Chinese term for these complex sentences *pianzheng fuju*. The *yinwei* adverbial clause is providing some information that helps explain the proposition in the main clause. It is acting in subordinate relationship to the main clause and is following a subordinate-main sequence, and is another fundamental principle of rhetorical organisation in traditional Chinese, although this relationship was not commonly signaled by the use of connectors, as we shall show below.

Further evidence that MSC exhibits a modifying-modified sequence is provided by Tai ("Two Functions"). While arguing that the word order of locatives in Chinese can be explained in terms of their semantic function, Tai points out that both preverbal and post-verbal locatives were placed after the main verb in classical Chinese. However, prior to the word order change that affected locatives, Tai states that classical Chinese had already exhibited the feature of modifier preceding head in that relative clauses, possessives and adjectives all preceded nouns as they do in modern Chinese. The shift from post- to preverbal locatives was patterned after this modifier-head sequence. In a later article on word order in Chinese, Tai argues for the "Principle of Temporal Sequence" (PTS) which he defines as: "the relative word order between two syntactic units is determined by the temporal order of the states which they represent in the conceptual world" ("Temporal Sequence" 50). So, for example, when two Chinese sentences are conjoined by certain temporal connectives, the action described in the first sentence / clause *always* takes place before the action described in the second. This is exemplified in (7).

7. *wo chi-guo fan, ni zai da dianhua gei wo*

   I eat-A food, you then phone give me

   Call me after I have finished the dinner.

The constraint of temporal sequence does not operate in English, as clause order is not determined by the sequence of events. For example, (7) could be translated into English as, "After I have finished dinner, call me." Tai also shows that PTS holds in a number of other constructions in Chinese such as action-result patterns and in serial verb constructions where no overt connectors are used. For example, the sentence

8. (a) *Zhang dao tushuguan na shu*

   Zhang to library take book,

must mean that Zhang went to the library to get a book, while the sentence

8. (b) *Zhang na shu dao tushuguan*

must mean that he took a book to the library.

Tai extends PTS to include the Principle of Temporal Scope (PTSC). PTSC is, "If the conceptual state represented by a syntactic unit X falls within the temporal scope of the conceptual state represented by a syntactic unit Y, then the word order is YX" (60). He then suggests that PTSC is part of an even more general principle in Chinese which is that constituents with a larger scope precede those with a smaller scope in both time and space. As an example of this he points out that the only acceptable way to report a time in Chinese is "1980 year, December, 22nd day, morning, 10 o'clock." This "big to small" sequence looks very much like the whole preceding part principle that operates in topic-comment constructions as in (5) above. We also see this principle operating in the way Chinese write addresses. The "English" "small-big" sequence becomes a "big-small" sequence in Chinese. For example, the "English" address,

> Flat 33b, Building 4, Beijing University, Haidian District, Beijing, China,

becomes, in Chinese ordering,

> China, Beijing, Haidian District, Beijing University, Building 4, Flat 33b.

The Principle of Temporal Sequence suggests that the essential strategy of Chinese grammar is to knit together syntactic units according to some concrete conceptual principles. Chinese is iconic, in Tai's view, and thus presents a case where word order corresponds to thought flow "in a genuinely natural way"(64). Chinese word order is, therefore, in Tai's terms, natural rather than salient, where "Because John went walking in the freezing rain he caught cold" is in natural order because it follows the chronological sequence whereby the cause precedes the effect, but "John caught cold because he went walking in the freezing rain" is in salient order, as the effect—seen as the most salient or important part of the message—is therefore placed first and before the cause. We now turn to consider principles of the sequencing of clause order in complex sentences in more detail.

CLAUSE SEQUENCING IN COMPLEX SENTENCES (PIANZHENG FUJU)

This next section considers the sequencing of clauses and the use of connectors in sentences that are called *pianzheng fuju* and which we translate as "complex sentences." The term *pianzheng* is used to describe the modifier-modified relationship as in the phrase *xin sushe* (new dormitory) and has been extended to describe sentences that have a "modifying" clause followed by a "modified" clause (Ma Zhong 234).

The use of the term subordinate clause, with reference to the components of a sentence, has been questioned for English (Schleppergrel) and the very nature of Chinese often makes it difficult to distinguish between subordinate and main clauses. We discuss this further below when we consider parataxis and hypotaxis in Chinese. Nevertheless, for ease of reference and because they approximate to the terms employed by Chinese linguists, the clauses in these complex sentences will be called subordinate clause (SC) and main clause (MC).

It is widely accepted that the normal order in *pianzheng fuju* sentences is that the *pian* clause or the subordinate clause precedes the *zheng* or main clause (e.g., Lin Yuwen). For example:

9. *Yinwei feng tai da,   suoyi bisai gaiqi-le*

   Because wind too big, therefore competition change time-A

   Because the wind was too strong, the competition was therefore postponed

A point worth making is that the English translation of (9) seems marked. To make the English translation mirror more accurately the meaning of the Chinese sentence, the clause order of the Chinese needs to be changed to give: "The competition was postponed because the wind was too strong." The Chinese version follows natural, logical order. The English prefers to follow an order in which the salient or more important message is placed first. As we have pointed out earlier, this means that the clause sequence in the *unmarked* Chinese version is the same as the clause sequence in the *marked* English version. Similarly, of course, the *unmarked* English sequence of main clause to subordinate clause becomes the *marked* Chinese sequence. As we shall show, the marked Chinese sequence has become increasingly common through the influence on Chinese from Western languages.

Ni Baoyuan agrees that the normal clause order in complex sentences is subordinate clause-main clause (77). He points out, furthermore, that this is relatively rigid. He extends the analysis of marked and unmarked order to include Subject-Predicate order, Verb-Object order Modifier-Modified order.

Ni states that these sequences are the unmarked, normal orders. Conversely, therefore, *marked* order in Chinese is:

- Predicate-Subject
- Object-Verb
- Modified-Modifier
- Main Clause-Subordinate Clause.

Li and Zhang also argue that the sequences identified above by Ni are the unmarked and marked orders respectively. They suggest that the marked order is used to give emphasis or prominence. As an example of marked predicate-subject order they give (10), a sentence taken from the twentieth-century writer, Lu Xun (77):

10. *Qu ba ye cao,   lian-zhe wo-de tici*

    Go P wild grass, join-A I-M   foreword.

    Go, wild grass, together with my foreword.

The authors suggest that the moving of the predicate (*qu ba*) to the front of the subject emphasises Lu Xun's hope for the swift decay of the "wild grass," a hope he has also expressed a few lines earlier in the foreword.

In addition to providing emphasis, Li and Zhang also suggest that a marked order can be used to prevent the sentence becoming too "sluggish" (*tuota*). This is particularly the case when the modifier is very long. Then the normal unmarked sequence of modifier-modified becomes inelegant. (11) is an example of a sentence that uses the marked order of modified-modifier. The modified (the animal) is in bold and is followed by the modifying phrases.

11. *Dazhi yikan, wuzi-li haishi kong xu*

    Roughly once look, room-in still empty,

    Dan ouran kandao dimian, que panxuan-zhe yi-pi xiao xiao-de dongwu

    But by chance look to floor but circle-A one-CL small small-M animal

115

Shouruo-de, bansi-de, manshen chentu-de ....

Weak, half dead, whole body dust

With his quick first look, the room still seemed empty, but, by chance he looked at the floor, where, going round and round, was a tiny animal, thin and weak, half dead and covered with dust....

Li and Zhang, therefore, suggest that this marked order of modified-modifier is used for two reasons, to emphasise the modifying phrases and to provide stylistic elegance.

Li and Zhang also consider clause ordering in complex sentences and give two reasons for using the marked main clause-subordinate clause order. The first is for emphasis, to provide prominence for the end placed subordinate clause.

12. *Zhe budan shi sha hai, jianzhi shi nuesha*

This not only be murder, simply be cruel murder,

Yinwei gunbang-de shanghen

because cudgel-M scar.

This is not just murder but murder of great cruelty because of the scars made by the cudgel

The marked order here, as the authors point out, stresses the evidence of the scars.

The second reason Li and Zhang give for using the marked MC-SC order is that the subordinate clause is fulfilling an explanatory function. By this they mean that the marked subordinate clause provides additional information for the justification for the proposition or event in the main clause. For example:

13. *yizhing ji aishang-de shengyin cong ta-de kou-li fachulai-le*

a very distressed-M sound from her-M mouth-in emitted

dixi erqie duanxu

low and intermittent

du you Dao Caoren tingdechu, yinwei ta tingguan-le ye

only Dao Caoren hear-R, because he, hear accustomed-A night-in

jian-de yiqie

everything

A very distressed sound emitted from her mouth. It was both low and intermittent and only Dao Caoren[17] heard it, because he was used to listening for anything at night.

In (13) the subordinate clause beginning *yinwei* (because) explains how Dao Caoren, and no one else, was able to hear the sound.

To sum up, Chinese linguists have given three reasons for using the marked MC-SC sequence: to give the subordinate clause prominence; for the subordinate clause to provide some additional information to justify the proposition or event in the main clause (the so called explanatory function); and for stylistic reasons.

There are circumstances, however, where using the marked MC-SC sequence is not possible. This is particularly the case when there are no conjunctions or logical connectors in the sentence. Lin Yuwen gives (14) as an example of a conditional *pianzheng fuju*.

14. *shei gezi gao,   shei pai diyi*

Who stature tall, who line up first

Whoever is the tallest stand at the end of the line.

The clause order here is fixed with the *pian* clause *shei gezi gao* having to come before the *zheng* clause. The reverse sequence *shei pai di yi, shei gezi gao* is impossible. The clause order is fixed because there are no logical connectors to show the reader what the logical relations between the two parts of the sentence are. The clauses must therefore follow the unmarked SC-MC order and argument for the reader to be able to interpret the sentence correctly. This reminds us of Tai's principles of temporal sequence and that unmarked Chinese follows natural, chronological or logical order. It also explains why, when following the unmarked order, connectors are not needed to signal the relationship or argument between the clauses, as this is understood.

The classification of these clauses as subordinate and main is problematic, however, as both appear to be of equal weight. We now turn to a brief discussion of parataxis and hypotaxis.

PARATAXIS AND HYPOTAXIS

The distinction between parataxis and hypotaxis is a distinction commonly made in any discussion on clause combining. There appears to be, however, some disagreement over the meaning of these terms in English. There is, in addition, a problem over the translation of these terms into Chinese, as the Chinese understanding of parataxis (*yihefa*) and hypotaxis (*xinghefa*) does not precisely parallel Western definitions of these terms.

A source of disagreement over the definitions of these two terms by Western linguists stems from the importance attached to the use or non use of conjunctions as a criterion for distinguishing between parataxis and hypotaxis. On the one hand, Crystal defines parataxis as a term that refers to "constructions which are linked solely through juxtaposition and punctuation/intonation and not through the use of conjunctions. Paratactic constructions are opposed to hypotactic ones where conjunctions are used" (221). Crystal clearly distinguishes paratactic and hypotactic constructions on the grounds of conjunction use. Lehmann, on the other hand, claims that the presence or absence of conjunctions has nothing to do with the distinction between hypotaxis and parataxis. Parataxis is defined by Lehmann as the coordination of clauses. It may be syndetic or asyndetic, by which he means the coordination may be explicitly signalled by the use of conjunctions or may not be so signalled. In contrast, hypotaxis is defined as the subordination of clauses and "the presence or absence of a connective device between two clauses has nothing to do with parataxis vs hypotaxis" (210). Lehmann, then, distinguishes paratactic constructions and hypotactic ones on the grounds of coordination or subordination while Crystal sees conjunction use as the determining factor.

Halliday defines parataxis as the "linking of elements of equal status" and hypotaxis as the "binding of elements of unequal status" (198). The use of the terms "equal status" and "unequal status" shows that Halliday agrees with Lehmann's coordinate vs. subordinate distinction. However, Halliday also uses the two different terms of "linking" and "binding" and this suggests that the way the elements of equal status are linked differs from the way the elements of unequal status are bound. In his discussion of "enhancing hypotaxis," which is the term he gives to those constructions that traditionally contain adverbial clauses and are thus similar to the constructions being considered in this chapter, he says that finite enhancing hypotactic clauses are introduced by a hypotactic (subordinating) conjunction, where the conjunction serves to express both the dependency and the circumstantial relationship. Indeed, the role of the conjunction is crucial here, as, according to Halliday, a finite clause is, in principle, independent, and can become dependent "only if introduced by a binding (hypotactic) conjunction" (216–17). Halliday argues, therefore, that the coordinate vs. subordinate distinction determines the difference between parataxis and hypotaxis. But he also stresses the importance of conjunctions in "enhancing hypotactic" constructions.

Curme's *A Grammar of the English Language. Volume II: Syntax* of 1931 helps put the parataxis vs hypotaxis debate in historical perspective. Curme points out that sometimes there is no apparent formal link that binds the elements of a sentence together since the logical connection forms a sufficient tie. Yet, one of the propositions often stands in some relation to the other, such as an adverbial relation of cause, purpose, result, concession or condition. For example, sentences such as, "Let him talk (concession), it'll do no harm," represent an older order of things. In the earliest stages of the languages from which Indo-European languages have come there were no subordinating conjunctions. The placing of a subordinate proposition alongside a principal proposition without a formal sign of subordination, was, Curme suggested, parataxis. He goes on to say that the development of a formal way of signalling subordination, either through relative pronouns or through conjunctions—hypotaxis —is "characteristic of a later stage of language life" (170). Curme, then, argues that parataxis can be seen as the juxtaposition of a subordinate proposition against a main proposition without the use of conjunctions. In other words, therefore, Curme is suggesting that it is, in the first instance, conjunction use, and not the coordinate vs. subordinate distinction, that determines hypotactic constructions.

This is interesting as the Chinese translation of these terms—*yihefa* (method of combination by meaning) for parataxis and *xinghefa* (method of combination by form) for hypotaxis—seem close to Curme's and Crystal's definitions. Furthermore, there is evidence that the person who is credited with coining the word *yihefa*, Wang Li, had read Curme. The *A Dictionary of Chinese Grammar and Rhetoric* defines the term *yihefa* as follows, "a complex sentence that has no connectors between the separate clauses but whose combination is established by a meaning relation and when this relation can be understood, is paratactic" (Zhang Dihua 482).

In this discussion, therefore, we will adopt the historical or Chinese view and take parataxis to mean the juxtaposition of clauses and propositions, both coordinate and subordinate, without the use of connectors; we will take hypotaxis to mean the subordination of one proposition to another by use of subordinating conjunctions. With this in mind, we now proceed to a discussion of parataxis and hypotaxis in MSC.

IS CHINESE PARATACTIC? THE CASE IN CLASSICAL CHINESE

Although Classical Chinese was paratactic, it was not exclusively so, and nor is it the case that the use of connectors was unknown. Compound sentences made up of coordinate clauses allowed freedom of clause movement without affecting the meaning. In *pianzheng fuju*, on the other hand, the clause order was much more rigid and followed the subordinate clause-main clause sequence. The meaning of these sentences was primarily established by the relationship between the two clauses with the clause carrying the main point coming at the end. Connectors, however, could be used. Example (15) shows the use of the therefore marker *gu* being used in the main clause of a classical cause-effect *pianzheng fuju* taken from the *Analects*.

15. *Qi yan bu rang,*   *shi **gu** shen zhi*

    This language N modest,   be therefore laugh him

    His language was very boastful and so I laughed at him.

On occasion, paired connectors could be used in both clauses. This was particularly true of conditional sentences such as (16). This use of paired connectors provides stylistic balance or *qian hou huying*, literally "front-back echo" (Ma Zhong 234). This stylistic preference explains why Chinese writers tend to use both pairs of connectors in complex clauses. The connectors are underlined.

16. <u>Ruo</u> fu yu,   <u>ze</u> qing chu zhi

    If N bestow,   then request eliminate him

    If you do not mean to give it to him, allow me eliminate him.

These examples show that, with its use of connectors, contemporary Chinese has not taken on a completely new grammatical structure. Furthermore, they show that the use of the marked MC-SC clause sequence in *pianzheng fuju* was, although rare, possible. MSC has, however, seen a substantial increase in use of these structures, primarily through influence from Western languages.

MSC AND INFLUENCE FROM THE WEST

Possibly the best known Chinese linguist of the twentieth century, Wang Li, argues that, traditionally, word order in Chinese was fixed (Chen, Shou-yi). In particular, in Chinese conditional, concessive and cause and effect sentences, the subordinate clause traditionally came before the main clause. In English, on the other hand, Wang Li points out that the so-called "if" clauses, the "because" clauses, the "though" clauses and the "when" clauses can go before or after the main clause. In Chinese, as we have seen, these clauses most frequently precede the main clause; and on occasion, must precede them.

Wang Li then argues that this comparatively rigid SC-MC clause order of Chinese means that connectors are not really necessary. In a crucially important insight into principles of rhetorical organisation in Chinese, Wang Li points out that, in Chinese, when two sentences are juxtaposed, even though there are no connectors, "we still know that the first sentence includes meanings such as 'although,' 'if,' 'because,' etc., because the subordinate component must come at the beginning" (97).

Wang Li also makes clear that, while it is a more paratactic language than English, Chinese has been influenced by English and other Western languages, especially since the Chinese literary revolution of the May 4th Movement in 1919. As we explain in more detail in Chapter 8, at this time enormous numbers of Western works were being translated into Chinese and published in China. Not only did this provide large numbers of influential works written in a kind of Europeanised Chinese, but their influence was also seen in the styles of contemporary Chinese writers. For example, since the May 4th movement of 1919, subordinate clauses appearing after their main clauses in the writings of Chinese authors have become frequent. Wang Li gives this example from the contemporary Chinese writer, Lao She, of a marked subordinate clause order in a conditional sentence. (372)

17. keshi wo dei sheng xie qian,   wan yi mama jiao
    wo qu

> But I must save some money,   10,000 one mother tell me go
>
> wo keyi pao jiaru wo shou-zhong you qian
>
> I can run if I hand-in have money
>
> But I must keep some money on the off chance that Mum tells me to go. I can run if 1 I have some money.

Here, the conditional clause introduced by *jiaru* (if) comes after the main clause. Note the use of the conjunction in the marked subordinate clause and the absence of one in the main clause. This use of a single conjunction in the subordinating clause in complex sentences that follow the marked MC-SC sequence, and without a "balancing" conjunction in the main clause, is representative of this "new" Westernised phenomenon of Chinese hypotactic constructions. Nevertheless, while admitting that contemporary Chinese uses more connectors than did classical Chinese, Wang Li argues that contemporary Chinese is still a far more paratactic language than English. It is his view that parataxis is abnormal or marked (*biantai*) in Western languages but normal and unmarked (*changtai*) in Chinese.

Xie Yaoji (7) agrees with Wang Li that it is Western linguistic influence, primarily the influence of the translation into Chinese of Western works, that has increased the use of the marked MC-SC clause order in modern Chinese. This, in turn, has given rise to the increased use of connectors as they are obligatory in such marked MC-SC clauses ordering, where they signal the subordinate clause. Xie gives a whole host of examples taken from Chinese writing after 1919 to demonstrate the recent use of conjunctions.

Gunn has suggested that although clause transposition (anastrophe) would have appeared strikingly new in Chinese in print in the 1920s, and although it was undoubtedly inspired by foreign language texts "the forms themselves probably existed in spoken Chinese already" (40). The point was made earlier that this structure was also possible in classical (written) Chinese.

The notion of a relatively rigid word or clause order in Chinese is further discussed by Chen Ping. He argues that, when there are no explicit conjunctions in Reason, Concession and Condition Predicates, an "adjunct preceding nucleus" (183) order is crucial for a clear indication of nucleus (main) vs. adjunct (subordinate) status of the propositions subsumed within the relational predicate. On the other hand, however, when connectives are present, the order is less rigid. In other words, then, paratactic constructions in complex sentences in Chinese will follow the subordinate -main clause order. The use of a subordinating conjunction allows the use of the marked MC-SC clause order. The use of at least one conjunction is *obligatory* in Chinese when the marked or "illogical" order is used in complex sentences.

In the next chapter, we turn to considering rhetorical organisation at the level of discourse and the extent to which the principles of sequencing identified and illustrated in this chapter also operate at the discourse and text level.

7 PRINCIPLES OF SEQUENCING AND RHETORICAL ORGANISATION: DISCOURSE AND TEXT

In this chapter we consider whether the principles of rhetorical organisation we have identified so far also operate at the levels of discourse and text. We first discuss some data collected by Young (*Crosstalk*; "Unraveling"), as these provide nice examples of the use of Chinese frame-main sequencing at the level of discourse and which is consequently misinterpreted by an American speaker, leading to a breakdown in communication. We then consider and analyse three examples of extended Chinese discourse and text.

Young relies primarily, but not exclusively, on data gained by recording Chinese speakers engaged in discussions in English and often in role play situations. She makes several judgements about the characteristics of Chinese discourse based on the data. She suggests that the use of the pair of connectors "because" and "so," that occur frequently in the data, appears to play an important role in discourse sequencing management. They signal, Young suggests, the topic-comment relationship working at the level of discourse. "Connective pairs such as 'because/as' and 'so/therefore' signal a topic-comment relationship between the ideas or events that they tie together" ("Unraveling" 161). She also suggests that these two connectors operate the whole-part principle. However, in arguing that "because" and "so" signal transition in the phases of argument she says: "The choice of 'because/as' to mark the introduction of one's case and 'so/therefore' to indicate a shift to the main point are examples of such transition markers" (150).

Here again topic is being used to describe two different concepts. On the one hand, the "because" connector is said to signal a topic and the whole, while the "so" connector is said to signal the comment and the part. On other hand, the "because" connector is said to signal the introduction of one's case and the "so" marker signals the transition to the main point. In other words, the "because" connector is claimed to be signalling these three items: the topic; the whole of a whole-part relationship; and the introduction of one's case. We have seen earlier that the whole of a whole-part relationship can be classified as topic (see example [5] in the previous chapter). But it seems that the "because" connector that signals the introduction to one's case can only be signalling a topic, if topic is defined as something that sets the framework in which the rest of the sentence is presented. We propose, therefore, that the "because" connector that introduces one's case is not signalling a topic but is signalling modifying or subordinate information from which the proposition in the principal clause can be understood, signalled by the "so" connector. In other words, it is signaling what we have earlier called a "frame-main" sequence.

We now consider some of Young's data and examine whether the "because" markers are indeed signalling topics or whether they are signalling subordinate information; and whether the "so" markers are signalling comments or a transition to the main point. Is the sequence one of subordinate/modifier to main/modified rather than one of topic-comment? The data here "comes from an audiotaped role play enacted in Hong Kong as part of a classroom discussion among members of Hong Kong's police force" (190ff). There are five participants in the role play, one of whom is a white male, a guest speaker to the classroom from the United States. He plays a member of the public. The police, working in pairs, have the task of stopping the American from approaching and going into his office because there has just been a fire in the building. Below are some excerpts.

1(a).   American: What's the matter? This is my office.

Chinese: Oh, because this on fire and this area is closed.

1(b).   American: Well, can you—can you call the other officer? You call the other officer and tell him that I have to get into my office. Can you do that?

Chinese: I'm afraid I can't do it. I'm afraid....

Chinese: Or... or we suggest you uh.... Because it is by the court order closed it, Close it by court order.

1(c).   American: But uh I have to find out what happened to my office. Uh, I—I've got to get in there.

Chinese: Uh, I'm sorry uh because this cl—this building is closed by court order uh I can't help you.

1(d). American: But why... why can't... I just want to go into my office. I have some important papers there.

Chinese: I'm sorry. Because the building is in a dangerous

American: Well...

Chinese: Nobody allowed to enter the building.

In her analysis of the data, Young suggests that the Chinese police officers are transferring their native discourse patterns into English. While this is certainly true, it is hard to argue that the utterances of the Chinese police are following a topic-comment structure when topic is defined as what the sentence is about. What all these "because" initial clauses are doing is setting a framework within which to present the main point the sentence or the principal clause of the sentence. Each of these "because" sentences provides information that will help to explain the information in the principal clause. The information presented by the Chinese police follows, therefore, a sequence that moves from subordinate to main or from frame to main. Thus they follow the principles of logical or natural rhetorical organisation identified earlier. What appears to be confusing the American is that he is expecting the information to follow a sequence which he is more familiar with in this context and which would be from main to subordinate. He is expecting a salient order in which the main or most important part of the message is presented first. In other words, the American might have been more prepared to accept what the police were saying had they sequenced their information in the following way, where the "because" clauses is placed after the main clause:

Chinese: This area is closed because there has been a fire

Chinese: (You can't go in I'm afraid) because the building is closed by court order.

Chinese: I'm sorry I can't help you because this building is closed by court order.

Chinese: I'm sorry, nobody is allowed to enter the building because the building is in a dangerous condition.

So, while we agree with Young's analysis of this interaction that the Chinese police are transferring their native discourse patterns to English, it is suggested that these discourse patterns are *not* those of topic-comment. Rather the discourse pattern being followed adheres to a subordinate /frame-main or modifying-modified information sequence. This "frame-main" or "because-therefore" sequence adheres to the fundamental principle of logical and natural sequencing in Chinese. We now demonstrate this with examples taken from naturally occurring Chinese discourse and text.

The three pieces of data to be analysed represent one relatively informal occasion (a university seminar) a more formal occasion (a press conference given by the Chinese Ministry of Foreign Affairs)[18] and a text from the author Lu Xun. The first example comes from the question and answer session which took place after the speaker had given a seminar at a well-known Australian university. The speaker would have not known what sort of questions he would be asked and had no time to plan his answers. This then represents an informal unplanned occasion. We include this, however, as the rhetorical organisation of the discourse follows the principles we have identified, even though it is informal and unplanned. The second piece of data is taken from a Foreign Affairs press conference. While this text was delivered orally, it was planned and pre-written. It is thus a written text delivered orally in a relatively formal setting. The third example comes from an essay written by possibly the most famous Chinese writer of the early twentieth century, Lu Xun.

THE UNIVERSITY SEMINAR

This was delivered in Modern Standard Chinese by a native speaker from Mainland China, and was entitled "The Peking Student Movement of 1989. A Bystander's View." The talk was attended by some thirty people. Although some of those who attended were not native Chinese speakers, all present were able to speak MSC and the entire proceedings—the talk and the question and answer session that followed it—were conducted in MSC. As indicated above, the atmosphere was informal. The speaker was not acting in any official capacity and was certainly not there to give the official line of the events of June 4th (the Tiananmen Massacre). Furthermore, the speaker had personal friends in the audience. Although a long time resident of Beijing, the speaker was living in Australia at the time of the seminar in Australia and has an Australian wife.

We here analyse the question and answer session rather than the talk itself, as the question and answer session was spontaneous in the sense that the speaker had no foreknowledge of any of the questions that he was asked. The speaker's answers therefore provided good examples of unplanned spontaneous spoken discourse. As explained earlier, we include this because, despite its spontaneous and informal nature, it still follows the fundamental principles of rhetorical organisation.

The first extract is taken from the speaker's answer to a question asking whether the Chinese students welcomed foreign participation in the Chinese student movement. This has been chosen because it shows a "because-therefore" sequence operating at sentence level. But as we shall see in the analysis of a second extract taken from this answer, this sentence level "because-therefore" sequence can itself be part of a piece of discourse whose overall sequence is also "because-therefore," or what we are calling the "frame-main" pattern. The first excerpt occurs thirteen lines into the answer dealing with foreign involvement in the June 4th "incident." In the previous twelve lines, the speaker has pointed out that some students were in favour of foreign involvement and that others were against it. He has raised the legal question but has also said that the law is a "fascist" one. He then says:

2. because (*yinwei*) we haven't faced this question, I and my wife both have Beijing residence permits, therefore (*suoyi*) I haven't more thoroughly investigated this problem.

The speaker explains that he has not thought very much about the question of foreign participation in the student movement because he and his wife are not foreigners. (Actually his wife is an Australian but, as he explains, she has a Beijing residence permit, so, for the purposes of the question presumably doesn't count as a foreigner). Note that "I and my wife both have Beijing residence permits" is itself a reason for why they have not faced the question of foreign participation. The *suoyi* is linking with the *yinwei* in line one of the example and is separated from it by the secondary reason. This shows that *suoyi* can refer back to reasons separated from it by other information. As we shall show, *suoyi* often operates as a discourse marker across lengthy texts. Note also that the information sequence follows the "because-therefore" sequence, and that the subordinate-main clause sequence is operating here at a level above the clause. This information sequence, with its overt and covert discourse markers, can be represented as:

Sequence	Connectors
Reason	*yinwei*
Reason for reason	no overt marker
Therefore	*suoyi*

Chapter 7

The second extract, (3), comes from this same answer. It demonstrates a more complex information sequence that includes what we call a "pregnant" "because-therefore" unit, which incorporates, among others, a concessional structure and lower level "because-therefore" structures. Where connectors in the translation are placed in brackets, it signifies that they are not present in the Chinese.

> 3. but because I N meet this question, although I-M, wife be Australia person, but she then in China have, Beijing permit, therefore she can-P for example even with parade troops walk one walk, because she have Beijing citizen status this we N enter one step discuss I N way again deep reply sorry-A.
>
> but because I haven't come across this question, (because) although my wife is Australian she had in China at the time a Beijing residence permit therefore she might for example even walk with the parading marchers because she has Beijing citizen status (so) we haven't further discussed this (so) I have no way in replying in any more depth, sorry.

The pregnant "because-therefore" unit starts with the "because" (*yinwei*), in line 1. The "this question" that the speaker mentions is the original question concerning foreign participation in the Chinese student movement. The "therefore" part of this "because" is not stated until later. That is to say, *because* the speaker and his wife haven't come across the question, (so) they haven't discussed it, and (so) the speaker cannot give an in-depth reply to the question. The reader will notice that there are no overt connectors introducing the "therefore" part of the discourse unit. The translation provides (so) in brackets.

Within this pregnant "because-therefore" unit lie:
> (i) a concessional although (*suiran*)-but (*danshi*), construction. This follows the normal unmarked sequence of subordinate clause-main clause. The pair of connectors, *suiran* and *danshi* are both present.
>
> (ii) The therefore (*suoyi*) represents the "therefore" part of a "because-therefore" sentence level construction. The *yinwei*, which could be placed either before or after the *suiran*, is not present. We have inserted (because) in the English translation. Notice how the "because" is restated later. The marked MC-SC sequence is used here as the speaker is emphasising the importance of his wife's Beijing residence status and citizenship.

(iii) a "for example" clause that is in parenthesis within the *suoyi* clause

These few lines of data provide a complex rhetorical structure and sequence that is presented as Figure 1, below.

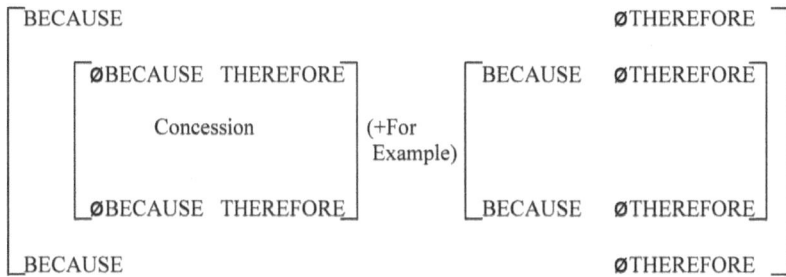

Figure 1. Complex rhetorical structure and sequence.

What this shows is that the discourse "because-therefore" or "frame-main" sequence can include within it, at lower levels of textual hierarchy, a complex of other propositions, among which can be lower level "because-therefore" relations. That is to say, the sequence can be realised at any level and that the lower level units can lie within the pregnant unit. Figure 1 also shows that (3) is characterised by what we shall call enveloping. This provides a clue that the answer is unplanned as enveloping often signals spontaneous speech. Enveloping is common in speech where a speaker's turn is determined only immediately prior to his turn, and the speech is, therefore, unplanned. Sacks, et al., also state a significant corollary of this, which is that a planned or pre- allocated turn will contain a "multiplication of sentence units" (Sacks, Schegloff, and Jefferson 730). Data from the more formal press conference should therefore provide more examples of coordinate structures with relatively few overt connectors.

"BECAUSE" CONNECTOR YINWEI AS A DISCOURSE MARKER

The "because" connector *yinwei* can act as a discourse marker. In (4) below, another example taken from the university seminar, the "because" connector controls a series of reasons that precede the "so" summary statement. Here, the speaker is answering the question "Why are you a bystander and not a playmaker?" The speaker initially responds by laughing and saying that, "this is a very good question." It is possible that he feels a little defensive about this as it would have been possible to infer that the questioner is disapproving of the speaker's role of mere bystander. As a result, the speaker feels that he is being called upon to justify his role.

He then says that there are, "two reasons..., two points, the first:":

> 4. because-P, I-P at middle school period-P, be at that, China also good world also good-P, then little red guards source-M in growing up-M students, I then read middle school-M time already then see-EXP armed struggle also participate-EXP small scale-M armed struggle, I also that time already also in rifle in tank under live-EXP, I have-EXP that kind one-M life experience, I perhaps NOM some things special some things see-R-trivial-P little, this one ques(tion)

> (the first point,)

> because, at the time I was at middle school, China was fine, the world was fine, the little red guards started, and students growing up, when I was at middle school I had already seen armed struggle and had taken part in small scale armed struggle, and also at that time I had lived with guns and tanks, I have had that experience of life, (so) I possibly trivialize things a little, that's one question.

In answer to the question of why he is a bystander and not a playmaker, the speaker says that there are two points to bear in mind. Example (4) gives his account of the first point which consists of a series of reasons why the speaker tends to trivialise things (and thus is content to be a bystander at the current time rather than a playmaker). The "because" connector *yinwei* controls a whole series of reasons. There is no overt discourse marker here that signals the start of the summary "so" statement. The rhetorical structure and sequence of (4) can therefore be represented as follows:

Because n (where n means any number of reasons)

Therefore

Having stated the first reason for why he is a bystander and not a playmaker, the speaker goes on to provide the second reason. His basic point is that he did not say that he was going to tell all in his talk, the inference being that he perhaps did play some active role, although he did not mention it in his talk. Having said this he comments:

> 5. therefore-P (*suoyi*) this question who knows I myself and other people-M one one question, thus (*yinci*) I N participate this these student movement-M any protest activity
>
> therefore this question, who knows, is a question for myself and other people, (and) so I didn't take part in this, in any of these student protest movements....

In (5) the speaker first provides the summary statement for his second reason for being a bystander. This is signalled by the use of the therefore marker *suoyi*. He then goes on to provide the summary statement of his entire answer to the question "Why are you a bystander and not a playmaker?" This, in turn, is signalled by another therefore marker *yinci*.

What this shows is a recursive information sequencing pattern of "because-therefore" occurring throughout the answer. This also prefaces the final summary "therefore." The speaker, in attempting to justify his role as a mere bystander, uses the "because-therefore" sequence at several levels of hierarchy, thus following a justification for statement-statement pattern in the form of a "frame-main" sequence.

"THEREFORE" CONNECTOR SUOYI AS A SIGNALLER OF A SUMMARY STATEMENT

The use of discourse marker "therefore" to signal the summary statement of an entire piece of discourse rather than the immediately preceding argument(s) can also be seen in (6) and (7) below. For (6), the speaker has been answering a question concerning the power of dialogue in the present situation in China. The questioner wants to know whether the speaker thinks that dialogue has a chance of success in the Chinese political climate of the time. In a long answer running to more than thirty lines of tapescript, the speaker cites several reasons why he thinks that dialogue has little chance of success in China at the moment. The main reason he gives is that, for dialogue to succeed, there has to be a workable balance of power between the parties. He cites several historical examples to back this up. He then ends his answer by saying:

6. now thus (*yinci*) I not think these dialogue can succeed because not exist one equal dialogue-M base is this way

   thus I don't think that these dialogues can succeed because an equal base for dialogue doesn't exist, that's the way it is.

Here, the "therefore" marker *yinci* is signalling the summary statement for the whole answer and its communicative purpose is to let the audience know that the answer is coming to a close. Interestingly, it is coupled with a "because" clause in the marked sequence of main clause-subordinate clause. The speaker has included this final because clause to emphasise the main point of the argument he has been making throughout the answer. He feels the point is of sufficient import to be restated and to be marked in this way. In general, however, the speaker's answer here provides another example of reasons preceding the statement, or of grounds preceding the claim and "frame-main."

The final piece of this seminar data (7) represents the closing words of the speaker's final answer. Here the "therefore" connector *suoyi* is being used to signal the summary statement, not just of the answer that the speaker has been giving, but of the entire session. Remember that the talk was entitled "The Beijing Student Movement of 1989. A Bystander's view."

7. this I therefore (*suoyi*) be bystander, this this say—this way, anybody anybody still have what this, therefore I'm a bystander, all this I've said is (about) this.

   And that's why I'm a bystander. Does anyone have anything else?

That nobody does raise a further question and the chairman of the meeting then calls the meeting to a close, suggests that the audience recognised the speaker's final summary statement for what it was.

This analysis of the university seminar has shown:

(i) that the "because-therefore" sequence is a common way of sequencing information at the level of discourse. This means, for example, that the speaker often precedes a statement or claim with the grounds for that statement or claim and thus follows a rhetorical structure of a "frame-main" sequence;

(ii) that enveloping occurs with unplanned speech and that a "because-therefore" unit can therefore act as a "pregnant" unit containing a number of lower level units;

(iii)   that the connector *yinwei* can function as a discourse marker, where it signals or controls a number of reasons; it need not be lexically marked;
(iv)   that the connector *suoyi* can signal a summary statement. On occasion when performing a summarising function, it need not be lexically marked.

THE TAIWAN AIRLINK PRESS CONFERENCE

The second piece of extended discourse to be analysed comes from a press conference held in Beijing. This data represents a planned piece, as the spokesman reads from a prepared written text before inviting questions from the assembled journalists. The press conference starts with the spokesman welcoming the journalists and then saying that he has several items of news that he wishes to impart before answering their questions. The third item of news concerns a proposed Soviet-Taiwan airlink. This is a topic that had occasioned some speculation (the press conference was held in 1990), and the aim of the spokesman is to quell the speculation by placing on record China's official position. Excerpt (8) below is the translator's version of the statement which was read out by the spokesman.

> 8. My answer to this question is it is our consistent policy that Taiwan is a part of the territory, China, and one of its provinces. We are resolutely opposed to the establishment of official relations or official contacts with Taiwan by countries which have diplomatic relations with China. To start an air service with Taiwan by any foreign air company. Governmental or non-governmental is by no means non-governmental economic and trade relations in an ordinary sense but rather a political issue involving China's sovereignty. **Therefore** consultation with China is a must before such a decision is taken. We hope that the countries will act with prudence on this matter.

These comments follow the by now familiar "because-therefore" and "frame-main" sequence, although, as predicted for planned discourse which follows the unmarked MC-SC sequence, there are no overt "because" markers in the text. Interestingly, in the original Chinese, the spokesman does not use an overt

Chapter 7

"therefore" marker either to signal the overall summary of the statement, only adding this when the interpreter fails to translate the final comment about the need for consultation. The spokesman actually repeats his final comment, adding the therefore marker in the way shown in (9) below.

9. *Bixu dou bixu shixian yu wo shangliang*

Must all must first with me discuss

(The interpreter fails to translate this in the first instance, so the spokesman repeats it, but, tellingly now also adds a "therefore" marker to explicitly signal that this is the conclusion of the statement.)

Suoyi *dou bixu shixian yu wo shangliang*

Therefore all must first with me discuss

Therefore consultation with China is a must before such a decision is taken.

For good measure he then adds:

Xiwang you guan guojia zai zhe shi-shang shenzhong xingshi

Hope have concern country in this matter-on prudent conduct.

We hope that the countries will act with prudence on this matter.

The spokesman's comments follow this rhetorical structure.

Because	therefore
Taiwan is a part of China	oppose others dealing with Taiwan
opening an airlink with Taiwan is political	China must be consulted and people must act prudently

The lack of any "because" or "therefore" discourse markers is evidence that these comments were prepared beforehand. Interestingly, they proved to contain too much information for the interpreter to manage, so the spokesman had to repeat his final point and added an explicit "therefore" in order to underline the argument.

The third example we analyse is taken from Wu Yingtian who provides it as an example of inductive reasoning. Wu (124) defines inductive reasoning as follows:

> The organisation of induction always places the material first, discusses the argument (*liyou*), and then puts forward the conclusion, making the thesis unequivocally clear.

To exemplify inductive reasoning, Wu uses this summary of a contemporary essay by Lu Xun in which he compares Hitler with the Qin emperor, Qin Shihuang (124ff).

> Xitele gen Qin Shihuang bi shi diji-de
>
> Hitler and Qin Shihuang than be low-M
>
> Xitele gen Qin Shihuang bi shi kechi-de
>
> Hitler and Qin Shihuang than be shameful-M
>
> Xitele gen Qin Shihuang bi shi geng duanming-de
>
> Hitler and Qin Shihuang than be even short-lived-M
>
> (er, diji, kechi, duanming shi kebei-de)
>
> (and low, shameful, short-lived is lamentable)
>
> *Suoyi* (Xitele bi Qin Shihuang shi kebei-de)
>
> *Therefore* (Hitler than Qin Shihuang be lamentable-M)
>
> raner Xitele zai Zhongguo-de ganr-men dou wei
>
> but Hitler in China-M follower-PI all for
>
> Xitele shang tai er xinggao cailie

Hitler gain power as happy delirious

Suoyi   Xitele zai Zhongguo-de ganr-men

Therefore, Hitler in China-M followers-Pl

shi gaoxing-de tai zao-le

be happy-R too soon-A

Hitler was of a lower status than Qin Shihuang. He was more shameful and he didn't even live as long as Qin Shihuang. (Now) being of low status, shameful and short lived is tragic and *therefore* Hitler was *a* more tragic figure than Qin Shihuang. Yet Hitler's followers in China were deliriously happy at his accession to power. They were *therefore* happy too soon.

The reasoning here runs that because Hitler is lower, more shameful and short lived (historically) than Qin Shihuang (the first emperor of China), he is therefore more pitiful. But because Hitler's followers in China were deliriously happy when Hitler assumed power, their happiness was therefore premature.

What is of interest here is that the reasons precede the conclusion and the argument follows a "because-therefore" or "frame-main" sequence. We can represent this piece of inductive reasoning in the following way:

<u>Inductive Reasoning</u>

<u>Individual Arguments (*fenlun*)</u>

  Ø BECAUSE 1

  Ø BECAUSE 2

  Ø BECAUSE 3

  Ø BECAUSE 4   THEREFORE

  Ø BECAUSE 5   THEREFORE

This can be summarised as:

Ø BECAUSE 1-4 — THEREFORE

Ø BECAUSE 5 — THEREFORE

This provides a further example of inductive reasoning in contemporary Chinese. The "because-therefore" sequence is followed and its propositional structure is similar to the propositional structures of the discourse and text presented above and in earlier chapters.

The next question is, therefore, whether inductive reasoning is common in Chinese and whether Chinese prefers to use inductive reasoning over deductive reasoning. In Chapter 2, we showed that Chinese traditionally used chain-reasoning and reasoning by analogy and historical precedent in preference to hypothetico-deductive reasoning. We have also seen that the propositional structures of arguments following these methods of reasoning have many similarities to the propositional structures of the examples of extended discourse and text analysed here. The argument here is that chain-reasoning is very similar in its propositional structure to inductive reasoning and we would thus expect Chinese to show a preference for inductive reasoning. As Sivin has pointed out, rational thought can be either inductive or deductive or a combination of both. In contrast to this flexibility, however, we argue that chain-reasoning, by its very nature, can only be inductive. It can never be deductive, using, as it does, a number of examples or pieces of information to establish a generalisation or conclusion. In its preference for chain-reasoning and reasoning by analogy and historical precedent, Chinese exhibits a consonant preference for inductive reasoning.

Before concluding this chapter we want to again stress that this preference for inductive reasoning does not imply that Chinese does not employ other types of reasoning. Indeed, in Chapter 2, we showed that Wang Chong, the Han dynasty scholar, used deductive reasoning when his aim was to make a controversial point and draw the attention of the audience and, in Chapter 3, we showed Chen Kui's support for a deductive sequence.

Wu also provides examples of what he calls *yangui xing*, which is simply a combination of inductive and deductive reasoning. This is interesting and, as we shall see in Chapter 8, Wang (108–9) also provides evidence for this type of combined reasoning in the paragraph organisation of Chinese writers and this confirms the point made by Sivin above concerning the organisation of rational thought. Wu (130) represents this type of reasoning in the following way:

Inductive-Deductive Reasoning (*yangui xing*)

1 General statement (*zonglun*)

2 Individual arguments (*fenlun*)

Conclusion (*jielun*)

In his summing up of methods of reasoning and textual organisation in Chinese, Wu concludes, using a typical "because-therefore" sequence (135), "Because in real life cause precedes effect, therefore to place the reason at the front (of the argument) also accords with logic."

This statement nicely encapsulates the main point we have been making, which is that Chinese prefers to follow this frame-main or because-therefore sequence in a wide range of texts, from the sentence level through complex clauses and to the level of discourse and text. This principle of rhetorical organisation is fundamental to Chinese rhetoric and writing, although it by no means excludes other types of rhetorical organisation.

SUMMARY

The following principles of rhetorical organisation have been identified and illustrated in this chapter.

(i) The "because-therefore" sequence operates at levels of discourse as well as at sentence level. It represents an important sequencing principle in MSC. For example, when MSC speakers are justifying a claim, they commonly posit the reasons for the claim before making it, following a "frame-main" sequence.

(ii) The "because-therefore" sequence can be recursive. This rhetorical structure is more likely to occur in planned speech than in spontaneous speech. Although, in more planned speech, the use of the because and therefore connectors is comparatively uncommon, a therefore connector, either *suoyi* or *yinci* is common, but not obligatory, when its communicative purpose is to signal a summary statement.

This rhetorical structure is represented in the diagram.

BECAUSE x n +THEREFORE x n

THEREFORE.

(iii) In more spontaneous speech, enveloping is likely. When this occurs a "because-therefore" unit can act as a "pregnant" unit and contain a number of lower level units within it. These lower level units can themselves be lower level "because-therefore" units. In more spontaneous speech, where there is enveloping, connectors are more common. This structure is represented in the diagram.

BECAUSE [LOWER LEVEL UNITS] THEREFORE

(iv) The structures in (ii) and (iii) can be used in combination.

(v) In addition to acting as sentence level connectors, both the "because" and the "therefore" connectors can act as discourse markers. They can introduce and control a series so that "because x n" and "therefore x n" are possible sequences.

(vi) The presence of explicit "because" and "therefore" discourse markers is less likely in formal planned speech than in informal and more unplanned discourse.

To date, we have suggested that Chinese traditionally followed a logical or natural order and that this is a fundamental principle of rhetorical organisation in Chinese. This logical order is contrasted with the preference English shows for salient ordering, where the important part of the message is presented early. This principle results in Chinese preferring sequences such as topic-comment, whole-part, big-small, modifier-modified, subordinate–main, and frame-main. We have called these the unmarked or preferred sequences in Chinese. This is not to say, however, that classical Chinese did not allow marked sequences in certain circumstances. A significant increase in the use of marked sequences, such as main–subordinate in modern Chinese is, nevertheless, largely the result of the influence upon Chinese of the rhetorical organisation and clause structure present in Western languages.

We have also argued that the rhetorical "frame-main" structure and sequence which we have identified at the clause, sentence levels also operates at the level of discourse and extended discourse, as illustrated in the examples above. We further propose that this "frame-main" principle of rhetorical organisation also shaped the structure of many of the texts of classical and traditional Chinese which were illustrated in earlier chapters.

In the next chapter, we look at the influence of Western rhetoric and writing on Chinese rhetoric and writing at the turn of the twentieth century and describe the historical context in which this influence developed.

8 THE END OF EMPIRE AND EXTERNAL INFLUENCES

Dear Mr. Chen:

In an earlier essay of yours you strongly advocated the abolition of Confucianism. Concerning this proposal of yours, I think that it is now the only way to save China. But, upon reading it, I have thought of one thing more: if you want to abolish Confucianism, then you must first abolish the Chinese language; if you want to get rid of the average person's childish, uncivilised, obstinate way of thinking, then it is all the more essential that you first abolish the Chinese language. (cited in Ramsey 3)

The letter above was written by Qian Xuantong, a member of the Chinese Language and Literature Department of the then Imperial Peking University (now Beijing University) in the early years of the twentieth century. It was written to a fellow member of the Department, Chen Duxiu, who is better known as one of the founding members of the Chinese Communist party.

While Qian's view that China needed to get rid of, not only Confucianism, but also the Chinese language was doubtless an extreme one, arguments for the replacement of the Chinese script with a phonetic script were common in the early years of the twentieth century. To help explain this it should be remembered that the percentage of Chinese who were literate at the time was low, possibly no more than 5% of the population. However, we must be careful here, as literacy can be defined in different ways. Rawski has suggested that between 30-40% of males were literate in that they could read and write to some extent. However, as Woodside and Elman (532) point out, the new education ministry that had been established in 1908 predicted that it would take until 1917 to make "even 5%" of the population literate, with literacy here being defined as "politically active literacy," "of the type needed to understand constitutions and parliamentary elections." At the same time, many scholars were jealous of their privileged literate status, and were therefore unlikely to encourage an increase in literacy numbers and the government had an interest in "controlling the growth of politically empowering literacy" (Woodside and Elman 531). Yet literacy and mass education were seen to be crucial for modernisation, so there was felt to be an urgent need to consider ways of increasing literacy levels and quickly. A further motivation was provided by Japan, as it had developed into a major power and had developed katakana and hiragana syllabaries, and these were seen to be key in increasing literacy levels in Japan (Li and Lee). Japan's status as a modernised country also explains why so many Chinese intellectuals chose to study in Japan at this time. An added impetus for the reform of the Chinese language was provided by Western missionaries developing alphabetic scripts for minority languages. For example, Samuel Pollard developed a script for the Miao people in 1905. While the primary reason for this was to ensure that the Miao could read the bible, "the new script expanded beyond its religious focus to cover all of Miao life and thought" (Woodside and Elman 538).

The desire to modernise needs to be seen in the context of a China which had been routinely humiliated by Western powers from the second half of the nineteenth century, with China's defeat in Opium Wars perhaps providing the nadir. Some scholars see China's defeat in the first Opium War (1838-1942) as marking the beginning of foreign imperialism (Hsu 246–7) and thus the beginning of China's realisation of the need to modernise in order to be able to withstand and repel the foreign powers that were carving up China's territory. The education system was held largely to blame for China's backwardness. In the early years of the twentieth century, Huang Yanpei pronounced the Qing imperial education system "bankrupt" (Woodside and Elman 525) and felt that only the adoption of Western educational practice could save China. His pro-Western prejudice can be seen from his characterisation of the Western and Chinese systems, as he paints the Western system as white and the Chinese as black. The Western system treated the sexes equally, encouraged individuality and creativity and taught people to do good and serve society. The Qing system segregated the sexes, demanded uniformity and focussed on the self (Woodside and Elman 525).

Although the official date of the reform movement is usually given as 1898, attempts at reform were seen earlier. One of the earliest was the establishment of the Tong Wen Guan in 1862. This is of linguistic significance, as it was a school for interpreters where English and other foreign languages were taught. The concerns about the ability of Chinese to act as a medium of modernisation also fuelled the need for China to learn foreign languages. There was a view that "traditional native literacy education was inadequate in the pursuit of national modernization" (You, *Writing* 6). Many of the Tong Wen Guan's teachers were Western missionaries and so introduced Western methods of learning, textbooks and styles of writing to the classroom. The Tong Wen Guan not only taught languages. It later introduced science subjects for which Western, primarily American, textbooks were also used. In this way, the Tong Wen Guan developed a comprehensive curriculum and at the time of the actual Reform Movement of 1898 became part of the new Imperial Peking University (Lin X. 27). Zhang Zhidong (1837-1909) developed the first curriculum and he attempted to integrate a holistic Confucian knowledge with Western disciplinary specialisations. It is perhaps not surprising to learn that he was the author of the famous saying *"zhongxue weiti, xixue weiyong"* (Lin 9), a phrase which translates as "studying from China for the essence, studying from the West for practical knowledge." This dichotomy between Chinese essence and Western practice became known as the *ti-yong* debate. As we shall show, this debate continues.

Zhang Zhidong's curriculum—modeled on those at the Imperial Tokyo and Kyoto universities—aimed at synthesising Chinese and Western learning. There is some debate about the precise number of disciplines (Lin 19ff) but they included history, Chinese language and literature, philosophy, education, law, political science and psychology. The university also opened a School of Translation (*Yixueguan*) in 1903, based on the Tong Wen Guan, whose aim was to train translators and diplomats and "to introduce Western learning into China" (Lin 27).

The Chinese Language and Literature Department played two major roles. Linguistics was seen as an important ally in justifying and promoting the Western-driven historicism movement on the one hand, and in providing the theoretical basis and practical skills for the reform of the Chinese language on the other. That is to say, one role was associated with history and the other with future reform. Both roles, however, were inspired by an agreed agenda for China's need to reform and both, historicism and the language reform movement, were clearly inspired by Western scholarship. One definition of historicism is:

> the belief that an adequate understanding of the nature of any phenomenon and an adequate assessment of its value are to be gained by considering it in terms of the place it occupied and the role which it played within a process of development (Mandelbaum, cited in Ankersmit 146 ff)

In the Chinese context, historicism thus allowed Chinese history to disavow the past and to break from the Confucian model. The past was now to serve as a *reference* for the past. It was not to serve as the *standard* for the present (Lin X. 90). As such, historicism argued that historical changes were not simply cyclical events in a largely unchanging world. Linguistics' role in this centred around philology, defined as "the textual exegesis and identification of the meaning of ancient words through pronunciation and word parts" (Lin 46). This was important in China's move to change as there was a desire to find primary historical sources that would allow scholars to contextualise Confucianism as a product of a particular time and thus allow for a debate as to its value for contemporary China. This also allowed scholars to question the dominant place given by the Qing court to the Neo-Confucianism of the Song dynasty. Philology was used politically to attack neo-Confucian orthodoxy (Woodside and Elman 553). The importance attached to philology can be seen in that two of the University's Chinese Language and Literature Department's three majors were philology and archaeology, with the third being literature.

The second role linguistics played was in language reform. As we have seen above, one member of the department considered going as far as calling for the abolition of Chinese altogether.

In this chapter we provide the context in which reform—particularly with regard to language and rhetoric—took place and summarise the major contributions to this reform by leading Chinese intellectuals. This is the period when the final dynasty of the Chinese imperial system collapsed and was replaced in 1911 by the new Republic of China. This was the period when, in 1905, the imperial civil service exams were finally abolished. This was the period which saw the famous May 4th Movement of 1919 when thousands demonstrated against the terms of the Versailles Treaty through which Chinese possessions previously held by European powers were handed over to Japan, in direct disregard of China's wishes. This was the period of the New Culture Movement, when many new ideas were circulated and many new authors began to be heard. It was a time of intellectual, political and social ferment.

Not surprisingly, this time of ferment and the importation of ideas caused significant changes. Before considering how Western rhetoric influenced Chinese at this time, however, we provide a brief review of various definitions of Western rhetoric in the same way that we showed, in Chapter 1, how concepts of Chinese rhetoric changed over time. Here we show how the concept of what constitutes "Western" rhetoric has changed and explain why, by the turn of the twentieth century, rhetoric had come to be primarily associated with writing rather than speech in the United States. This is important as it was this "written" view of rhetoric that the Chinese intellectuals who studied in the States at the turn and beginning of the twentieth century came across.

WESTERN DEFINITIONS AND CONCEPTIONS OF RHETORIC

At the 2007 Fuzhou Forum on Rhetoric organised by Liu Yameng at Fujian Normal University, John Gage provided a list containing a selection of conceptions or definitions of rhetoric within the Western tradition starting from Gorgias (425 BCE) through to Wayne Booth. Gage's list (reproduced below) neatly illustrates how these conceptions have changed over the periods. Gorgias was considered the first formulator of the art of rhetoric (Corbett and Connors 490). He devised a system of pleading civil cases in the law courts brought by citizens after the expulsion of the tyrants from Syracuse in 467 BCE. Thus "Western" rhetoric has its origins in the law courts. This gave it specific characteristics: it was primarily oral—although speeches were written and then delivered orally; and the competing participants were equals who were presenting arguments before a judge. These two characteristics—oral and equal –represented significant differences between Western and Chinese rhetoric of the same period.

Gorgias' definition was:

> "The power of using words to persuade, or to affect the condition of the soul by producing belief."

Others in Gage's list are:

> Plato (*Gorgias,* 360 BCE), "Rhetoric is not an art but a knack, a kind of flattery, dangerous because it is useful only to make the worse appear the better."

> Aristotle (*On Rhetoric,* 332 BCE), "Let rhetoric be defined as an ability (faculty) for perceiving the available means of persuasion in each particular case."

> *Rhetorica ad Herennium* (87 BCE), "The art of persuasion, consisting of invention, arrangement, style, memory and delivery."

> Cicero (*De Oratore,* 55 BCE), "The art of effective disputation, as practiced by the good man in speaking."

> Quintilian, (*De Institutione Oratoria,* 93 CE), "The knowledge and ability to speak well, thus forming the basis of the complete education of an ideal statesman."

Augustine *(On Christian Doctrine*, 426 CE), "The art by which the Christian orator acquires, through exercise and habit, skilful use of words and abundance of verbal devises to teach the truth of scriptures."

Boethius (*On Topical Differences*, 510 CE), "The method of argumentation."

Agricola (*Dialectical Invention*, 1480 CE), "The art of inquiry by means of dialectic."

Erasmus (*De Copia*, 1500 CE), "The practice of eloquence; verbal abundance and variety."

Peter Ramus (*Dialectique*, 1555 CE), "Style (figures and tropes) and delivery (voice and gesture), invention and arrangement belong to dialectic)."

Henry Peacham (*Garden of Eloquence*, 1577 CE), "Figures and schemes of verbal ornamentation."

Francis Bacon (*Advancement of Learning*, 1605 CE), "Rhetoric is subservient to the imagination, as Logic is to the understanding; and the duty and office of rhetoric is no other than to apply and recommend the dictates of reason to imagination, in order to excite the appetite and will."

Bernard Lamy (*L'arte De Parler*, 1675 CE), "Speaking so as to affect the passions of the mind."

George Campbell (*The Philosophy of Rhetoric*, 1776 CE), "That art or talent by which discourse is adapted to its end, using all the powers of the mind "to enlighten the understanding, to please the imagination, to move the passions, and to influence the will."

Hugh Blair *(Lectures on Rhetoric and Belles Lettres*, 1783 CE), "The cultivation of good taste to prepare oneself for speaking or composition."

Samuel Taylor Coleridge (*Biographica Literaria*, 1817 CE), "Rhetorical caprices" are at worst inorganic artifice and as such are dissociated from powerful thought and sincere feeling, constituting "the characteristic falsity in the poetic style of the moderns."

Richard Whately (*Elements of Rhetoric*, 1846 CE), "Addressing the Understanding to produce conviction and the will to produce persuasion."

Alexander Bain (*English Composition*, 1866 CE), "Writing instruction, based on the study of stylistic means of provoking and combining associations according to the mental laws uncovered by psychology."

I.A. Richards (*The Philosophy of Rhetoric*, 1935 CE), "Rhetoric is 'the study of misunderstanding and its remedies' through knowledge of the semantic functions of metaphor."

Kenneth Burke (*A Rhetoric of Motives*, 1950 CE), "...rhetoric as such is not rooted in any past condition of human society. It is rooted in an essential function of language itself, a function that is wholly realistic, and is continuously born anew; the use of language as a symbolic means on inducing cooperation in beings that by nature respond to symbols."

Wayne C. Booth (*Modern Dogma and the Rhetoric of Assent*, 1977 CE), "... rhetoric: the art of discovering warrantable beliefs and improving those beliefs in shared discourse. The 'philosophy of good reasons.'"

Of particular relevance is the explicit mention of "writing instruction" in Alexander Bain's definition. Bain was extremely influential in the United States where, at around the beginning of the twentieth century, rhetoric had become associated with written composition. This is the time when Hu Shi and other Chinese intellectuals went to study in the United States.

RHETORIC AND WRITING IN THE UNITED STATES

While at Oxford rhetoric had become more a historical study than one of contemporary practice by the end of the nineteenth century, the situation in the United States was quite different (Corbett and Connors 518). The increasing democratisation of the United States, along with people's increased access to reading and writing as education became more widely available, led to the development of new rhetorics, particularly in the area of writing instruction. Four books which were of great influence were:

- Alexander Bain's 'English Composition and Rhetoric (1866),
- A.S. Hill's 'Principles of Rhetoric (1878),
- John Genung's 'Practical Elements of Rhetoric' (1886), and,
- Barrett Wendell's 'English Composition' (1890).

The major reason why these books were so influential is that they announced a shift from a rhetorical focus on oral discourse to a focus on written discourse (Corbett and Connors 525). It is, for example, Alexander Bain who describes a paragraph as a "collection of sentences with unity of purpose" and the notion that a "topic sentence" is followed by subsidiary sentences that develop or illustrate the main idea, contained in the topic sentence. Coherence is obtained by ensuring that all the sentences in a paragraph are related to those around them and to the topic sentence (Corbett and Connors 527). We shall see this advice reiterated in Chinese textbooks of rhetoric and composition. While Bain was himself not American—he was Professor of Logic and Rhetoric at Aberdeen University in Scotland—his work was stimulated by the need to provide a course in remedial English to cater to the increasing number of Scottish students who had not received a traditional education. This was particularly important in Scotland, as there education was seen as a public and state responsibility and the universities offered a more general education that the traditional education available at Oxford and Cambridge (Ferreira-Buckley and Horner 196). This role was mirrored to a certain extent in the new redbrick universities that sprung up in England at around this time. The relative massification of education led to a need for the teaching of writing (Ferreira-Buckley and Horner 195).

A.S. Hill, Boylston Professor of Rhetoric and Oratory at Harvard developed Bain's ideas and it is Hill all American undergraduate students have to thank for the first year writing requirement. His exasperation at the perceived poor quality of people's writing is strikingly familiar:

> Those of us who have been doomed to read manuscripts written in an examination room—whether at a grammar school, a high school or a college—have found the work of even good scholars disfigured by bad spelling, confusing punctuation, ungrammatical, obscure, ambiguous, or inelegant expressions. Everyone who has had much to do with the graduating classes

of our best colleges has known men who could not write a letter describing their own Commencement without making blunders that would disgrace a boy twelve years old. (cited by Corbett and Connors 529)

The influence of this new rhetoric was not universally appreciated, as it encouraged a universal adoption of principles of composition. Barrett Wendell synthesised these new principles into three main themes:

1. unity (composition should have a central idea);
2. mass (chief components must catch the eye);
3. coherence (relationship between the parts must be unmistakeable).

He later became convinced, however, that the wholesale adoption of these three main principles meant, in his own view, that he had "exerted a more baleful influence upon college education in America than any other man in his profession" (Corbett and Connors 533). Some scholars, most notably Fred Newton Scott, a friend of John Dewey's, argued strongly against the mechanical tendencies of the time and established a PhD course in rhetoric at Michigan in an ultimately unsuccessful attempt to offer a counter to the contemporary style.

One reason for this was the strength of the opposition. In the late eighteenth century, Harvard had shifted from Latin to English as the primary focus of rhetorical instruction and the writing of formal English became the primary concern (Wright and Halloran 221). In the eighteenth century paper also became cheaper and this is when our contemporary notion—heightened immeasurably by the advent of computer technology—of writing "as continuous process of revision" develops (Wright and Halloran 225). Mirroring the increased opportunities for education in Scotland, there was also the need to teach composition to large classes of people, so the old systems of oral recitation and disputation became unworkable. The influence of Francis James Child, A.S. Hill's predecessor as Boylston Professor of Rhetoric and Oratory at Harvard is hard to overestimate as he "held a largely undisguised contempt for rhetoric in both its traditional and more literate forms" (Wright and Halloran 238) and his focus was on correctness, reducing, in the minds of some, including Scott, English studies to composition drudgery. Composition courses of the late nineteenth century became courses in mechanical correctness with writing being constrained within set down formulae and templates. Wright & Halloran ask whether classical rhetoric could not have been adapted to the needs of widening democracy and suggest that it could. In the event, however, it was virtually abandoned "in favour of a socially and politically unaware rhetoric of composition" (240).

It was into this rhetorical environment with its focus on the "correct" way to write a composition that young Chinese scholars, such as Hu Shi, were immersed on their arrival in the United States.

RHETORIC AND WRITING IN CHINA

It is now time to return to the situation in China at the turn of the nineteenth century. We have seen how many of the educated elite felt the creation of a national language was a crucial aspect of nation building (Gunn 1). The notion of language in the Chinese context, especially with regard its written form, needs brief explanation at this point. The literate elite wrote in a stylised form of Chinese known as *wen yan*. This was unintelligible to all but the most highly educated. The "common people" used a form of vernacular called *bai hua*, which had a written form. Indeed the most popular novels of Chinese history, such as *The Dream of the Red Mansions* and *Journey to the West*, owed their great popularity to being written in *bai hua*. However, scholarship—and this included the civil service exams and the eight-legged essays—were written in *wen yan*. So, a major aspect of language reform at this time centred around the use of *wen yan* and how to reform it. There were, of course, many schools of thought on what this new national language should be, of which the Tong Cheng school was perhaps the most famous. The school was named after an area in Anhui Province where the supporters came from, the best known of whom was Yao Nai (1731-1815), and who will be referred to again in the next chapter. The school was characterised by three main features, namely the promotion of the Neo-Confucian doctrine developed during the Song Dynasty and which still held sway in the Qing court, a didactic view of writing and the espousal of the *guwen* writing style (Chow 184). We have discussed the *guwen* style in earlier chapters, but it is important to remember that the name of this style did not imply that its proponents had to adopt a classical style. On the contrary, they promoted a writing style that was clear, unadorned and accessible to contemporaries. This was called *guwen* because this had been the style of classical prose. This was the style promoted by Chen Kui, as we saw in Chapter 3.

Their wish to establish a national form of the language raised, however, contradictions that could not be resolved. One of their members, Wu Rulun, who held a senior position at Imperial Peking University, advocated providing mass education through a form of standardised Mandarin. He was, however, unwilling to abandon *wen yan* (Gunn 32). Wu died in 1903 and, the civil service exams—the great maintainer of *wen yan*—were abolished in 1905. It would be tempting to see the abolition of the civil service exams as a triumph for the reform-minded. While people were happy to see the end of the proscriptive and stultifying eight-legged essays, it was not necessarily because they were against a form of centralised control. Rather, they were happy to see the end of the exams because they felt they were not doing their job in producing scholars of the right (i.e., orthodox) moral stature. Zhang Zhidong himself, the author of the Imperial University's curriculum, was among the number who was critical of the civil service exams for this reason. For such critics, "the abolition of the examinations in 1905 was not a blow struck against the centrality of moral indoctrination in education but an effort to reconfirm it" (Woodside and Elman 552).

Somehow the "new" language had to accommodate the new vocabulary and concepts that were flooding in from aboard. At the time, there were many different groups all advocating different styles but all claiming to serve "the cause of *ti-yong*" (Gunn 37). This is why "all intellectual groups sooner or later gave in to the ready-made compounds invented in Japan to translate Western-language terms" (Gunn 33). It is also why the Tong Cheng school lost favour at Beijing University and its members and followers were replaced in 1914, somewhat ironically, by classical scholars. The reason for the appointment of these classical scholars was, however, that they were supporters of language reform and keen to spread literacy (Lin X. 46). But it was Hu Shi, also a member of the University's Chinese Language and Literature Department who became the most influential. His proposal of adopting *bai hua* as a medium of educated discourse "had the effect of finally dropping the notion of *ti*, of essence, as futile enterprise, in favour of considering first and foremost what was of utility, *yong*" (Gunn 38). And, although the Tong Cheng school lost its influence, Hu Shi felt that it had cleared "the way for the literary revolution whose goal was to teach the Chinese to write simple and unadorned prose" (Chow 205). In this way, Hu Shi credited the Tong Cheng school with an influence it perhaps did not deserve.

As You ("Alienated Voices") has pointed out, Hu Shi was influenced during his five years as Boxer indemnity scholar at Cornell, where he enrolled in 1910. He himself wrote that he was most influenced by John Dewey and Instrumentalism (Pragmatism), so much so that he moved from Cornell to Columbia and completed, in 1917, a PhD "A Study of the Development of the Logical Method in Ancient China" under Dewey's supervision (You). Dewey was also hugely influential among many Chinese intellectuals at the time, many of whom had also studied with him at Columbia. His educational theories were particularly attractive, as they fitted well with historicism, centring as they did around the inevitability of change and the non-existence of any universal or everlasting truth. Dewey spent some two years between 1919-1921 on a lecture tour of China, during which Hu Shi acted as his interpreter (Haffenden 439).

While there is no doubt that Hu Shi's thinking was influenced by his time in America and by educational philosophers such as Dewey, we want to suggest that his ideas for the reform of language—in particular writing and the rhetoric of writing—may also have been influenced by Chinese scholars, not only by people such as Yao Nai of the Tong Cheng school, but possibly also by those of a much earlier period, in particular by Chen Kui of the Southern Song dynasty, whose *"Rules of Writing"* we reviewed in Chapter 3. The historical contexts in which the two men were writing hold some interesting parallels. Both were times of great literary change. The development of printing during the Song period saw the popularisation of reading and education. This rapid expansion of education was not without its critics, among whom was Chu Hsi, the leading Neo-Confucian philosopher of the time. He published his "Rules of Reading" in response to what he saw were the sins of book culture (Cherniack). These sins included the desire to gobble down as many books as possible, speed-reading and superficial reading. He recommended that people read less and more slowly and with greater concentration, one book at a time. His twelfth-century concerns about the growth of the exam culture resonate today. Walton quotes him:

> Scholars must first make a distinction between the two separate things, the examinations and the learning, as which to value as more weighty. If learning occupies 70% of the will, and the examinations 30%, then it is all right. But, if the examinations are 70%, and learning is 30%, then one will surely be defeated (by being focused on external reasons for learning, rather than the self); how much more if the will is entirely set on the examinations! (13).

However, given the extraordinary increase in education and in the number of boys and young men sitting a series of examinations, it is perhaps not surprising that Chen Kui felt the need to write "The Rules of Writing." While we might suspect that he was partly motivated by the same concerns that led Chu Hsi to write "The Rules of Reading," as we argued in Chapter 3, his major motivation was to provide a helpful handbook for students. The book is full of practical hints and advice. By way of recapping, we summarise them as four major principles:

1. Texts should be natural. The words of a text must be suitable to the time, occasion and context. The length of sentences should

be determined by the needs of the content. Clinging blindly to a model must be avoided.
2. Texts should be clear. A text must make its meaning clear.
3. Texts should be succinct and straightforward. Being succinct, texts must also be complete. Being succinct does not imply omitting important information. And while a straightforward approach is to be preferred, at times, the content may require more complex forms of expression.
4. Texts should be written in popular and common language. They should not be difficult to understand, but accessible.

In comparison, below are the eight guidelines Hu Shi penned in the context of promoting the vernacular *bai hua* as the medium of educated discourse:

1. Language must have content
2. Do not (slavishly) imitate classical writers
3. Make sure you pay attention to grammar and structure
4. Do not complain if you are not ill—in other words, don't overdo the emotion
5. Cut out the use of hackneyed clichés
6. Don't cite or rely on the classics
7. Don't use parallelism
8. Embrace popular and vernacular language

The similarity between these four principles and Hu Shi's eight guidelines are remarkable. Chen Kui was also insistent that meaning was more important than form. People should use language that would be easily understood by contemporaries. We do not know whether Hu Shi read Chen Kui. Given the similarity between his eight guidelines and Chen Kui's four principles, however, it is at least possible that Hu Shi and others were influenced by the Chinese rhetorical tradition in the context of adopting the vernacular and a simple, clear style as a medium of educated discourse. We conclude this section of this chapter by suggesting that the U.S. in the nineteenth century also saw an exponential increase in the number of people seeking an education and this, along with technological reform, especially the increasing availability of paper, led to a rhetorical and literary reform represented by the rise in the importance of written rhetoric and composition. Hu Shi and other Chinese intellectuals looking for inspiration for language reform arrived in the United States at this time. They happened upon an America itself undergoing literary reform with the focus upon composition and writing.

We now turn to briefly review the publication of early twentieth-century Chinese texts on language and rhetoric which introduced Western ideas to the Chinese. Probably the best known and certainly the most influential of these texts was Chen Wangdao's *Introduction to Rhetoric (Xiucixue Fafan)* first published in 1932. Chen was one of the many thousands of Chinese students who studied overseas in Japan in the early years of the twentieth century and his book is largely influenced by Japanese sources which were themselves influenced by Western sources (Harbsmeier 119), including Alexander Bain's 1866 *Modes of Discourse* (Wang Chaobo 169). In his discussion of *youdao wen,* or writing that seeks to persuade readers to alter their views, Chen W. (*Xiuci Xue Fafan* 130) argues that the author must observe these seven conditions, some of which seem to echo both Chen Kui and Hu Shi. This suggests that Chen was also himself influenced by both Chinese and Western traditions:

1. Do not use too much abstract language
2. Be tactful, mild and indirect
3. Be serious, but not overly so
4. Do not over-elaborate
5. Make sure your choice of language suits the readers
6. Avoid monotony, use variety
7. Use a light (*qing*) to heavy (*zhong*) sequence

By "light" to "heavy," we argue that Chen means adopt the inductive or "fame-main" sequence, advising that the writer lead the reader to the main point. Chen Wangdao also asserted that an argumentative essay should have three parts: the thesis statement; the proof; and conclusion and be formulated "in concrete and assertive terms" (You, *Writing in the Devil's Tongue* 53).

It will be noted that Chen advises his writers to be "indirect." We return to a discussion of what "indirect" might mean in this context below, but suggest it refers to the Chinese preference for frame-main argument which we proposed earlier.

Chen and his work were very influential, not least because he was director of the Shanghai chapter of the Chinese Communist Party and later became President of one of China's most prestigious universities, Shanghai's Fudan University. That he was appointed to this position in 1952 by Mao himself will naturally have added to his personal and intellectual influence (Wu Hui). Fudan remains a leading centre for the study of rhetoric (Harbsmeier 118).

The early 1920s saw a flood of books on rhetoric written by Chinese who had studied overseas. *Rhetorical Style (Xiuci ge)* was published in 1923 and introduced Anglo-American rhetoric to China. This led Chen Wangdao to call it China's first scientific book on rhetoric (Wu Hui).

This was also a period when other types of writing—in particular creative writing—flourished. The New Culture Movement saw, in addition to translations of Western novels, the publication of many new literary journals and the emergence of many novelists, essayists and poets writing in the vernacular *bai hua*. These included such luminaries as Ba Jin, Lao She, Mao Dun, Bing Xin and Lu Xun, the latter a candidate for the title of the greatest writer never to have won the Nobel Prize.

One recurring question surrounding this period of imperialism and reform is the extent to which the changes were enforced by the West or sought by the Chinese. It would be naïve to argue that imperialism was anything other than the dominating factor in this, but the extent to which Chinese intellectuals actively sought and campaigned for reform should not be overlooked. We have seen, for example, how strongly many Chinese intellectuals felt that the Chinese language had to be reformed, if not abandoned. One quirky example of where this tension between imperialism and reform can be seen is in the introduction of Basic English to China by I.A. Richards. Basic English (BE) was developed by two Cambridge scholars, Ogden and Richards, and was a reduced version of the language containing only 850 words and eighteen verbs. The impetus for its development came from the chaos and tragedy of the First World War, which Richards saw as the consequence of an error "produced by a crucial misunderstanding of language" (Koeneke 14). Ogden and Richards designed BE to be "a logical medium of fostering better understanding between different cultures" (4). Ogden hoped that it would become "an international auxiliary language for the benefit of science and peace" (Haffenden 305).

In 1929, Richards accepted a lectureship at the newly established Tsing Hua University in Beijing. Tsing Hua had, unlike many of the other missionary-run tertiary institutions being founded at the time, a secular curriculum with a focus on science and Western languages. The notion of BE seemed to offer some Chinese scholars, given their antipathy to their own language which we have described earlier, "an ideal solution to their country's problems" (Koeneke 5). Richards undertook several visits to China—the last being as late as 1979—and assiduously promoted the idea of BE. In 1933, he established the Orthological Institute of China, with an American, Jim Jameson, as director (Haffenden 437). The major aim of the Institute was to develop and promote BE. This required, for example, the writing of textbooks in BE and the translation of major works from their original English into BE. Richards had even translated Homer's Iliad into BE. He achieved such success that, in 1937, the Ministry of Education agreed to institute BE throughout the school curriculum. Success was short-lived, however, as the Japanese invaded two months later and brought an end to the BE experiment in Chinese schools.

Was BE an imperialist construct designed to get the Chinese (and others) to think in English and thus think like the English? Churchill thought so, as he viewed BE as a possible tool for disseminating English across the world. Or was it, as Richards himself maintained, "fundamentally anti-imperial" and "multicultural" (Koeneke 9)? Today the answer seems clear—that it was a naïve and ill-conceived product of cultural imperialism—naïve and ill-conceived in that no simplified form of a language has ever been successful in taking on the role of a language of international communication. Neither Ogden nor Richards apparently understood how a whole host of historical, political and socio-cultural factors influence the development of any language. Yet there is no denying that many Chinese intellectuals took BE seriously and saw in it, a possible solution to China's backwardness. BE was seen by many Chinese as a way of "defying the legacy of empire and a step towards Chinese autonomy" (Koeneke 215). Richards remained a "friend" of China until his death. Indeed his final visit in 1979 was at the invitation of the Chinese government itself and was viewed as a "gesture of rapprochement" with the West after the years of the Cultural Revolution and China's period of isolation from the West (Koeneke 8).

In this chapter we have argued that Chinese language reform—and thus contemporary Chinese writing—was influenced both by traditional Chinese rhetoric and by Western—particularly Anglo-American rhetorical styles. We argue, therefore, that the position argued by Kaplan ("Cultural Thought Patterns"), which has been so influential among scholars of contrastive rhetoric, that writers from different cultures necessarily use rhetorical structures which are particular to their culture, is difficult to support.

In concluding this chapter, we consider this further and review two important studies which compare the rhetorical organisation of paragraphs in Chinese and English academic writing. The first is a study of paragraph organisation in English and Chinese academic prose by Wang Chaobo. Rightly insisting that contrastive rhetoric must compare the writing of people who are writing in their first language—it will be remembered that Kaplan and many other contrastive rhetoricians have drawn their conclusions from the writing in *English* of people from different linguistic and cultural backgrounds—Wang analysed the paragraph structures of articles taken from Mainland Chinese and American academic journals. He found that English writers heavily favoured deductive patterns but that Chinese writers were far more diverse, with some showing a preference for deductive patterns, some for inductive patterns, and some for paragraph structures which combined deductive and inductive patterns. He summarised his findings in the following way (108–9):

1. Almost all paragraph types can be found in both English and Chinese writing.

2. The deductive paragraph is predominant in English.
3. The three styles—deductive, inductive and mixed—are evenly split among Chinese writers.

He also argues (110) that reasoning and ideas are developed in one of three ways:

1. claim-elaboration and/or justification (the deductive pattern);
2. reasons/elaboration-generalisation/claim (the inductive pattern);
3. combinations of 1 and 2.

While method 1 is most common in English, both Chinese and English use all three, but Chinese use is more evenly distributed. What this also shows, however, is that both Chinese and English writers use linear patterns of reasoning. There is nothing circular about Chinese reasoning in these texts. The often expressed frustration that Chinese writers writing in English "never get to the point" or that Chinese students rarely place the subject of a sentence first" (You, *Writing in the Devil's Tongue* 72) can perhaps be explained by their relatively frequent use of the inductive pattern through which Chinese writers will present a series of arguments—which may not be explicitly linked—leading to the main point. This pattern, of course, follows the "frame-main" and logical and natural order that we earlier identified as fundamental principles of reasoning and rhetorical organisation in Chinese.

Wang also sought to explain why contemporary Chinese academic writing was more diverse than English academic writing. As he felt that traditional Chinese rhetoric may have influenced the writing of some of the Chinese writers, he analysed a total of fifty paragraphs taken from ten classical argumentative texts. He then compared the percentages of deductive, inductive, mixed and "double-faced" (explained below) paragraphs in the English, Chinese and Classical Chinese texts. The results are shown in the table below, adapted from Wang (179).

Table 8.1

Paragraph type	English	Chinese	Classical Chinese
Deductive	81%	40%	31%
Inductive	7%	24%	40%
Mixed	12%	36%	29%
Double-faced	0.55	10%	12%

Wang defines double-faced paragraphs as those in which "a sentence or group of sentences functions as conclusion to the previous communicative act, but something else to the subsequent one" (98).

The table shows the overwhelming preference for the deductive pattern in English writing and the low use of the inductive pattern. It also shows that both the deductive and inductive patterns are attested not only in modern Chinese but also in Classical Chinese, as, indeed, we have ourselves earlier shown. He concludes that the diversity of use seen in modern Chinese writing can be explained by a combination of Classical Chinese and Western influences, the latter introduced during the reform period of the early twentieth century. Indeed Wang goes as far to say that the Western influence during this period was so great that, "modern Chinese academic writing... has its roots more in the tradition of Western science than in that of classical Chinese learning" (161).

The second study we review is by Yang and Cahill. They analysed the rhetorical organisation of Chinese and American students' expository essays. They studied four different groups of students: two classes of native speakers of English in an American university; one class of Chinese majors at a Chinese university; two classes of Chinese first year English majors at a Chinese university; and two classes of Chinese third year English majors at a Chinese university. They conclude that Chinese students, like the Americans, prefer directness, but that "U.S. students tend to be significantly more direct than Chinese students" (123). They also noted that the more advanced the Chinese EFL writer was, the more direct was their writing.

In this, their study supports the findings of Wang summarised above. To quote again from Yang and Cahill, "Chinese students also prefer directness in text and paragraph organization, but they are significantly less direct than American students" (124). Yang and Cahill, however, also point out that many Chinese classical texts followed a deductive pattern so the use of the deductive pattern in contemporary Chinese academic writing was not simply due to Western influences. As the table above shows, Wang also identified a relatively high percentage of deductively organised paragraphs in Chinese classical texts. And as we showed in earlier chapters, the deductive style has always been an option for Chinese writers. Our argument is that it was traditionally used for particular effect. We would sum this up by reverting to the use of the terms "marked" and "unmarked" and say that the *deductive* style is *unmarked* in *English* but *marked* in *Chinese*. By the same token, the *inductive* style—as often realised by a frame-main sequence—is *unmarked* in *Chinese* but *marked* in *English*.

Yet, as we argued earlier, the sheer volume of translations from Western languages into Chinese influenced Chinese linguistic and rhetorical structures. By 1904, 533 books had been translated into Chinese (Wang Chaobo). Two direct consequences were the introduction of loan words and an increase in sentence length. Other consequences of the Westernisation of Chinese included the Europeanisation of the use of connectives and a corresponding increase in a main clause—subordinate sequence in complex clauses (Xie 75), which also encouraged a tendency towards adopting a deductive style in paragraph and text organisation.

All this linguistic change took place at a time of remarkable and profound political and socio-cultural change. We started this chapter by quoting Chinese scholars who saw the Chinese language as being inadequate for the modernisation of China and who disparaged Chinese education on the one hand and glorified Western education on the other. We end by citing Woodside and Elman who argue that those reformers who saw Western–style schools and education as the basis for modernisation and power were over-simplifying an immensely complex situation. What was actually happening was "one form of educational expansion, oriented towards the reproduction of Confucian values... was (being) displaced by another form of educational expansion based—haltingly—on the production of new kinds of knowledge..." (554–5). The language and ways of writing had to change in order to accommodate this new knowledge. But, as we have argued, the Chinese rhetorical tradition was able to provide the foundation for this change.

9 PARTY POLITICS, THE CULTURAL REVOLUTION AND CHARTER 08

In this chapter we shall first briefly discuss the effect the writing of Chairman Mao has on Chinese rhetorical style. Those interested in in-depth treatments of contemporary Chinese political writing are directed to Schoenals' 1992 monograph, *Doing Things with Words in Chinese Politics*. The second part of the chapter will be more anecdotal as the authors will recount their own experiences in learning to write "academic" Chinese. This encompasses the period directly after the Cultural Revolution to the 1980s. Those who are interested in the rhetoric of the Cultural Revolution itself should consult Xing Lu's 2004 study *Rhetoric of the Chinese Cultural Revolution*. The chapter concludes with a rhetorical analysis of recent petitions, including Charter 08, where we consider from where the authors may have drawn their inspiration and influence.

While the texts analysed in this chapter are taken from political, rather than academic, writing, they are all persuasive texts and thus are relevant to argumentative writing. We start by considering examples from Mao's political writing, which was influenced by translations into Chinese of Western writers, most notably translations of Marxist theoreticians, including Engles and Marx themselves. In a break from traditional Chinese writing styles, he wrote long sentences and, as these followed the modifier-modified principle, we tend to get long modifying elements and subordinate clauses preceding the head and main clauses. We previously pointed out that Wang Li had identified the Europeanisation of Chinese caused by translations of Western works into Chinese. One consequence was the Chinese "Europeanised" long sentence (*Zhongguo Yufa Lilun* 281) leading to an increase in sentence length in Chinese. Examples of these long sentences, which also illustrate this modifier-modifying or subordinate-main sequence, are provided by Cheng Zhenqiu (120), where he discusses issues connected with the translation of Mao's work into English.

Example 1 below is the Chinese pinyin version of a Mao passage. Example 1a is the "poor" translation of this passage into English, "poor" in that it follows the original Chinese sequence. It is worth noting at this early stage, therefore, that although the sentence length shows Western influence, the sequencing patterns remain Chinese. Example 1b represents a translation which alters the original Chinese sequence to better conform to the preferred English sequence. The relevant sections of each of these passages are italicised.

> Zai zhe yi nian zhi liang nian nei keneng fasheng liang zhong qingkuang: yi zhong shi women tuanjie duo shu guli shaoshu de shangceng tongzhan zhengci fasheng le xiaoli, xizang qunzhong ye zhujian kaolong women, *yiner shi huai fenzi ji zangjun bu juxing baoluan;* yi zhong....

> 1a. Two things could happen in the next year or two: one is that our united front policy towards the upper stratum, a policy of uniting with the enemy, will take effect and that the Tibetan people will gradually draw closer to us, *so the bad elements and the Tibetan troops will not dare to rebel;* the other....

> 1b. Two things could happen in the next year or two: One is that *the bad elements and the Tibetan troops will not dare to rebel* as our united front policy towards the upper stratum, a policy of uniting with the enemy is taking effect and the Tibetan people are drawing closer to us; the other....

The first of the translations, (1a) follows the Chinese sequence. This follows the unmarked "BECAUSE-THEREFORE" sequence which places the subordinate clause(s) before the main clause. So the English translation (1a) follows the Chinese propositional sequence of "BECAUSE our united front policy is taking effect, THEREFORE the bad elements and the Tibetan rebels will not dare to rebel." Cheng criticises this translation on the grounds that it does not provide the readers with the main point of the argument first, as preferred in English. This is why he recommends altering the order as it occurs in the Chinese and translating the passage as in (1b), where the main point, the fact that the Tibetans won't dare rebel, is placed at the front and thus follows the preferred English placement.

In other words, then, the English translation in (1a) follows the normal Chinese unmarked "because-therefore" sequence. This results in a translation in which the main point of the piece, that the bad elements and the Tibetan rebels will not dare to rebel, gets placed after subordinate detail. For a more effective English translation, the sequence of the propositions as expressed in Chinese needs to be reversed when translated, as in (1b). This ensures that the main point occurs towards the beginning of the piece, its normal unmarked position in English.

A further example of the need to reverse the normal unmarked Chinese "because-therefore" sequence when translating Chinese into English is provided in (2), also taken from Mao's work. The main point, which occurs towards the end in the normal Chinese order, needs to be moved to the front to provide an accurate English translation (2a). The excerpt in the Chinese that has the dotted lines under it is represented in italics in both the pinyin version and the English translation.

> lao zhong nong zhongjian de xia zhong nong, youyu tamen de jingji diwei yuanlai jiu bu fuyu, youxie ze yinwei zai tudi gaige de shihou bu zhengdang de 'shou le yixie qinfan, zhexie ren zai jingji diwei sheng he xin zhong nong zhongjian de xia zhong nong da ti xiang si, *tamen duiyu jiaru hezuoshe yiban de gandao xingqu.*
>
> 2a. *They (the lower-middle peasants) are generally interested in joining the cooperatives,* because in economic status they are more or less similar to the lower-middle peasants among the new middle peasants, as they were not well off to start with and the interests of some were improperly encroached upon at the time of the agrarian reform.

The original Chinese follows the "because-therefore" sequence of:

> "BECAUSE the economic status of the lower-middle peasants was similar to the lower middle peasants among the new middle peasants, ... THEREFORE they are interested in joining the co-operatives."

The English translation follows the opposite sequence, however, and needs to transpose the final part or main point of the Chinese text to the front in order to get the correct balance. For, if an English translation were to follow the original Chinese sequence, as in (2b), it would have the main point at the end and preface it with a great deal of subordinate information. It would read:

> 2b. The lower middle peasants among the old middle peasants, because their economic position was not prosperous, and some (of them) because they suffered oppression at the time of the land reform, (therefore) their economic status was more or less similar to the lower middle peasants among the new middle peasants, (therefore) *they are generally interested in joining the cooperatives.*

This translation follows the clause sequence of the original and clearly shows the unmarked "because-therefore" sequence being followed throughout the text.

This is further evidence that the sequencing principle for complex sentences that we have discussed earlier also operates at a level above the sentence. This may also help explain why people have classified Chinese as being indirect, as this inductive sequence allows the main and salient points to be made towards the end of an extended piece of text, with the subordinate information preceding it, in the ways illustrated in these two examples taken from the writing of Mao. When the texts become long, readers may well feel that they have to wait a long time for the main point while having to process a great deal of subordinate information while waiting.

Mao's use of long sentences of the type illustrated above also made him difficult to read for the Chinese themselves. One reason for the publication of the famous *Little Red Book* was to provide a simplified version of his ideas that could be read and understood by the masses. In the previous chapter, we discussed the question of literacy and pointed out that the estimates for literate people ranged from 5% to as high as 40%, depending on how literacy was defined. While the evidence in the next section of this chapter is anecdotal, Kirkpatrick's experience as a postgraduate student of Chinese literature at the prestigious Fudan University in the years 1976-1977 would suggest that the lower percentage rates were more accurate. In 1982, UNESCO reported that some 32% of the Chinese population was illiterate, although the figures for rural areas were much higher. The problem was recognised by the Chinese government which criticised primary education in rural areas for not providing adequate training even to teach children how to read and write (Seeberg 425). It also needs to be remembered that the period of the Cultural Revolution—which is usually considered to span the ten years from 1966-1976—denied many intellectuals an education while attempting to educate many who were illiterate. This explains why, even at a university as prestigious as Fudan, many of the local students of Chinese literature were illiterate, as they had been recruited from the so-called *gong nong bing* or workers, peasants, and soldiers. This meant that many of Kirkpatrick's fellow students not only had never heard of famous contemporary Chinese writers such as Lao She and Ba Jin—their works had been proscribed by this time—but they were also unable to read or write about the writers that were still approved, most notably Lu Xun and Mao himself. There were, of course, exceptions. Kirkpatrick's two roommates were both highly literate and well-educated, one being the son of an army general, the other the son of a high-level cadre. This was, presumably, why they were thought to be suitable roommates for a foreign student. They were both educated and politically trustworthy, both red and expert, as it were. Kirkpatrick also became aware of their literate ability when they confessed to him that they had been asked by the university authorities to translate into Chinese the articles he had written for the Far Eastern Economic Review, a weekly magazine then based in Hong Kong. As they had no English, not unnaturally they found the task of translating the articles into Chinese quite beyond them. But with the help of the original author, they managed most successfully, and were thus able to fulfill their duty.

As part of the course at Fudan, foreign students were required to undertake two weeks each of "learning from the peasants" and "learning from the workers." The first took place in a People's Commune and the second in a machine tool factory. While at the commune, Kirkpatrick discovered that, while his peasant hosts were able to read the slogans in the Little Red Book and those which were displayed in vast numbers around the commune, they were unable to identify the individual characters which made up the slogans. Thus, if the order of the characters in the slogan were altered, the peasants were unable to read them. Mao was routinely described as the *weida-de lingxiu* 伟大的领袖 or *great leader*. The peasants would happily read off the standard phrase "*Women weida-de lingxiu Mao zhuxi,*" *Our great leader Chairman Mao*. But Kirkpatrick discovered that, when the characters *ling* 领 and *xiu* 袖 were presented separately to the peasants, they were unable to read them.

While at the factory, all the foreign students were assigned to political study groups, one foreigner to each study group. These study groups met three times a week for two hours each time. Tools were downed and the machines silenced as we sat in our groups to study the prescribed texts. At the time in question, the groups were studying Mao's essay "On the Ten Great Relationships." The routine was that the political advisor would read a paragraph of the text while the rest of the group followed in their copies. After completing the paragraph, he would then invite comments from the rest of the group, an invitation that was invariably met by deathly silence, apart from the occasional embarrassed shuffling of shoes against the stone floor. After what always seemed a painfully long period of silence, he would then identify the key points, and then would direct a member of the group to read the next paragraph. During these political study sessions it quickly became clear that very few of the workers were able to read at all, as it was rare for one of the workers to be able to read his or her paragraph. This was acutely uncomfortable for Kirkpatrick, as the political as advisor would often ask him to read the paragraph on behalf of the poor worker who was unable to.

The modern literature course in which Kirkpatrick was enrolled was assessed by an end- of- course assignment, comprising a short dissertation of twenty-thousand Chinese characters. Choice of author and topic was limited to those approved by the authorities. The title of Kirkpatrick's dissertation was "The Effect of his Hometown upon Lu Xun's Short Stories." As recalled earlier in the introduction to this book, the dissertation was returned with the instruction to add more references to authority in order to bolster the argument. In the context, it was clear that "authority" meant Chairman Mao himself. Kirkpatrick then spent the next two weeks or so plowing through Mao's works looking for apposite quotes which could then be interspersed at appropriate points through the dissertation. Once the arguments presented in the dissertation had been buttressed—or, more accurately framed—by quotes from Mao, the dissertation was passed.

The importance attached to finding the apposite quote in order to justify one's position is nicely captured in an account given by Schoenals (24–5). In July 1972, the Communist Party's major propaganda organ, the People's Daily newspaper, published an article in which it stated that, "there has to be praise as well as criticism, although there should mainly be praise." A secretary of Yao Wenyuan, a member of the infamous Gang of Four, then phoned the People's Daily office to ask for the reference. Schoenals quotes the person who had written the People's Daily article:

> [I felt that] the passage might create a major problem, because I honestly could not think what the scriptural basis for this statement might be.... I discovered that Lin Biao of all people had remarked in 1964—in his "Instructions to the Entire Army on Organization Work"—that "in dealing with soldiers, there has to be praise as well as criticism, although there should mainly be praise." At the time [in 1972] the entire Party was in the midst of the anti-Lin Biao rectification campaign, but here was I—an editor with the People's Daily—propagating the point of view of Lin Biao. Outrageous! Was this not tantamount to disseminating Lin Biao's remnant poison? I became even more nervous.

The author of the article alerted other people in the People's Daily office to his problem and they joined in a frantic search for the original reference. The author continues the story:

Just before lunch, a Comrade came running into the office… mad with joy, saying: "We are saved! I've got a reference. In his 1964 "Conversation at the Spring Festival," Chairman Mao said exactly the same thing." Everyone was as if relieved of a heavy burden. All that needed to be done now was to use the quote from Mao as a reference, and then pass on a report to those on high.

The concern, if not downright panic, felt by the author of the People's Daily article at not being able to find the reference and then discovering that it had been said by the discredited Lin Biao serves to remind us just how difficult life was for intellectuals during the Cultural Revolution. It was not a time for academic writing. It was a time of an extremely confrontational style (Lu Xing, *Revolution* 192ff). As we mentioned at the beginning of the chapter, we shall not here discuss this in any detail (see Lu Xing *Rhetoric of the Chinese Cultural Revolution* for an in-depth study), but as Lu Xing herself points out, this confrontational and aggressive style is still seen today. As an example she cites the official language used to attack the Falun Gong. She quotes one of the people she interviewed:

The language used to attack Falun Gong is exactly the same language as that used to attack "cow ghosts and snake spirits" during the Cultural Revolution. On hearing such language, I felt like the Cultural Revolution had returned. (196)

This confrontational style has spread to the language of the dissidents. Xing Lu quotes another of her interviewees:

There is definitely a trace of the cultural-revolutionary style, even in the writings of political dissidents…. The language they use to attack the CCP is very similar to the Red Guard style. They use Mao's style of verbal aggression to condemn Mao. (196)

Here are two translated excerpts from Mao which show his confrontational and direct style.

I am hated by many, especially comrade Pang Dehuai, his hatred is so intense that he wished me dead. My policy with Pang Dehuai is such: You don't touch me, I don't touch you;

you touch me, I touch you. Even though we were once like brothers, it doesn't change a thing. [Source: "Minutes of Lu Shan Meetings" (1959), Mao Zedong]

A commune makes one mistake, there are 700,000 plus brigades, then we have 700,000 plus mistakes. If we let all these mistakes be published in newspaper, it takes forever to print them. What shall be the end result? The end result would be the collapse of this nation. Let's say the imperialists would leave us alone, our own people would rise to start a revolution, every one of us will be kicked in the arse. To publish a newspaper which specializes in saying bad words... once 700,000 bad incidents are published, and nothing else, I will be surprised to see our nation survive! No need to wait for an American or Chiang Kai-shek's invasion, our nation will be exterminated, this nation would deserve to be eliminated.... If communists do ten tasks, and nine are bad and published in newspaper, this nation will be eliminated, and deserved to be eliminated. [Source: "Minutes of Lu Shan Meetings" (1959), p. 136 Mao Zedong]

In the final section of this chapter we provide further support for Xing Lu's argument that the cultural-revolutionary style of aggression and confrontation is still very much in evidence, and that this is at great cost to public and civil discourse in China. In doing this we analyse Charter 08, the open letter issued in 2008 by a group of 303 Chinese authors to the Chinese Communist Party. In this open letter, the authors, the most well-known of whom is the Nobel Laureate, Liu Xiaobo, called for a reaffirmation of the following fundamental concepts: freedom, human rights, equality, republicanism, democracy, and constitutionalism. They also set forth nineteen specific demands.

We shall argue that the authors of Charter 08 must have realised that their letter would cause disdain, if not downright fury, among the Party elite, not least because of the way the argument and demands are framed. As will be shown, far from using a "bottom-up" form of persuasion as advised by Gui Guzi more than two thousand years ago and many others since, the authors chose to use language and a rhetorical structure representative of "top-down" rhetoric, reminiscent of the imperial edicts we included in Chapter 1. The translation below comes from the online forum Human Rights in China (http://www.hrichina.org/public/index) and can be seen at http://www.hrichina.org/public/

contents/press?revision_id=89851&item_id=85717). The Chinese text can be accessed at http://www.2008xianzhang.info/chinese.htm.

In the preamble, the authors write:

> After experiencing a prolonged period of human rights disasters and a tortuous struggle and resistance, the awakening Chinese citizens are increasingly and more clearly recognizing that freedom, equality, and human rights are universal common values shared by all humankind, and that democracy, a republic, and constitutionalism constitute the basic structural framework of modern governance. A "modernisation" bereft of these universal values and this basic political framework is a disastrous process that deprives humans of their rights, corrodes human nature, and destroys human dignity.

They then seem to offer some praise by noting that the government did sign two human rights treaties in 1997 and 1998 and that the government has also promised "to formulate and implement a National Human Rights Action Plan." But they go on:

> However, this political process stops at the paper stage. There are laws but there is no rule of law. There is a constitution but no constitutional governance.... The power bloc continues to insist on maintaining the authoritarian regime, rejecting political reform. This has caused corruption in officialdom, difficulty in establishing rule of law, and no protection of human rights, the loss of ethics, the polarisation of society, warped economic development, damages in the natural and human environments, no systematic protection of the rights to property and the pursuit of happiness, the accumulation of countless social conflicts, and the continuous rise of resentment. In particular, the intensification of hostility between government officials and the ordinary people, and the dramatic rise of mass incidents, illustrate a catastrophic loss of control in the making, and the anachronism of the current system has reached a point where change must occur.

This preamble does not represent yin-yang persuasion as advocated by Gui Guzi and which we considered in Chapter 1. It is a withering attack on the current government and its policies. Neither is the advice, which we repeat below, of Han Feizi heeded.

> Men who wish to present their remonstrances and expound their ideas must not fail to ascertain their ruler's loves and hates before launching into their speeches.... If you gain the ruler's love, your wisdom will be appreciated and you will enjoy favour as well. But, if he hates you, not only will your wisdom be rejected but you will be regarded as a criminal and thrust aside. ...The beast called the dragon can be tamed and trained to the point where you may ride on its back. But on the underside of its throat it has scales a foot in diameter that curl back from the body, anyone who chances to brush against them is sure to die. The ruler of men too has his bristling scales. Only if a speaker can avoid brushing against them will he have any hope of success.

The authors then go on to call for the reaffirmation of six fundamental concepts, listed above. Here they spell out each concept and there is the frequent use of modals of obligation. For example, in the statements on human rights and equality they write:

> To ensure human rights **must be** the foundation of the first objective of government and lawful public authority, and is also the **inherent demand** of "putting people first."

> The principle of equality before the law and a citizen's society **must be** implemented; the principle of equality of economic, cultural, and political rights **must be** implemented.

This authoritative tone is maintained, if not strengthened, in the language of the nineteen "basic standpoints." Imperatives and "shall be" modals abound, as indicated in bold type. There is not space here to include all nineteen points. The first four are representative of the tone:

1. Amend the Constitution: Based on the aforementioned values and concepts, **amend** the Constitution, **abolishing** the provisions in the current Constitution that are not in conformity with the principle that sovereignty resides in the people so that the Constitution can truly become a document for guaranteeing human rights and [appropriate use of] public power. The Constitution **should be** the implementable

supreme law that any individual, group or party **shall not** violate, and lay the legal foundation for the democratization of China.
2. Separation and balance of power: A modern government that separates, checks, and keeps balance among powers guarantees the separation of legislative, judicial, and administrative power. The principle of governing by laws and being a responsible Government **shall be** established. Over-expansion of executive power **shall be** prevented; the Government **shall be** responsible to the taxpayers; the separation, checking and keeping balance of powers between the central and local governments **shall be** set up; the central power authority **shall be** clearly defined and mandated by the Constitution, and the local governments **shall be** fully autonomous.
3. Democratise the lawmaking process: All levels of the legislative bodies **shall be** directly elected. **Maintain** the principles of fairness and justice in making law, and democratise the lawmaking process.
4. Independence of the judiciary: The judiciary **shall be** nonpartisan, free from any interference. **Ensure** judicial independence, and **guarantee** judicial fairness. **Establish** a Constitutional Court and a system of judicial review; **maintain** the authority of the Constitution. **Abolish** as soon as possible the Party's Committees of Political and Legislative affairs at all levels that seriously endanger the country's rule of law. **Avoid** using public tools for private objectives.

Charter 08 concludes with the authors accusing China as being alone "among the great nations of the world" of remaining authoritarian and of causing untold suffering and holding back the progress of civilisation itself.

> China, as a great nation of the world, one of the five permanent members of the United Nations Security Council, and a member of the Human Rights Council, should contribute to peace for humankind and progress in human rights. But to people's regret, among the great nations of the world, China, alone, still clings to an authoritarian political way of life. As a result, it has caused an unbroken chain of human rights disasters and social crises, held back the development of the Chinese people, and hindered the progress of human civilization. This situation **must** change! The reform of political democratization **can no longer be** delayed.
>
> Because of this, we, with a civic spirit that dares to act, publish the "Charter 08." We hope that all Chinese citizens who

> share this sense of crisis, responsibility and mission, without distinction between the government or the public, regardless of status, will hold back our differences to seek common ground, actively participate in this citizens' movement, and jointly promote the great transformation of the Chinese society, so that we can establish a free, democratic and constitutional nation in the near future and fulfill the dreams that our people have pursued tirelessly for more than a hundred years.

The overall tone of Charter 08 is one of command. The use of imperatives and modals recalls the *yang* rhetorical style of the imperial edicts exemplified in Chapter 1. There is also ample use of hyperbole and metaphor, typical of powerful discourse, and a marked absence of mitigated expressions, typical of powerless discourse (Van Dijk 184–5). "We do tend to leave implicit all propositions that we believe to be known or derivable by the recipients" (184–5). This tenet is also clearly breached, as the authors explicitly list the "fundamental concepts." The nineteen "basic standpoints" are presented as explicit demands.

The use of pronouns further demonstrates an extremely antagonistic adversarial stance. The authors (we) are associated with "civic spirit." "Because of this, we, with a civic spirit that dares to act, publish the 'Charter 08.'" The explicitly addressed audience, the Chinese Community Party, is an inanimate "it," the opposition, as exemplified in this excerpt from the preamble.

> The "New China" established in 1949 is a "people's republic" in name only. In fact, it is under the "Party's dominion." The ruling power monopolizes all the political, economic and social resources. It created a string of human rights catastrophes such as the Anti-Rightist Campaign, the Great Leap Forward, the Cultural Revolution, June 4, and attacks on non-governmental religious activities and on the rights defense movement, causing tens of millions of deaths, and exacted a disastrous price on the people and the country.

Rhetorically, Charter 08 is not a petition. It is a demand. A Chinese academic remarked that, "My first impression of Charter 08 was that it is full of the scent of gun powder (火藥味) followed by bullets (or bullet points) out of a machine gun (衝鋒槍)." The provocative and antagonistic nature of the document must have been understood by the authors, so we assume that their real aim was never to persuade the Communist Party of the need to change. Instead, the two primary aims of the Charter must have been to gain an international audience for their demands and to embarrass the Party. In the first of these they were successful. In the second, less so, as despite international protests, the government has imprisoned those it sees as the key players in the writing of Charter 08.

While, as we indicated earlier, the style here owes much to the Cultural Revolution, it is hard to see what language and rhetorical style a dissident in contemporary China can adopt. To recall Jullien's question from Chapter 1, "In the name of what, therefore, can the Chinese man of letters break free from the forces of power, affirm his positions, and thus speak openly?". Yet, Jullien also argues that "With such obliquity, dissidence is impossible" (137). But perhaps obliquity offers a possible rhetorical style for dissent. Would Charter 08 have been more persuasive had it been written in a traditional "bottom-up" *yin* style, as exemplified in the critical *baguwen* of Zhou Youguang which we illustrated in Chapter 4?

Charter 08 is commonly thought to have been inspired by Charter 77, the document published in January 1977 criticising the Czechoslovakian government (http://libpro.cts.cuni.cz/charta/docs/declaration_of_charter_77.pdf). One of its principal authors was Vaclav Havel, who, as is well-known, became the first President of the new Czech Republic. As Charter 08 was inspired by Charter 77, it is instructive to compare their rhetorical styles. While space forbids including all of Charter 77, we here provide some excerpts, along with a rhetorical analysis of the type we conducted on Charter 08. The opening paragraph of Charter 77 recounts the Czechoslovakian government's signing of pacts concerning rights. In this, it sets the frame within which the signatories of the Charter can argue for these rights to be upheld. This differs in style from Charter 08, where the opening paragraph records that China has "suffered a prolonged period of humans rights disasters and a tortuous struggle and resistance...." The opening paragraph of Charter 77 reads:

> On 13.10.1976, there were published in the Codex of Laws of the CSSR/no. 120 an "International Pact on Civil and Political Rights" and an "International Pact on Economic, Social and Cultural Rights," which had been signed on behalf of Czechoslovakia in 1968, confirmed at Helsinki in 1975 and which came into force in our country on 23.3.1976. Since that time our citizens have had the right and our state the duty to be guided by them.

The second and third paragraphs of Charter 77 provide further background and welcomes the government's signing of the pacts, but then points out the signing is "completely illusory."

> The freedom and rights of the people guaranteed by these pacts are important factors of civilization for which, throughout history, many progressive forces have been striving and their enactment can be of great assistance to the humanistic development of our society. We therefore welcome the fact that the Czechoslovak Socialist Republic has expressed adherence to these pacts.
>
> But their publication reminds us with new urgency how many fundamental civil rights for the time being are—unhappily—valid in our country only on paper. Completely illusory, for example, is the right to freedom of expression, guaranteed by article 19 of the first pact.

Contrast the comparatively measured tone here with the second paragraph of Charter 08, the first sentence of which reads:

> "The monumental historic transformation in the mid-nineteenth century exposed the decay of the traditional Chinese despotic system and ushered in the most "unprecedented and cataclysmic change in several thousands of years" in all of China."

Charter 08 then describes a series of reforms that were put in place during the end of the nineteenth and early twentieth century. The failure of these and the "Party's dominion" over the post 1949 "catastrophes" is clearly spelled out in the final section of paragraph 3.

> The "New China" established in 1949 is a "people's republic" in name only. In fact it is under the "Party's dominion." The ruling power monopolizes all the political, economic and social resources. It created a string of human rights catastrophes such as the Anti-Rightist Campaign, the Great Leap Forward, The Cultural Revolution, June 4, and attacks on non-governmental religious activities and on the rights defense movement, causing tens of millions of deaths and exacted a disastrous price on the people and the country.

The paragraphs following the opening three paragraphs of Charter 77 itemise areas where the pacts signed by the Czechoslovak government have been broken. However, the passive voice is used, and usually no agent is explicitly mentioned (although of course it is implicitly understood that the government is the agent of these breaches of the pact and the "authorities and social organizations" are named as agents in one instance). Paragraph 4 of the charter provides a good example of this "agent-less passive" style.

> Tens of thousands of citizens are not allowed to work in their own branches simply because they hold opinions which differ from official opinions. At the same time, they are frequently the object of the most varied forms of discrimination and persecution on the part of the authorities and social organizations; they are deprived of any possibility of defending themselves and are virtually becoming the victims of apartheid.

The direct agency of some part of the government is not mentioned again until paragraph 11, and even here it is the Ministry of the Interior which is named, not the government as a whole. The opening sentence of the paragraph reads:

> Other civil rights, including the express banning of "arbitrary interference in private life, the family, home and correspondence" (artArt.17 of the first pact), are hazardously violated by the pact , too, that the Ministry of Interior by various means controls the life of its citizens, for example by the "bugging" of telephones and flats, control of posts, a watch on persons, the searching of homes, the creation of a network of informers from the ranks of the population (often recruited by impermissible threats or, on the contrary, promises), etc.

Agency is also attributed in paragraph 12.

> In cases of politically motivated criminal proceedings, the investigating organs violate the rights of the accused and their defence counsels, guaranteed by Article 14 of the first pact and by Czechoslovak legislation.

The style then reverts to a measured description of a list of violations against the pacts, again using the agent-less passive. Then, however, in paragraph 15, the tone shifts and the active mood is employed. And in further stark contrast to the tone of Charter 08, the signatories indicate that they and "everyone of us has a share of the responsibility." The paragraph reads:

> Responsibility for the observances of civil rights in the country naturally falls, in the first place, on the political and state power. But not on it alone. Each and every one of us has a share of responsibility for the general situation and thus, too, for the observance of the pacts which have been enacted and are binding not only for the government but for all citizens.

Paragraph 16 continues with this notion of shared responsibility.

> The feeling of co-responsibility, faith in the idea of civic involvement and the will to exercise it and the common need to seek new and more effective means for its expression led us to the idea of setting up CHARTER '77, the origin of which we are publicly announcing today.

The following paragraphs then further describe the origins and aims of the Charter, often in terms of what it is not. For example, "CHARTER '77 is not an organization, it has no statutes, no permanent organs and no organised membership."

The final paragraph concludes:

> We believe that CHARTER '77 will contribute towards all citizens in Czechoslovakia working and living as free people.

Our argument here is simply that the rhetorical style and tone of Charter 77 is more measured and calm than its counterpart in Charter 08. Charter 77 describes, almost dispassionately, the violations of the pacts signed by the Czechoslovak government. The government itself is only rarely mentioned and then only specific organs of it (The Ministry of the Interior and "investigating organs"). Charter 77 also points out that the responsibility for observing human rights lies with the citizens as well as with the government. The tone of Charter 77 thus contrasts starkly with the far more authoritarian and imperial *yang* style of Charter 08.

Only time will tell whether Charter 08 will be successful in bringing about political change in China. But its adoption of a top-down rhetorical style and aggressive *yang* antagonistic tone will guarantee its official dismissal by the current regime. However, official dismissal does not necessarily mean that the political changes the Charter demanded will not be implemented at some time. After all, the People's Charter of nineteenth-century Britain was presented to the British parliament on three occasions (1836, 1842 and 1848). It was not supported because its demands for universal suffrage and the abolition of the property requirement for politicians was seen as a threat to the status and privileges of the wealthy and propertied elite who made up the members of parliament at the time. However, all but the sixth of the demands made in the People's Charter have long since been implemented (Nash 10ff). The six demands of the People's Charter were:

The Six Points of the People's Charter

1. A VOTE for every man twenty-one years of age, of sound mind, and not undergoing punishment for crime.

2. THE BALLOT—to protect the elector in the exercise of his vote.

3. NO PROPERTY QUALIFICATION from Members of Parliament—thus enabling the constituencies to return the man their choice, be he rich or poor.

4. PAYMENT OF MEMBERS, thus enabling an honest tradesman, working man, or other person, to serve a constituency, when taken from his business to attend to the interests of the country.

5. EQUAL CONSTITUENCIES, securing the same amount of representation for the same number of electors, instead of allowing small constituencies to swamp the votes of large ones.

6. ANNUAL PARLIAMENTS, thus presenting the most effectual check to bribery and intimidation, since though a constituency might be bought once in seven years (even with the ballot), no purse could buy a constituency (under a system of universal suffrage) in each ensuing twelvemonth; and since members, when elected for a year only, would not be able to defy and betray their constituents as now.

It is worth stressing that, although the People's Charter did not adopt a "bottom-up" rhetorical style, it is also somewhat less imperious of tone than Charter 08. As we argue further below, only when the Chinese are able to negotiate a reform of political and public discourse and rhetorical style which will allow the leaders and the governed to engage in critical, civic and constructive debate, will real political change be likely.

THE OPEN LETTER

The second text we analyse here is the 2010 open letter written by the mothers of those who died in Tiananmen. This letter carried 127 signatories with a further nineteen names added of those who had signed in the past, but had since themselves died. This is also taken from the Human Rights in China website and it is also their translation. We first provide the complete text and then discuss it. We have numbered the paragraphs for ease of reference when we discuss the text.

Please Show Courage, Break the Taboo, Face "June 4" Head on.

The Honorable Deputies of the Eleventh Session of the Second Plenary of the National People's Congress and Committee Members of the Chinese People's Political Consultative Conference:

This year marks the 20th Anniversary of the "June Fourth" Massacre.

(1) In the last century, on June 4, 1989, the Chinese authorities launched a massacre against peaceful demonstrators and civilians in the capital, seriously violating our country's constitution and breaching their duty, as leaders of a sovereign state, to protect the people. This was an unconscionable atrocity that grew from a longstanding contempt for human rights and civil rights.

(2) Over this long stretch of time, government authorities deliberately played down "June Fourth," forbade discussion among our people of "June Fourth," and prohibited the media from touching on "June Fourth." China has become like an airtight "iron chamber," and all the demands of the people about "June Fourth," all the anguish, lament, and moaning of the victims' relatives and the wounded of "June Fourth," have

been sealed off from this "iron chamber." Today, as the deputies and committee members of these "Two Meetings" are stately seated in this assembly hall, can you hear the cry from "June Fourth"? Can you hear the painful sighs of the families of the victims of "June Fourth"? But now, the bloodstains of that time have long been washed away and the bullet marks rubbed out, and the site of the massacre is now decorated with exotic plants and flowers and has become a scene of peace and prosperity.

(3) But can all this conceal the sins of that time? Can it erase the sorrow of the relatives of the victims that deepens year after year?

(4) No! It absolutely cannot. The "June Fourth" massacre has long secured its place in history's hall of shame. It absolutely cannot be diminished as a "political disturbance" or even a "serious political disturbance." It was nothing short of an unconscionable atrocity. No amount of force can negate the bitter reality of the hundreds and thousands of lives snatched away by guns and tanks twenty years ago.

(5) Twenty years are not a short time; they are enough for a whole new generation to emerge. This new generation never experienced the bloodshed of that time, nor has it ever felt the desolate calm that settled on a killing field. It has passed; it seems that everything has passed. "Play not the songs of former dynasties; listen instead to the new tune of the 'Willow Branch.'"[19] In these wenty years, generations of our country's leaders have succeeded the one before, from the second generation to the third, and then the fourth. You deputies and committee members of the "Two Meetings" have also changed from session to session. The passage of time and the shift of circumstances seem to have given the party and country leaders a kind of opportunity to minimise "June Fourth" and push it to a distant corner of history.

(6) Even so, China's Tiananmen Mothers cannot consent. On the question of defining "June Fourth" we feel that we cannot afford to be the least bit vague. Whether to adhere to the initial interpretation or to change it, we must base it on facts and let

the truth do the talking. If Deng Xiaoping, then Chairman of the Central Military Commission of the Communist Party of China, was wrong in "suppressing the counterrevolutionary rebellion," then we must overturn it and correct it through established legal procedures and publicly announce it to the whole society, and should not explain it away with the vague term of "political disturbances."

(7) The Tiananmen Mothers have always held one belief, and that is: act and speak according to the facts; accept no lies. From the start of our inquiry activities, we would repeatedly check and verify our data regarding the person of interest. As of now, not a single one of the 194 dead that we have examined had any history of violence. They are all among the innocent victims of that massacre. They gave their lives for the sake of justice and all we can do is return justice to them, to pursue the justice that comes late to them. Otherwise, we would not be able to face the spirit of the dead.

(8) Since 1995, our group of "June Fourth" victims and loved ones return here every year to write to the "Two Meetings" with three requests for officially acknowledging "June Fourth." They are: start new investigations on the "June Fourth" incident, publicly announce death tolls, release a list of the names of the dead; clarify each case to the family members of the dead and compensate them according to law; investigate "June Fourth" cases to determine those responsible and punish them. To summarize, our three requests are: "Truth, Compensation, Responsibility."

(9) We have always upheld the principles of peace and reason. We appeal to the two committees and government authorities to utilize the methods of democracy and open dialogue to come to a just resolution. Yet our requests have not been discussed in the "Two Meetings."

(10) In 2006, we suggested the following in order to end the stalemate over "June Fourth" and ensure that the situation can develop along a steady path: use the principle of tackling the simpler problems first. The divisive issues that cannot be

resolved or agreed upon easily can be set aside temporarily. Instead, first solve the issues that involve the basic rights of the victims and their personal interests. These issues include: 1) remove all monitoring of and restrictions on the movements of "June Fourth" victims and their families; 2) allow families of the dead to openly mourn their loved ones; 3) stop intercepting and confiscating both domestic and international humanitarian aid contributions, and return all the aid money that was previously frozen; 4) relevant government departments should, in humanitarian spirit, help the victims who are facing hard times to find employment and guarantee them a basic livelihood, without any political conditions; 5) remove political biases against the disabled victims of "June Fourth" such that they are treated as all other disabled persons in regards to communal participation and treatment by society, etc.

(11) In 2008, we again proposed to the deputies of the "Two Meetings": in the world today, dialogue has replaced confrontation. The Chinese government advocates using dialogue to resolve differences and conflicts on international issues. Thus we have an even stronger basis to ask that the government authorities resolve the internal differences and conflicts in the same way. If we are able to use dialogue to replace confrontation on the problem of "June Fourth," it would benefit the whole country and be a blessing for all our people. The more dialogue we have, the more civility and law and order, and the less ignorance and tyranny. Dialogue does not lead society towards opposition and hatred, but rather, towards tolerance and reconciliation. Using dialogue to solve the problem of "June Fourth" is an imperative path toward societal reconciliation.

(12) Another year has passed now, yet we have heard nothing.

(13) We note that President Hu Jintao said the following in public not long ago: In determining every single policy, we start and end with whether the people endorse it or not, agree with it or not, are happy with it or not, and consent to it or not. We welcome these words. If this is so, then we suggest to the NPC and CPPCC: why not eliminate the taboo of "June Fourth"

and conduct a broad survey of the people's attitudes towards "June Fourth" countrywide, especially in Beijing, to find out what exactly the people endorse? What they agree with? What they are happy with? Consent to? We believe this should not be difficult to do.

(14) But the people of China know very well that the tragic case of "June Fourth" is an "ironclad case" created single-handedly by the second generation leader, Deng Xiaoping. As long as Deng Xiaoping enjoys any lingering prestige in our country from top to bottom and in future history, it would be an extremely formidable task to overturn the conclusion that has "already been decided on by the Party and government," and to discard the new "Whatever" policy.[20] Even if "suppressing the counterrevolutionary rebellion" is relabelled as a "serious political disturbance," the judgment, in essence, still has not changed.

(15) This then will require each deputy to demonstrate extraordinary courage and resourcefulness, political courage and wisdom, to break the taboo and face head-on the unspeakable tragedy that took place twenty years ago and resolve "June Fourth" with the truth. If this should happen, you will have brought a great blessing upon our people and your achievement will go down in history.

This is an open letter written to the deputies of the National People's Congress (NPC) and the committee members of the Chinese People's Political Consultative Conference (CPPCC). These are annual meetings held in Beijing and which run concurrently. They are often referred to as "Two Meetings," as is the case at one point in the letter. The adjective in the address term for the deputies and committee members is "honorable" (*zunjing* 尊敬) and is the standard polite term. This is the last iota of respect and the only nod towards *captatio benovolentiae* or facework that is shown in this letter. The two opening paragraphs use extremely forceful language to set out what the authors of the letter believe to be the true interpretation of what happened on June 4, 1989 and the authorities' role in it. The opening line presents as indisputable fact that the "Chinese authorities launched a massacre (*tusha* 屠杀) against peaceful demonstrators and civilians in the capital, seriously violating our country's constitution...." This action is then described as an "unconscionable atrocity" (*buzhebukou-de fan rendao baoxing* 不折不扣的反人道暴行), which was caused by "a longstanding contempt of human rights and civil rights." This gives the opening paragraph a highly confrontational tone, even though the authors later claim (paragraph 11), rather curiously given the circumstances, that "in the world today, dialogue has replaced confrontation." The term "massacre" is used five times in the letter, including in the frame-setting opening line. Needless to say, this is not the term favoured by the official authorities, who prefer a range of far more neutral descriptions such as "incident" (*shijian* 事件), or "political disturbance" (*zhengzhi fengbo* 政治风波).

Throughout the opening two paragraphs, the Chinese authorities are in subject/actor position. They "launched a massacre....seriously violating.... breaching their duty", "deliberately played down June 4th", "forbade discussion", and "prohibited the media". In contrast the demonstrators are described as "peaceful", "victims", and "innocent victims".

The tone that the letter writers' position is the indisputable truth is further underlined by their "one belief, and that is: act and speak according to the facts; accept no lies" (paragraph 7). While "they" (the authorities) have "forbade discussion," etc., "we" (the authors) "have always upheld the principles of peace and reason" (paragraph 9). As was noted with the use of pronouns in Charter 08, this use of pronouns is also adversarial here. Simply speaking, "they" are all bad, "we" are all good.

In paragraph 6, the authors also directly challenge the authority and interpretation of Deng Xiaoping, the "paramount" leader at the time, saying that if he was wrong in suppressing "the counterrevolutionary rebellion, then we must overturn it and correct it."[21] This challenge to Deng Xiaoping's interpretation is repeated in paragraph 14, where they also appear to recognise that to overturn his interpretation would be "an extremely formidable task."

The direct and forthright condemnation of the authorities is followed by the first mention of the request (paragraph 8). The authors recall that, since 1995, they have written every year "with three requests," which they then list. The authors then summarise the three requests as: "truth, compensation, responsibility".

From paragraph 9, the tone of the letter changes appreciably, as the authors say that "we have always upheld the principles of peace and reason." In paragraph 10, the authors repeat a suggestion they made in an earlier letter for adopting the principle of "tackling the simpler problems first," and they call for the use of dialogue as "[t]he Chinese government advocates using dialogue to resolve differences and conflicts on international issues" (paragraph 11). Paragraph 11 also contains a general plea for the use of dialogue as this "would benefit the whole country and be a blessing for all our people."

The authors also attempt to buttress their argument by referencing authority when they cite President Hu on the importance of pleasing the people and then suggest that the President's advice be followed in the investigation of June 4th. They conclude paragraph 13 with the sentence, "We believe this should not be difficult to do." This is somewhat contradicted, however, by the reference to Deng Xiaoping in the next paragraph and the description of "June 4th" as an "ironclad case."

The final paragraph attempts to persuade the deputies and committee members to call for a new investigation by appealing to their "courage and resourcefulness" and indicating that, were they to proceed, "you will have brought a great blessing upon our people and your achievement will do go down in history." It should be noted that the "you" is not in the original Chinese. Rather, the final paragraph begins "This will require each deputy to..." In phrasing the final paragraph in this way and emphasising "each of the deputies," the authors are attempting to distinguish between the "authorities" and the "Chinese government" from the individual deputies attending the "two meetings." As such, they are acknowledging that the real power still lies in the hands of a very small elite, and consequently that the likelihood of their requests being granted—or even discussed—remain miniscule.

The authors' realisation that their case is, in effect, hopeless, may explain the adversarial and confrontational tenor of the opening paragraphs in which they baldly state that the authorities are responsible for a "massacre" and for committing an "unconscionable atrocity."

As with the case of Charter 08, these Chinese citizens clearly feel a sense of hopelessness when it comes to finding a way of conducting civilised and constructive discussions with the Chinese government. There simply is no agreed form of public discourse or rhetoric which would allow such debate. The realisation of this is what gives the following excerpt from paragraph 11 of the Open Letter such poignancy:

> If we are able to use dialogue to replace confrontation on the problem of "June Fourth," it would benefit the whole country and be a blessing for all our people. The more dialogue we have, the more civility and law and order, and the less ignorance and tyranny. Dialogue does not lead society towards opposition and hatred, but rather, towards tolerance and reconciliation.

Sadly, there remains little chance of this.

In this chapter we have discussed political writing in modern Chinese, using examples from Mao's writing and more recent dissident writing. We showed that, although Mao's writing was influenced by European translations in that he wrote long sentences he also retained the traditional sequencing pattern of because-therefore or frame to main. We also showed that an unfortunate influence Mao's more confrontational style is that it has been adopted for contemporary political writing, as evidenced by the rhetorical style adopted by dissident groups. We consider the possible implications of this in the final chapter but, in the next chapter, we return to academic writing and consider the advice given in recent and contemporary composition textbooks to Chinese writers.

10 A REVIEW OF CONTEMPORARY CHINESE UNIVERSITY WRITING (COURSE) BOOKS

In this chapter, we review a number of contemporary Chinese university writing books so that readers may know what input and instructions Chinese university students receive in terms of Chinese writing. In Chapter 8 we argued that Chinese writing has been influenced by its own tradition and by the West. Here we again argue that the writing of Chinese students has certain "blended" features and these are inherited from Chinese writing traditions and Western influence. For example, the modes of argument are diverse, and "deductive reasoning has always existed alongside inductive reasoning" (Kirkpatrick, "Chinese Rhetoric" 246).

There is currently a wide range and variety of Chinese writing books for university students. These books can be briefly classified into: 1) writing course books, e.g., Wang and Li; Qiao; Zhou, Li, and Lin; Ye; Ma Zhengping; and Wu Hanxiang; 2) applied writing guides on different genres, e.g., Huo; Lu, Zhan, and Zhang; Yu, Chen, and Wu; Liu Zhuang; Cheng, Fan, and Ma; Huang and Liu; Gao, Sun, and Zhao; Gao et al.; 3) Chinese rhetorical studies, e.g., Zong (*Chinese Rhetoric, Parts 1 & 2*), and studies of specific genres and topics such as Lu and Pu's *Thesis Writing in Chinese*; Duan and Li's *New Edition Schema Writing Ccoursebook*, Yu and Huang's *Schema Writing*; and Wang Zelong's *An Exploration on Chinese Writing Studies*; 4) collections of essays on writing by well-known authors, e.g., Liang's *Liang Qichao's Introduction to Composition*; Xia and Ye's *72 Lectures on Speech and Writing* and Yue, Zhan; and Zhao's *Writing Masters on How to Write Papers*.

We shall, in the main, review the first category of the above mentioned books, namely, writing course books. These include Wu Hanxiang; Ma Zhengping; Ye; Wang and Li; Qiao; and Zhou, Li, and Lin. These are the commonly selected books for Chinese writing courses.

UNIVERSITY WRITING COURSE (WU HANXIANG)

Wu's *University Writing Course* comprises three major sections including narrative writing, argumentative writing, and practical writing. What is worthy of special attention in this book are the two chapters (Chapter 9 and Chapter 10) as these discuss ways to present and strengthen an argument. These include two major categories: 1) setting up and defending one's arguments; and 2) describing and attacking others' arguments. Seven specific ways are listed for setting up and defending one's arguments. This can be done with the use of a. facts; b. theories; c. cause-effect relationships; d. analogies; e. contrasts and comparisons; f. metaphors; and g. indirect argumentation. The second category includes ways to attack the others' themes, their supporting details or evidence, and their means of argumentation. There are also direct and indirect ways of attacking others' arguments, e.g., revealing or disclosing the mismatch or gap between the others' viewpoints or arguments and supporting details; the breaching of logic and rules for argumentation; arguing by contradiction; and setting a person's own spear against his own shield (a Chinese expression which means refuting somebody with his own argument).

Kirkpatrick ("Chinese Rhetoric" 248–9) reviewed Wu's *University Writing Course* and a number of other coursebooks published in 1980s and 1990s and concluded that argumentative texts (or *yilunwen* in Chinese) must contain three essential components, namely the thesis, the argument and the proof (*lundian, lunju,* and *lunzheng*). In terms of thesis or *lundian*, "in the context of Chinese, Wu advises that the argument must be clear and explicit. In the debate between form and meaning, Wu's position is clear: facts conquer eloquence." In terms of argument or *lunju*, Wu proposes factual material and statistical material, including arguments from classical writers, appeals to authority, and scientific truths and axioms. Wu places scientific truths alongside the classics and authority. Kirkpatrick (248) also quotes Wu by saying that the *lunju* can be placed "either at the beginning or summed up at the end." In terms of the third essential component of argumentative texts, "the *lunzheng* or proof must show that there is a necessarily true link between thesis and argument" (Kirkpatrick 248).

ADVANCED COMPOSITION STUDIES COURSEBOOK SERIES (MA ZHENGPING)

As far as writing course books for Chinese college students are concerned, one series (edited by Ma Zhengping) plays a significant role. This series comprises seven course books on Chinese composition studies, including *Introduction to*

Advanced Composition Studies (*Gaodeng xiezuo xue yinlun*), *A Training Course for Advanced Composition Thinking* (*Gaodeng xiezuo siwei xunlian jiaocheng*), *A Training Course for Advanced Stylistics I: Basic Writing* (*Gaodeng wenti xiezuo xunlian jiaocheng I: jiben wenti xiezuo*), *A Training Course for Advanced Stylistics II: Practical Writing* (*Gaodeng wenti xiezuo xunlian jiaocheng II: shiyong wenti xiezuo*), *New Thinking for Teaching Secondary School Writing* (*Zhongxue xiezuo jiaoxue xin siwei*), *Advanced Composition: Exemplars and Analyses* (*Gaodeng xiezuo: liwen yu fenxi*), and *References for Teaching Advanced Composition* (*Gaodeng xiezuo jiaoxue cankao ziliao*). Ma's series on writing has become a "landmark of contemporary Chinese composition studies" (Sun 1). This series serves as a "milestone", indicating that Chinese composition studies is no longer a "marginalised" subject but a "conventional scientific" discipline (Sun 9). Sun (8–9) further argues that composition studies should be given status equal to that given to linguistics and literature, pointing out that, since the 1990s, Chinese composition studies has not been categorised as a distinct degree strand or a discipline in Chinese undergraduate and postgraduate studies.

A WRITING COURSE FOR COLLEGE STUDENTS (YE)

Ye's *A Writing Course for College Students* contains ten chapters. The first chapter is an introduction, and includes definitions of writing and a discussion of the essential skills required of writers. Ye (1) defines "writing" as "creative mental work that a writer engages in to express thoughts with words. The writing process includes collecting material, refining themes, considering structure and discourse, draft writing, revising and editing." The essential skills (12–24) include "the abilities to use language, to observe, to think critically, to imagine, and to express oneself." The remaining chapters of the book deal with the collection of material for writing and conceiving ideas; expressing and refining/revising; writing poetry, prose, novels and drama; *yingyong* writing (practical writing), e.g., writing a proposal/plan, a summary, regulations, reports, briefings, news, and advertisements; business writing; writing administrative documents; writing academic papers; writing speeches. The final chapter on *Shenlun* writing is of particular interest. *Shenlun* refers to argumentative essay writing, and this forms an integral part of the current Chinese examination for selecting State civil servants. The *Shenlun* examination comprises four sections, namely: reading; summarising; writing a proposal; and defending arguments. The Chinese characters of *Shen* and *Lun* respectively refer to explaining, demonstrating, proposing arguments and defending oneself. According to Ye (406), the words *shen lun* are found in the Confucian Analects *"shen er lun zhi,"* meaning "explaining, expounding, arguing, and reasoning." *Shenlun* essay writing, as an examination format or item, was introduced into the Chinese Examination for State Civil Servants in 2000. The purpose of including *Shenlun* essay writing is to test the participants' abilities to "analyse, summarise, refine, and process texts", in addition to their abilities to comprehend reading material, analyse material comprehensively, propose arguments, and use the Chinese language skillfully.

Shenlun essay writing has three characteristics. The first characteristic is its flexibility and variety. Since *Shenlun* essay writing contains three sections, i.e., summarising, making a proposal, and argumentative writing, its writing involves a variety of styles and genres, including narrative writing, expository writing, and argumentative writing. The second characteristic is its wide ranging content, which includes politics, economics, culture, education and other social issues, hot topics and current affairs. The third characteristic is its explicit focus on examining the participants' abilities to summarise and analyse text materials, and to argue sensibly and practically in light of contextual realities. The participants are expected to read and comprehend the given materials, to tease out the logical relationship of the ideas, and to work out the major issues embedded in the materials. At the same time, the participants are also expected to be able to make a proposal, and to support their arguments (Ye 408).

Ye (409) compares *Shenlun* essay writing with the policy essay (*celun*), required in the imperial civil service exam. *Celun* was different from the *bagu* essay in that its candidates were asked to address policy questions relating to social change. The essay required creative thinking on contemporary issues, rather than the simple reproduction of knowledge. Ye concludes that there are similarities between the *Shenlun* essay writing and the policy essay writing and that these include:

1. the policy essay of the ancient Chinese examinations required the candidates to "reflect deeply and thoroughly on the needs of the government and administration, to be far-sighted in their argumentation, to be practical and feasible in their proposals, and to be forceful and convincing in the use of words and rhetorical devices." The *Shenlun* essay writing also has these requirements;
2. both the policy essay and the *Shenlun* were/are used for selecting state civil servants;
3. they both touch upon contemporary and topical issues, i.e., policy essay writing concerned government and administration, and *Shenlun* writing encompasses politics, economics, law, culture and current affairs. However, one essential difference between the two

types of writing is that the *Shenlun* writing is more closely related to the actual work of contemporary civil servants, where they make and implement policies based on investigating and analysing realistic issues, putting forward their opinions, making proposals to solve current problems.

The *Shenlun* essay examination takes 150 minutes (with 40 minutes for reading, and 110 minutes for writing). The writing part comprises these three sections:

1) summarising the major problems or issues covered in the reading section in approximately 150 words;
2) making a proposal to solve or deal with the problems or issues in approximately 300 words. The proposal has to be stated clearly, with a focus on the problems or issues, and the solutions proposed have to be feasible;
3) writing an argumentative essay in approximately 1,200 words, with a self-defined topic, to address the problems or issues in the reading material and to justify the proposed solutions. The essay should be clear in its theme(s) and in-depth and convincing in its arguments.

Ye (412–413) also summarises three essential components for a well-constructed and well-written argumentative essay. These are:

1. an appropriate structure with logical presentation of content and a good combination of detail and brevity;
2. explicit and focused themes supported by detailed and specific content; and
3. fluent language with appropriate expressions and a coherent and cohesive argument.

Ye (412) proposes that the opening of the essay should be "short, brisk, and impressive"; the middle section should be "structurally sound, logically clear, rhetorically appropriate, and provide relevant supporting evidence"; and the conclusion should be forceful, striking, positive and inspirational. The conclusion should neither be a "snake tail (with a tiger head)", nor with "feet added to the drawing of a snake." (Both "*hu tou she wei*", i.e., "tiger head, snake tail", and "*hua she tian zu*", i.e., "adding feet when completing the drawing of a snake" are four-character Chinese proverbs). In the context of writing, "*hu tou she wei*" can be used to refer to an essay with a powerful and convincing opening, but a weak and incompatible concluding section, while "*hua she tian zu*" means unnecessary additions to an already well-written essay, particularly at the end of it.

UNIVERSITY WRITING COURSE: NEW EDITION (WANG AND LI)

Wang and Li's writing course book claims to be original in that it promotes a pattern of discovering—conceiving—expressing. The book has two sections: writing theories; and common types of writing, including writing for the public civil servant selection examinations. In Section One, Wang and Li define writing from a pedagogical point of view, arguing that writing entails creativity (or originality) and productivity. "Writing is transformation or generation of value-added information" (3). The value-added information is the result of discovery in the writing process. Wang and Li (4) also point out that traditional writing is text-based, comprising eight key elements: *zhuti* (theme), *cailiao* (material), *jiegou* (structure), *biaoda* (expression), *yuyan* (language), plus *xulun* (introduction), *xiugai* (revision), and *wenfeng* (style). They (9) further define writing as an activity of expressing and improving the content and form in relation to four key elements including *keti* (object), *zhuti* (subject), *zaiti* (medium), and *shouti* (readership). They summarise the characteristics of writing as possessing "individuality" and "originality" (13).

The theoretical sections, Chapters 2, 3, and 4, are about "writing discovery", "conceiving / mind-mapping", and "expression". They argue that "writing is to express what has been discovered, therefore, discovery is one of the essential steps in writing" (49). In terms of approaches to discovery, they propose *fasan* (divergent) approaches, *juhe* (convergent) approaches, *huanyuan* (substitution) approaches, *nifan* (opposite, or counter-factual) approaches, *xiangbei* (conflict) approaches, and *qianyi* (transfer) approaches. In terms of "conceiving / mind-mapping", they propose outlining, conceptual mapping, accumulative thinking, and conceiving ideas. They categorise means of expression into the following genres: "narration", "description", "prose writing", "argumentation" and "expository writing". Section two of the book is about writing a range of genres. These include news writing (news, correspondence, reports), practical and documentary writing (official documents, summary writing, applications), literary writing (prose, novels, poetry, drama and plays), and theoretical writing (critiques, essays and papers).

This comprehensive writing course book combines writing theories with practice, and makes students aware of the need for appropriate form and content. For example, of the eight key elements of writing introduced in the book, theme, introduction, and material are about content, while structure, expression, language, and style are primarily about form. Revision is related to both form and content. As we have illustrated earlier, the debates between form and content have continued for hundreds, if not thousands, of years in China.

UNIVERSITY COMPOSITION: NEW EDITION (QIAO)

Qiao's book on university writing has eight chapters: the introduction; summative writing; deductive writing; petition writing; evaluative writing; research writing; entertainment writing; and story writing. Qiao emphasises the importance of "establishing a thesis statement", "material selection and arrangement", and "process writing, including drafting and revising". The thesis statement should be positive, in-depth, and appropriate. In terms of the selection and arrangement of material, it is important to select useful and relevant materials, and arrange them so that the structure is complete (and the structure can be the *qi cheng zhuan he* structure we discussed and exemplified in Chapter 2). Qiao cites a metaphor from classical Chinese to describe an appropriate rhetorical structure: "the opening should be as attractive as the head of a phoenix; the body should be as rich as the body of a pig, and the closing should be as forceful and strong as the tail of a leopard (凤头, 猪肚, 豹尾)." In the remaining chapters, Qiao defines the different types of writing, and gives specific samples to illustrate a number of key points in writing. For example, "theme is the soul of writing" (52) and it is determined by means of "writing purpose", "writing style", and the "careful selection of material and genre" (53–8). In terms of the relationship between "theme" and "material" (63–4), Qiao argues that "material forms the basis for theme development", "material is the content, while the theme is the core", "material centers around the theme, serving to verify the theme", "material is a collection of objective facts and other's viewpoints, while theme is the result of the writer's independent thinking", and "material is the means for deepening the theme, while theme serves as the end for material selection and use". In terms of language use, Qiao places much attention on "conciseness" and "expressiveness".

In deductive writing, Qiao (85) points out that the central themes should be clearly thought out in the pre-writing stage. The establishment of a gist, a theme or a thesis, and choice of an appropriate form (including the discourse structure, and outline of the writing) are of primary importance. The central themes should then be sensibly explored or developed in a clear, concise, linear and logical manner (101–2). Rhetorical devices can be adopted in the deductive writing process, for example, the use of metaphors. What is also important for deductive writing is that the beginning (the central themes) and the ending (the conclusions) should cohere.

In petition writing, Qiao suggests that the writers set a clear target, use appropriate approaches (linguistically accurate, concise, and unambiguous, and culturally appropriate), and adopt an appropriate mindset, which refers to sensible and realistic expectations in relation to petition writing. In passing, we would stress that "sensible and realistic" aims are highly subjective terms in this context, as can be seen from the two petitions we analysed in the previous chapter, Charter 08 and the Open Letter.

In terms of evaluative writing, Qiao emphasises the importance of avoiding empty and worthless comments. With regards research writing, Qiao argues that it should focus on the significance of the research, the source and authenticity of the data, the values of the viewpoints, and the need to document the sources clearly. It is worth stressing here the importance he attaches to citation. The language used in research writing should be clear and unambiguous. Puns and inaccurate expressions should be avoided. Qiao also stresses the importance of developing outlines, saying that it helps with structural coherence, overall progression, time management, and appropriate material selection.

Qiao's university writing coursebook focuses on both form and content, and while embracing Western ideas, also honours the Chinese rhetorical tradition. For example, there is mention of the traditional *qi-cheng-zhuan-he* pattern. Linguistic clarity, succinctness, and cultural appropriateness are also stressed. "Empty words" should be avoided.

ADVANCED COURSEBOOK ON COMPOSITION STUDIES (ZHOU, LI, AND LIN)

Zhou, Li and Lin summarise three stages of contemporary writing pedagogy that have been in use since the Revolution of 1911, which saw the end of the imperial system and the birth of the Chinese Republic. These stages comprise:
1. the 1920s-1940s: with the focus on the teaching of writing at Beijing University, particularly on the promotion of writing in *baihua* (the vernacular style);
2. the 1950s-1970s: based on the writing courses in a number of higher institutions, and the introduction of former Soviet literary theories, and the studies in linguistics, rhetoric, and logic. In this period, the most widely adopted theoretical framework was that of the eight key elements, mentioned earlier by Wang and Li, namely: *zhuti*

(theme); *cailiao* (material); *jiegou* (structure); *biaoda* (expression); *yuyan* (language); *xulun* (introduction); *xiugai* (revision); and *wenfeng* (style);
3. the 1970s—present: the milestones of this stage include the College Entrance Examination system, the establishment of the first national writing society (1980), and the first issue of the national journal *Writing* (*Xie Zuo*). Changes during this stage include the shifts from static to dynamic writing, from micro- to macro-level writing, and from text based to human oriented writing.

Other representative works on writing include: He Jiakui's *Talks on Basic Writing Knowledge;* the two key writing course books written by academic staff in the Chinese Departments at Beijing and Fudan Universities respectively in the 1960s; and Zhu Boshi's 1983 *Introduction to Writing*.

Importantly, Zhou, Li, and Lin also point out that modern Chinese writing, in addition to adapting ideas from the West, should be based on theories inherited from classical Chinese rhetorical tradition. Of the classical texts they cite, they include Liu Xie's *Wenxin Diaolong* and Chen Kui's *Wen Ze* (Kirkpatrick) discussed earlier in Chapters 2 and 3 respectively.

It is worth mentioning here a brief note about the infamous Chinese university exam, the *gao kao* (literally meaning "high examination"). The *gao kao* has far-reaching influence on the students' career path and personal and professional development. The *gao kao* was established in 1955, although it ceased to function during the ten years of Chinese Cultural Revolution (1966-1976), re-emerging in 1977. Over the years, the *gao kao* has been changed and modified. It is still called the nationwide standard examination, but the test papers are administered regionally at the provincial level. Three subjects are compulsory: Chinese (*Yuwen*), Mathematics (*Shuxue*), and Foreign Language(s) (*Waiyu*). In addition, Arts students are examined on politics, history and geography, while Science students are examined in biology, chemistry and physics. As far as the Chinese subject is concerned, the test item on writing has a particular washback effect on the students' writing and literacy development. In the Chinese subject examination, students are required to do a series of exercises on Chinese vocabulary, grammar, reading comprehension, and their general knowledge of Chinese. They must also write an essay. The essay topics vary from year to year and here we give some sample topics and tasks which have been set since 1980. The topic for 1980 was a *du hou gan* (reaction to a reading) about a story describing Leonardo Da Vinci's attempts to draw a perfect egg. The topic and task for 1990 was to write a *yilun* (argumentative) essay on given reading material entitled "Beneath Every Flower There Is a Thorn". The topic and task for 2000 was a written response to four graphs given as visual stimuli, whereby students were required to express their own perspectives, their different understandings, approaches and solutions to real life issues. The essay topics also vary from region to region. The various essay topics on the one hand show that Chinese students, despite the mention of the *qi-cheng-zhuan-he* structure in some textbooks do not have to learn traditional Chinese text styles, in the same manner as the Chinese ancient *Shuyuan* students did, in order to enter universities. Contemporary Chinese students "are encouraged to be inventive and original in their writing" (Kirkpatrick "Are They Really so Different?" 50–1).

BOOKS ON CHINESE COMPOSITION PRIOR TO THE 1990s

Prior to the 1990s, Chinese composition courses and course book writing at the tertiary level were given more emphasis than they are today. For example, in the late 1970s, the Ministry of Education organised a number of meetings to discuss composition teaching and course book writing. One resultant course book was *Fundamentals for Writing* (*Xiezuo jichu zhishi*) (Liu X. et al.). This book was reviewed by prominent Chinese linguists including Lü Shuxiang, Zhu Dexi and Zhang Zhigong. It comprises chapters about definitions and the social functions of writing and attitudes towards writing; the collection of writing material; theme development; composition structure; language; narration; description and dialogue; argumentation and exposition; revising and editing; and writing styles. As far as language is concerned, this book advises that "language should be used to communicate and exchange ideas", and that the use of language should be "precise, concise, vivid, and simple" (Liu X. et al. 147–54). The book also pointed out eight common "sins" in contemporary writing, namely "fake writing", "empty writing", "irrational or unreasonable writing", "rigid writing", "insinuation writing", "invariable writing", "brainwashing writing", and "writing for fame and benefits" (Liu X. 298–9).

Other course books on writing published in the 1980s focused on fundamental writing skills training, and the relationship between writing and reading. Lu, Shi, and Fan's *A Writing Course Book* contains chapters on developing the basic skills needed for writing (e.g., observing, investigating, developing topic and theme, selecting material, developing structure, using language and appropriate writing styles, distinguishing speech and writing, imitating and being creative, and drafting and revising), and the training of writing in different genres, e.g., narration, argumentation, exposition, and practical writing. The book advocates the collection of empirical data for writing. For example, the authors (7–8) list six ways of collecting data: focus group interviews; individual interviews; field work; the writer's first-hand experience; observations; and literature, reference and archive searches.

Hu's *University Writing* contains not only a variety of topics on writing *per se*, but also a chapter which provides twenty sample readings, including a selection from the Chinese classics. One such piece is the *Memorial Expressing My Feelings* by Limi (224–87 CE) (translated and discussed in Chapter 2). The readings also contain contemporary masterpieces from both home and abroad. "Medicine" by Lu Xun (1881-1936), "Friendship or invasionInvasion?" by Mao Zedong (1893-1976), "The Cop and the Anthem" by O'Henry (1862-1910), and "On Authority" by Friedrich Engels (1820-1895) are examples. According to Hu (382), reading just twenty sample articles is far from sufficient and students need to consult other classical and modern collections in order to improve their writing skills.

In Chapter 8, we reviewed two important studies on paragraph development and arrangement. Hao identified eleven different ways in which paragraphs can be organised (Kirkpatrick, "Chinese Rhetoric" 251–5). The first of these is the juxtaposition of coordinates, *binglie guanxi*. The second way of organising a paragraph is through sequencing, *chengjie guanxi*. Paragraphs that follow this pattern are chronologically sequenced and are straightforward. The third method is *dijin guanxi*, and this is defined as a linguistic style that follows sequential ordering based on size, height, number, depth or weight. The fourth organisational method is the *xuanze guanxi*, literally "choosing relation". The fifth method is the *jieshuo guanxi* where the function of the latter part of the paragraph is to provide an explanation or example of what has been expressed earlier. The sixth organisational principle is the *zhuanzhe guanxi*, the transitional or contrastive relation. The seventh is the *yinguo guanxi*, or the cause and effect relation, which, in our view, is of greatest significance for the organisation of text in Chinese. The eighth and ninth organising principles or logical relations are *jiashe* or hypothetical, and *tiaojian* or conditional, respectively. The tenth method of paragraph organisation is the *mudi guanxi*, or purpose, or "in order to" type connection. The eleventh is the *zongfen* or whole-part organisational principle. "This eleventh principle is closely linked to inductive and deductive methods of argument, with whole-part linked to deductive argument and part-whole to inductive" (Kirkpatrick 2002: 254).

In his review of a sample of Chinese composition books written in the 1980s and 1990s, Kirkpatrick (246) points out that "the influence of European and English rhetoric should not be overlooked. The May 4th Movement of 1919 saw a flood of translations of European and English texts of a variety of different types and these translations had a stylistic influence on contemporary Chinese writing". He also points out that "by the 1980s a wider range of examples [for writing compositions] is evident. This more liberal trend is discernible into the textbooks of the 1990s."

In addition to academic writing as such, the majority of Chinese university writing books focus on practical writing (*yingyong* writing), i.e., business and official document writing, and various other practical genres. "*Yingyong* writing" is very common (Liu Yancheng 1). Although the nearest English equivalent of "*yingyong* writing" is practical writing, the term refers to a range of official documents, notices, receipts and so forth. Some of the modern genres of practical writing correspond to the classifications found in earlier classification. For example, Yao Nai (1731-1815), whom we discussed in Chapter 8 as a leading supporter of the Tong Cheng school of writing, listed thirteen genres.[22]

Huo classifies the different genres of contemporary practical writing into office documents, advertisements, public relations documents, business writing, law and court related writing, news writing, foreign affairs related writing, and academic writing. Thus academic writing is just one genre of the many listed under practical writing.

A more comprehensive classification of practical writing is provided by Lu, Zhan, and Zhang (*A Course on Practical Writing*). He lists the different genres, sub-dividing each. We provide his full list here to give readers an idea of how sophisticated and complex this list of genres is. The sub-genres, many of which are themselves sub-divided, are listed after the main genre.

1. *xingzheng gongwen* (administrative documents): a. *mingling* (administrative order, order), *jueding* (decision); b. *gonggao* (pronouncement), *tonggao* (announcement), *tongzhi* (notification), *tongbao* (circular, notice); c. *yian* (bill, proposal), *qingshi* (referendum, instructions), *pifu* (response to requests/memorials), *baogao* (report); d. *yijian* (suggestion), *han* (letter);
2. *gongguan wenshu* (public relations (PR) documents): a. *yaoqing xin* (letter of invitation), *ganxie xin* (letter of thanks, letter of gratitude), *weiwen xin* (letter of support), *qingjian* (invitation card); b. *daoci* (eulogy, memorial speech), *fugao* (obituary), *yanhan* (letter or message of condolence), *beiwen* (epitaph); c. *zhengming xin* (a letter prepared by an organisation to prove the identity of someone or for the convenience of contact), *jieshao xin* (letter of introduction, letter of reference); d. *qingjia tiao* (written request for leave), *liuyan tiao* (written) message; e. *tuijian xin* (letter of recommendation), *qiuzhi xin* (letter of application), *geren jianli* (resume, curriculum vitae);
3. *shiwu wenshu* (routine matters, affairs, work documents): a. *jihua* (plan, scheme, programme); b. *zongjie* (summing-up report,

summary); c. *diaocha baogao* (report of findings, investigation report); d. *guizhang zhidu* (rules and regulations);
4. *falu wenshu* (legal documents): a. *qisu zhuang* (pleading, administrative statement of claim); b. *shangsu zhuang* (petition for appeal); c. *shengsu zhuang* (appeal for revision); d. *dabian zhuang* (replication);
5. *caijing wenshu* (finance and economics documents): a. *chanpin shuoming shu* (product specifications), *guanggao wenan* (advertisement); b. *zhaobiao shu yu toubiao shu* (request for proposal, and tender/bidding document), *hetong* (contract); c. *shichang diaocha yu yuce baogao* (market investigation report, and market prediction report), *kexingxing yanjiu baogao* (feasibility study report); d. *jingji juece fangan* (economic decision/plan), *shenji baogao* (audit report);
6. *huiyi wenshu* (meeting/conference documents): a. *kaimu ci* (opening speech/address), *bimu ci* (closing speech/address); b. *jianghua gao* (text of a talk), *yanjiang gao* (text of a speech); c. *huiyi jilu* (minutes of a meeting), *huiyi jiyao* (summary of a meeting), *jianbao* (briefing, bulletin);
7. *keyan wenshu* (science and research documents): a. *xueshu lunwen* (academic paper); b. *biyelunwen* (thesis, dissertation); c. *shiyan baogao* (test/experiment report);
8. *shenlun* (the *Shenlun* exam): a. *yilun wen* (argumentative writing/paper); b. *shuoming wen* (expository writing, exposition).

The explicit focus on *yingyong* writing or practical writing among contemporary university composition books and academic writing's place as just one of many genres to be learned implies that Chinese composition instruction is currently more concerned with the needs of the bureaucracy than the university.

In addition to reviewing a number of contemporary Chinese texts on composition, we also conducted a focus group survey among university graduates, who majored in Chinese and Chinese-related degree strands, for example, Chinese Studies and Chinese Journalism. The survey shows that the majority of the Chinese Departments in Chinese universities use books on both writing theory and practical writing. The students are generally required to write short pieces between 100 and 500 words for the purpose of practicing writing a particular genre, e.g., argumentation, narration, and to practice using a particular rhetorical device. Such teaching approaches may also indirectly influence how composition textbooks for university students are designed and compiled. It is worth reiterating, however, that in the current tertiary curriculum, it is not common for non-Chinese majors to receive explicit instruction on Chinese writing. They usually get more instruction in English writing (and in other foreign languages, e.g., Japanese, Russian, German or French) than in Chinese. Chinese writing instruction and practice form only a part of the curriculum for Chinese and linguistics majors.

In this chapter, we have reviewed a selection of contemporary writing course books for Chinese university students. These books include writing course books which cover theoretical aspects of writing, and applied writing guides which instruct students on how to write a range of different "bureaucratic" genres. These writing books bear the influence, both of the Chinese tradition and Western theory and practice.

Writing at the tertiary level experienced a revival period immediately after the Cultural Revolution in the late 1970s, and 1980s. However, since the 1990s, the development of writing as an academic discipline has not been given sufficient emphasis especially among non-Chinese majors. In attempt to redress this, writing specialists and educators have recently compiled many course books in composition and rhetoric which aim to integrate Chinese writing traditions with the theories on writing introduced to China from the West. In this, however, they are revisiting an established practice. The review of the major currently adopted university composition books in China enables us to draw the following conclusions or observations: the focus of Chinese university composition books appears to be more on practical writing rather than on training students to develop skills in argumentative essay writing for the academy. A typical Chinese undergraduate (via the *gao kao*) may be well-equipped with writing short articles with memory-based historical facts or evidence, but not research-based academic essays; and a typical Chinese university major will be trained to write a wide variety of practical "bureaucratic" genres. Non-Chinese majors, however, who comprise the great majority of Chinese university students, will receive little instruction in Chinese writing and composition once they have entered the university. Many will receive more instruction in writing in a foreign language, particularly in English. We consider the implications of this in the concluding chapter, where we also summarise the main points we have made throughout the book.

CONCLUSION

In this book we have described a selection of rhetorical and persuasive styles in China, drawing a particular distinction between "top-down" and "bottom-up" persuasion. We have illustrated these and also exemplified a number of traditional Chinese text structures which were used as clothing in which to dress "persuasions." In so doing, we have also argued that similar styles have been adopted at different times in other cultures, including Ciceronian Rome and Medieval Europe, thus suggesting that, while there are clearly distinctive aspects of Chinese rhetoric, it is not the absolute other. We have elucidated a number of linguistic principles of argument and rhetoric in Chinese, showing how these principles work together to help construct the unmarked, default "frame-to-main" sequence and rhetorical structure of Chinese argument and persuasion, while showing that a marked sequence and structure is also commonly used when there is a specific motivation for such a marked form. We here recap the principles we presented in the conclusion to Chapter 7:

1. The "because-therefore" operates at levels of discourse as well as at sentence level. It represents an important sequencing principle in MSC. For example, when MSC speakers are justifying a claim, they commonly posit the reasons for the claim before making it, following a "frame-main" sequence.
2. These "because-therefore" and "frame-main" sequences can be recursive. This rhetorical structure is more likely to occur in planned speech than in spontaneous speech. Although, in more planned speech, the use of the because and therefore connectors is comparatively uncommon, a therefore connector, either *suoyi* or *yinci* is common, but not obligatory, when its communicative purpose is to signal a summary statement.

This rhetorical structure is represented in the diagram.

BECAUSE x n +THEREFORE x n

THEREFORE.

3. In more spontaneous speech, enveloping is likely. When this occurs a "because-therefore" unit can act as a "pregnant" unit and contain a number of lower level units within it. These lower level units can themselves be lower level 'because-therefore' units. In more spontaneous speech, where there is enveloping, connectors are more common. This structure is represented in the diagram.

BECAUSE [LOWER LEVEL UNITS] THEREFORE

4. The structures in (ii) and (iii) can be used in combination.
5. In addition to acting as sentence level connectors, both the 'because' and the 'therefore' connectors can act as discourse markers. They can introduce and control a series so that "because x n" and "therefore x n" are possible sequences.
6. The presence of explicit "because" and "therefore" discourse markers is less likely in formal planned speech than in informal and more unplanned discourse.

In addition, we have also illustrated related principles of sequencing and these include a preference for big-small sequencing or whole-part sequencing, often realised as topic-comment constructions, and James Tai's Principle of Temporal Sequence (PTS) defined as "the relative word order between two syntactic units is determined by the temporal order of the states they represent in the conceptual world" (50).

A further related principle we identified and illustrated was that Chinese follows logical or natural order so that the sequence in which the following two clauses are presented, "he fell over, he hurt his ankle", *must* mean that "because he fell over he hurt his ankle". The cause always precedes the effect. This, in turn means, that the use of explicit connectors which demonstrate the relationship between the clauses is not required. However, as we have also shown, influence from Western languages, particularly through the translations of Western texts into Chinese at the turn on the twentieth century, has meant that the use of explicit subordinating conjunctions in hypotactic clauses are now frequent in Chinese so that the sentence sequence, "He fell over because he hurt his ankle" are now possible (and common) in Chinese.

In the early chapters, we showed that an inductive method of argument represented the unmarked arrangement of ideas, not least because the official or 'persuader' was almost always persuading "up." It will be remembered that this 'bottom-up' persuasion was termed *yin* by the philosopher Gui Guzi and required speaking "in forked tongue", while persuading from above to below encouraged "straightforward speaking" (Tsao 103). Thus many methods of reasoning in Chinese adopted an inductive sequence, as this was safer when persuading "up." The key textual patterns of *qi-cheng-zhuan-he* and the *ba gu wen* both lend themselves to inductive and "indirect" argument. But, as we also pointed out, this did not mean that Chinese were not able to use deductive or mixed methods of argument. We provided examples of texts where writers adopted a deductive arrangement of ideas. We argue, therefore, that the socio-political context, in particular the relative relationship between speaker/writer and listener/hearer, is at least as important as culture in determining the ways in which people arrange argument and persuade. This is as true of Chinese rhetoric as of any other rhetoric.

We also showed that the Chinese rhetorical tradition was diverse and dynamic. On occasion the flowery *pianwen* style was promoted, while at others, the *guwen* classical style of plain speaking was required, as exemplified in Chen Kui's *Rules of Writing*. The debate between content and form has a long history in China.

We also argued that some of the rhetorical features which have been ascribed to Western influence since the turn of the twentieth century and since the development of rhetoric as a discrete discipline in China can, in fact, be found in traditional Chinese rhetoric. Contemporary evidence for this can be found in the advice given in contemporary texts on Chinese writing and composition which we analysed in Chapter 10. It is important to note, however, the irony that the majority of Chinese university students are now given more instruction on how to write in English than in how to write in Chinese. Only Chinese majors currently obtain in-depth knowledge of the Chinese rhetorical tradition.

This is one reason why we suggested in Chapter 9 that contemporary Chinese, whether they represent the government or its critics, have failed to create a new rhetorical style suitable for twenty-first-century public and political discourse in which citizens and the government can engage in critical debate. Instead, both sides have adopted a style that combines the imperious "top-down" style along with an agonistic "cultural-revolution" approach. We provided the examples of *Charter 08* and the Tiananmen mothers' *Open Letter* as examples of this aggressive accusatory style. These documents follow a "top-down" or *yang* style, and thus more likely to inflame than persuade the Chinese authorities. The current lack of an accepted rhetorical style of public discourse means that it is currently impossible for civic-minded Chinese to engage in constructive public debate. As we write (March 2011) several more "dissidents" have been arrested for "subversion." The practical writing taught to Chinese majors aims to serve the State and bureaucracy rather than constructively challenge it. As well as being an introduction to Chinese rhetoric and writing, this book also represents a plea that the extraordinarily rich and diverse rhetorical tradition of traditional China be re-instated into school and university curricula. A knowledge of the precepts of traditional Chinese rhetoric, an understanding of the principles of information and argument sequencing, along with a study of textual and rhetorical styles could lead to the development of new rhetorical styles "with Chinese characteristics" which would be appropriate for constructive and critical public discourse.

In conclusion, we hope that this book has offered insights into and an understanding of the Chinese rhetorical tradition. We hope that we have demonstrated that, as well as differences, there are many similarities between the Chinese rhetorical tradition and the Western rhetorical tradition.

In the Introduction to the book, we expressed the hope that it would encourage debate about what we referred to as the "primacy" of Anglo-American rhetoric. As the world becomes increasingly pluricentric, we argue that it is crucial that we learn about the rhetorical traditions of other cultures and that we consider ways in which the dissemination of knowledge can become increasingly multilateral. In the specific case of China, as China becomes increasingly powerful and important, it would seem no more than wise, to repeat Shi-Xu's admonition we quoted in the Introduction, to stress that we cannot understand China "without also understanding what it says, how it says things, how its current discourses are connected with its past and those of other cultures" (224–45). This has been the aim of this book.

WORKS CITED

Ammon, Ulrich. "Towards More Fairness in International English: Linguistic Rights of Non-Native Speakers?" *Rights to Language: Equity, Power and Education.* Ed. Robert Phillipson. Mahwah, New Jersey: Lawrence Erlbaum Associates, 2000. 111-116.
Ankersmit, Frank R. "Historicism: An Attempt at Synthesis." *History and Theory* 34.3 (1995): 143-61. Print.
Aristotle. *The Art of Rhetoric.* Trans. John Freese. London: Heineman, 1947. Print.
Bloch, Joel, and Lan Chi. "A Comparison of the use of Citation in Chinese and English Academic Discourse." *Academic Writing in a Second Language: Essays on Research and Pedagogy.* Ed. Diane Belcher and George Braine. Norwood: Ablex, 1995. 231-74. Print.
Bloom, Alfred. *The Linguistic Shaping of Thought: A Study in the Impact of Thinking in China and the West.* New Jersey: Lawrence Erlbaum, 1981. Print.
Bol, Peter K. *This Culture of Ours'. Intellectual Transitions in T'ang and Song China.* Stanford: Stanford University Press, 1992. Print.
Bolton, Kingsley. "English in Asia, Asian Englishes, and the Issue of Proficiency." *English Today* 23 (2008): 3-12. Print.
Cahill, David. "Contrastive Rhetoric, Orientalism and the Chinese Second Language Writer." Diss. University of Illinois at Chicago, 1999. Print.
Cai, Zong-qi, ed. *A Chinese Literary Mind: Culture, Creativity, and Rhetoric in Wenxin Diaolong.* Stanford: Stanford University Press, 2001. Print.
Camargo, Martin. *Medieval Rhetorics of Prose Composition.* Binghamton: State University of New York Press, 1995. Print.
Canagarajah, Suresh C. *A Geopolitics of Academic Writing.* Pittsburgh: University of Pittsburgh Press, 2002. Print.
—. "Reconstructing Local Knowledge, Reconfiguring Language Studies." *Reclaiming the Local in Language Policy and Practice.* Ed. Suresh C. Canagarajah. Mahwah: Lawrence Erlbaum Associates, 2005. Print.

Chafe, Wallace L. "Givenness, Contrastiveness, Definiteness, Subjects, Topics and Point of View." *Subject and Topic*. Ed. Charles N. Li. New York: Academic Press, 1976. 27-55. Print.

Chaffee, John N. *The Thorny Gates of Learning in Song China: A Social History of Examinations*. Cambridge: Cambridge University Press, 1985. Print.

Chai, Winberg, ed. *A Treasury of Chinese Literature*. New York: Thomas Y. Crowell, 1974. Print.

Chen, Jianping. "An Investigation into the Preference for Discourse Patterns in the Chinese EFL Context." *International Journal of Applied Linguistics* 18.2 (2008): 188-211. Print.

Chen, Ping. "Referent Introducing and Tracking in Chinese Narratives." Diss. University of California at Los Angeles, 1986. Print.

Chen, Pingyuan. *Lishi, Chuanshuo Yu Jingshen: Zhongguo Daxue Bainian (历史,传说与精神:中国大学百年) (History, Legend, and Spirit: China's University in a Century)*. Hong Kong: Joint Publishing (H.K.) Co. Ltd., 2009. Print.

Chen, Shou-yi. *Chinese Literature: A Historical Introduction*. New York: The Ronald Press, 1961. Print.

Chen, Wangdao. *Xiuci Xue Fafan (修辞学发凡) (An Introduction to Rhetoric)*. Shanghai: Dajiang Shupu, 1932. Print.

Chen, Zhenqiu. *Fanyi Wenti Tansuo (翻译问题探索) (on the Problems of Translation)*. Beijing: Shangwu Yinshuguan, 1980. Print.

Cheng, Duanli. "Dushu Fennian Richeng (读书分年日程) (the Annual Schedule of Reading)." *Siku Quanshu (四库全书) (the Complete Books of the Four Imperial Repositories) Vol. 709*. Shanghai: Shanghai Guji Publishing House, 1987. 487. Print.

Cheng, Fangyin, Qinlin Fan, and Qijun Ma, eds. *Xinbian Yingyongwen Xiezuo Jiaocheng (新编应用文写作教程) (A New Course on Practical Writing)*. 1st ed. Beijing: Foreign Language Teaching and Research Press, 2008. Print.

Cherniack, Susan. "Book Culture and Textual Transmission in Sung China." *Harvard Journal of Asiatic Studies* 54.1 (1994): 5-125. Print.

Chow, Kai-wing. "Discourse, Examination, and Local Elites: The Invention of the T'Ung-Ch'Eng School in Ch'Ing China." *Society and Education in Late Imperial China: 1600-1900*. Ed. Benjamin A. Elman and Alexander Woodside. Berkeley: University of California Press, 1994. 183-219. Print.

Corbett, Edward P. J., and Robert J. Connors. *Classical Rhetoric for the Modern Student*. Fourth Edition. New York: Oxford University Press, 1999. Print.

Crump, James. *Intrigues: Studies of the Chan-Kuo Ts'e*. Ann Arbor: Michigan University Press, 1964. Print.

Crystal, David. *A Dictionary of Linguistics and Phonetics*. Oxford: Basil Blackwell, 1985. Print.

Cua, Antonio S. *Ethical Argumentation: A Study in Hsun Tzu's Epistemology*. Honolulu: Hawaii University Press, 1985. Print.

—. "Ethical Uses of the Past in Early Confucianism: The Case of Hsun-Tzu." *Philosophy East and West* 35.2 (1985): 133-56. Print.

Curme, George O. *A Grammar of the English Language. Volume II: Syntax*. Boston: Heath, 1931. Print.

Dai, Lei. "Lun Yuti De Fenlei (论语体的分类) (the Classification of Styles) " *Xiuci Xuexi (The Study of Rhetoric)* 1 (1988): 5-21. Print.

Di, Chen. "Pianzhang Xiuci Chutan (篇章修辞初探) (A Preliminary Discussion on the Rhetoric of Text)." *Xiucixue Lunji (修辞学论集)(Collected Works on Rhetoric)*. Ed. Chinese Rhetoric Society. Fuzhou: Fujian People's Publishing, 1984. 289-306. Print.

Duan, Jianjun, and Wei Li. *Xinbian Xiezuo Siweixue Jiaocheng (新编写作思维学教程) (A New Course on the Studies of Thinking for Writing)*. Shanghai: Fudan University Press, 2008. Print.

Durrant, Stephen. "Creating Tradition: Sima Qian Agonistes?" *Early China/Ancient Greece: Thinking through Comparisons*. Ed. Steven Shankman and Stephen Durrant. New York: State University of New York Press, 2002. 283-311. Print.

Elman, Benjamin A., and Alexander Woodside, eds. *Education and Society in Late Imperial China: 1600-1900*. Berkeley: University of California Press, 1994. Print.

Elman, Benjamin A. "Changes in Confucian Civil Service Examinations from the Ming to the Ching Dynasty." *Education and Society in Late Imperial China: 1600-1900*. Ed. Benjamin A. Elman and Alexander Woodside. Berkeley: University of California Press, 1994. 111-49. Print.

Faulhaber, Charles B. "The Summa Dictaminis of Guido Faba." *Medieval Eloquence: Studies in the History and Practice of Medieval Rhetoric*. Ed. James Murphy. Berkeley: University of California Press, 1978. 85-111. Print.

Feng, Youlan. *Zhongguo Zhexue Shi Xin Bian (中国哲学史新编) (A New History of Chinese Philosophy)*. Vol. 3. Beijing: People's Publishing, 1984. Print.

Ferreira-Buckley, Linda, and Winifred B. Horner. "Writing Instruction in Great Britain: The Eighteenth and Nineteenth Centuries." *A Short History of Writing Instruction: From Ancient Greece to Modern America*. Ed. James J. Murphy. Mahwah, New Jersey: Lawrence Erlbaum Associates, 2001. 173-212. Print.

Foley, William, and Robert Van Valin. *Functional Syntax and Universal Grammar*. Cambridge, New York: Cambridge University Press, 1984. Print.

Forke, Alfred. "The Chinese Sophists." *Journal of the Royal Asiatic Society (North China Branch)* XXXIV (1901): 1-100. Print.

"Four Examination Essays of the Ming Dynasty." *Renditions* 33 & 34 (1990): 167-81. Print.

Gale, Esson M. *Discourse on Salt and Iron.* Leyden: E. J. Bull, Ltd., 1931. Print.

Gao, Hong, et al, eds. *Yingyongwen Xiezuo Xinjiaocheng (应用文写作新教程) (A New Course on Practical Writing).* 1st ed. Beijing: Tsinghua University Press, 2009. Print.

Gao, Po, Qiuling Sun, and Liguang Zhao, eds. *Yingyong Xiezuo Jiaocheng (应用写作教程) (A Course on Practical Writing).* 1st ed. Beijing: Tsinghua University Press, 2010. Print.

Garrett, Mary M. "The 'Mo-Tzu' and 'Lu-Shih Ch'Un-Ch'Iu': A Case Study of Classical Chinese Theory and Practice of Argument." Diss. University of California 1983. Print.

Graham, Angus C. *The Disputers of the Dao: Philosophical Argument in Ancient China.* Chicago and La Salle, Illinois: Open Court Press, 1989. Print.

—. *Later Mohist Logic, Ethics and Science.* London: School of Oriental and African Studies, 1978. Print.

—. *Yin Yang and the Nature of Correlative Thinking.* Singapore: Institute of East Asian Philosophies, 1986. Print.

Gunn, Edward M. *Rewriting Chinese: Style and Innovation in Twentieth-Century Chinese Prose.* Stanford: Stanford University Press, 1991. Print.

Haffenden, John. *William Empson, Volume I: Among the Mandarins.* Oxford: Oxford University Press, 2008. Print.

Halliday, Michael A. K. *An Introduction to Functional Grammar.* London: Edward Arnold, 1985. Print.

Hao, Changliu. *Yuduan Zhishi (语段知识)(Knowledge of Discourse).* Beijing: Beijing Publishing Company, 1983. Print.

Harbsmeier, Christoph. "Chinese Rhetoric." *T'oung Pao, Monographies.* 85 (1999): 114-27. Print.

Hatim, Basil. *Arabic Rhetoric: The Pragmatics of Deviation from Linguistic Norms.* Munich: Lincom GmbH, 2010. Print.

Hayhoe, Ruth. *China's Universities 1895-1995: A Century of Cultural Conflict.* New York, London: Garland Publishing, Inc., 1996. Print.

Her, One-soon. "Topic as Grammatical Function in Chinese." *Lingua* 84 (1991): 1-23. Print.

Hightower, J.R. *Topics in Chinese Literature.* Cambridge: Harvard University Press, 1965. Print.

Hockett, Charles F. *A Course in Modern Linguistics.* New York: Macmillan, 1958. Print.

Holzman, Donald. "Confucius and Ancient Chinese Literary Criticism." *Chinese Approaches to Literature from Confucius to Liang Ch'i-Ch'Ao.* Ed.

Adele A. Rickett. Princeton, N.J.: Princeton University Press, 1978. 21-41. Print.

Hsu, Chung Yueh Immanuel. *The Rise of Modern China*. Hong Kong: Oxford University Press, 1976. Print.

Hu, Shi. *The Development of the Logical Method in Ancient China*. Shanghai: Oriental Books, 1923. Print.

—. "Wenxue Gailiang Chuyi (文学改良刍义)(an Initial Discussion on Literary Innovation)." *Hu Shi Wencun (胡适文存) (A Collection of Hu Shi's Works)*. Ed. Shi Hu. Taipei: Yuandong Tushu Gongsi, 1953. 5-16. Print.

Hu, Yushu, and Xiu Yan. *University Writing*. Fudan University Press, 1985. Print.

Huang, Gaocai, and Huiqin Liu, eds. *Xinbian Yingyongxiezuo Jiaocheng (新编应用写作教程) (A New Course on Practical Writing)*. 1st ed. Beijing: Higher Education Press, 2008. Print.

Huo, Ran. *Daxue Yingyong Xiezuo (大学应用写作) (University Practical Writing)*. Zhejiang: Zhejiang University Press, 2006. Print.

Jenner, William F. J. *The Tyranny of History: The Roots of China's Crisis*. London: Allen Lane, Penguin Books, 1992. Print.

Jia, Yuxin, and Cheng Cheng. "Indirectness in Chinese English Writing." *Asian Englishes* 5.1 (2002): 64-74. Print.

Jullien, Francois. *Detour and Access: Strategies of Meaning in China and Greece*. Trans. Sophie Kawkes. New York: Zone Books, 2004. Print.

—. *The Propensity of Things: Toward a History of Efficacy in China*. Trans. Janet Lloyd. New York: Zone Books, 1995. Print.

Kao, Karl S. Y. "Chinese Rhetoric." *The Indiana Companion to Traditional Chinese Literature*. Ed. William H. Nienhauser. Bloomington: Indiana University Press, 1985. 121-37. Print.

Kaplan, Robert B. *The Anatomy of Rhetoric: Prolegomena to a Functional Theory of Rhetoric*. Philadelphia: Center for Curriculum Development, 1972. Print.

—. "Cultural Thought Patterns in Inter-Cultural Education." *Language Learning* 16 (1966): 1-20. Print.

Kennedy, George A. *Classical Rhetoric and its Christian and Secular Tradition from Ancient to Modern Times*. Chapel Hill: University of North Carolina Press, 1980. Print.

Kent Guy, Robert. "Fang Pao and the Ch'in-Ting Ssu-Shu-Wen." *Education and Society in Late Imperial China 1600-1900*. Ed. Benjamin A. Elman and Alexander Woodside. Berkeley: University of California Press, 1994. 150-82. Print.

Kinney, Anne B. *The Art of the Han Essay: Wang Fu's Ch'Ien-Fu Lun*. Tempe, Ariz: Center for Asian Studies, Arizona State University, 1990. Print.

Kirkpatrick, Andy. "Are They Really so Different? The "Chinese" Genre of University Entrance Essays." *Open Letter: Australian Journal for Adult Literacy Research and Practice* 5.2 (1995): 43-52. Print.
—. "The Arrangement of Letters: Hierarchy Or Culture? from Cicero to China." *Journal of Asian Pacific Communication* 17.2 (2007): 245-58. Print.
—. "China's First Systematic Account of Rhetoric: An Introduction to Chen Kui's *Wen Ze*." *Rhetorica* 23.2 (2005): 103-52. Print.
—. "Chinese Rhetoric by the Book: What the Textbooks and Handbooks Say." *Chinese Communication Studies: Contexts and Comparisons*. Ed. Xing Lu, Wenshen Jia, and Ray D. Heisey. Westport, CT: Ablex Publishing, 2002. 245-60. Print.
—. "Chinese Rhetoric: Methods of Argument." *Multilingua* 14.3 (1995): 271-95. Print.
—. "Information Sequencing in Mandarin in Letters of Request." *Anthropological Linguistics* 33.2 (1991): 1-20. Print.
—. "Information Sequencing in Modern Standard Chinese in Genre of Extended Spoken Discourse." *Text* 13.3 (1993): 422-52. Print.
—. "Traditional Chinese Text Structures and their Influence on the Writing in Chinese and English of Contemporary Chinese Students." *Journal of Second Language Writing* 6.3 (1997): 223-44. Print.
Knechtges, David. "Han and 6 Dynasties Parallel Prose." *Renditions* 33-34 (1990): 63-110. Print.
Koeneke, Rodney. *Empires of the Mind: I. A. Richards and Basic English in China, 1929-1979*. Stanford, California: Stanford University Press, 2004. Print.
Kracke, Edward A. *Civil Service in Early Sung China, 960-1067*. Vol. 13. Cambridge: Harvard University Press, 1953. Print.
Kroll, Jurij L. "Disputation in Ancient Chinese Culture." *Early China* 11-12 (1985): 118-45. Print.
Lanham, Carol D. "Writing Instruction from Late Antiquity to the Twelfth Century." *A Short History of Writing Instruction: From Ancient Greece to Modern America*. Ed. James Murphy. Mahwah: Erlbaum/Hermagoras Press, 2001. 79-121. Print.
Lasswell, Harold D., and Nathan Leites, eds. *Language of Politics: Studies in Quantitative Semantics*. New York: George Stewart, 1949. Print.
Lehmann, Christian. "Towards a Typology of Clause Linkage." *Clause Combining in Grammar and Discourse*. Ed. John Haiman and Sandra A. Thompson. Amsterdam, Philadelphia: John Benjamins, 1988. 181-225. Print.
Lewis, Mark E. *Writing and Authority in Early China*. Albany: State University of New York Press, 1999. Print.
The Li Ki (the Book of Rites). Trans. James Legge. New York: University Books, 1967. Print.

Li, Charles N., and Sandra A. Thompson. *Mandarin Chinese: A Functional Reference Grammar*. Berkeley: University of California Press, 1981. Print.

Li, David C. S., and Sherman Lee. "Bilingualism in East Asia." *The Handbook of Bilingualism*. Ed. Tej K. Bhatia and William C. Ritchie. Oxford: Blackwell Publishing, 2004. 742-79. Print.

Li, Xilan. "Weiqu Wanzhuan Mianli Cangzhen (委曲婉转绵里藏针) (Indirectness and Diplomacy: A Needle Hidden in Silk)." *Xiuci Xuexi (The Study of Rhetoric)* 3 (1985): 14-24. Print.

Li, Yunhan, and Weigeng Zhang. *Xiandai Hanyu Xiucixue (现代汉语修辞学)(the Rhetoric of Modern Chinese)*. Hong Kong: Shangwu Yinshuguan, 1984. Print.

Liang, Qichao. *Liangzhu Zuowen Rumen (梁著作文入门) (Liang's Introduction to Composition)*. Beijing: China Workers' Press, 2007. Print.

Lin, Xiaoqing Diana. *Peking University: Chinese Scholarship and Intellectuals 1898-1935*. Albany: State University of New York Press, 2005. Print.

Lin, Yuwen. *Pianzheng Fuju (偏正复句) (Compound Sentences)*. Shanghai: Shanghai Education Publishing, 1984. Print.

The Literary Mind and the Carving of Dragons (Liu Hsieh). Trans. Vincent Yu-chung Shih. New York: Columbia University Press, 1959. Print.

Liu, Xiqing, et al. *Fundamentals for Writing*. Beijing: Beijing Press, 1979. Print.

Liu, Yameng. "Three Issues in the Argumentative Conception of Early Chinese Discourse." *Philosophy East and West* 46.1 (1996): 33-58. Print.

—. "To Capture the Essence of Chinese Rhetoric: An Anatomy of a Paradigm of Contrastive Rhetoric." *Rhetoric Review* 14.2 (1996): 318-35. Print.

Liu, Yancheng. *Wen Ze Zhuyi (文则注译) (Commentary and Modern Chinese Translation of the Wen Ze)*. Beijing: Shumu Wenxian Chubanshe, 1988 Print.

Liu, Zhuang. *Zhongguo Yingyongwen Yuanliu Yanjiu (中国应用文源流研究) (A Study on the Origin of Chinese Practical Writing)*. Beijing: Beijing Library Press, 2007. Print.

Lu, Deqing, Yaxi Shi, and Peisong Fan. *A Writing Course Book*. East China Normal University Press, 1982. Print.

Lu, Xing. *Rhetoric of the Chinese Cultural Revolution*. Columbia, South Carolina: University of South Carolina Press, 2004. Print.

—. *Rhetoric in Ancient China: Fifth to Third Century BC*. Columbia, South Carolina: University of South Carolina Press, 1998. Print.

Lu, Yaping, Dan Zhan, and Biao Zhang. *Yingyongwen Xiezuo Jiaocheng (应用文写作教程) (A Course on Practical Writing)*. Shanghai: Fudan university press, 2008. Print.

Lu, Zhuoqun, and Lihua Pu. *Zhongwen Xueke Lunwen Xiezuo (中文学科论文写作) (Thesis Writing in Chinese)*. 1st ed. Beijing: China People's University Press, 2008. Print.

Ma, Zhengping. *Advanced Writing Training Course (高等写作思维训练教程) (A Course on the Training of Thinking for Advanced Writing)*. Beijing: China Renmin University Press, 2002. Print.

Ma, Zhong. *Gudai Hanyu Yufa (古代汉语语法) (Classical Chinese Grammar)*. Shandong: Shandong Jiaoyu Chubanshe, 1983. Print.

Mair, Victor. "Buddhism in the Literary Mind and Ornate Rhetoric." *A Chinese Literary Mind: Culture, Creativity, and Rhetoric in Wenxin Diaolong*. Ed. Zong-qi Cai. Stanford, California: Stanford University Press, 2001. 63-81. Print.

McDonald, Edward. *Learning Chinese, Turning Chinese: Challenges to Becoming Sinophone in a Globalised World*. London: Routledge, 2011. Print.

McMullen, David. *State and Scholars in Tang China*. Cambridge: Cambridge University Press, 1988. Print.

Miyazaki, Ichisada. *China's Examination Hell: The Civil Service Examinations of Imperial China*. New Haven: Yale University Press, 1981. Print.

Moloughney, Brian. "Derivation, Intertextuality and Authority: Narrative and the Problem of Historical Coherence." *East Asian History* 23 (2002): 129-48. Print.

Murphy, James J., ed. *Three Medieval Rhetorical Arts*. Berkeley: University of California Press, 1971. Print.

Murphy, James. "Rhetoric, Western European." *The Dictionary of the Middle Ages*. Ed. Joseph R. Strayer. New York: Charles Scribner's Sons, 1988. 351-64. Print.

—. *A Short History of Writing Instruction from Ancient Greece to Twentieth Century America*. Davis, California: Hermagoras Press, 2001. Print.

Nan Song Guan Lu (南宋管录) (Official Records of the Southern Song). Ed. Fuxiang Zhang. Beijing: Zhonghua Shuju Chubanshe, 1988. Print.

Nash, David. "The Chartists: Charting a Future Democracy." *History Today* 60.5 (2010): 10-17. Print.

Ni, Baoyuan. *Lianju (炼句)(Refining Sentences)*. Shanghai: Shanghai Education Publishing, 1983. Print.

Oliver, Robert T. *Communication and Culture in Ancient India and China*. Syracuse, New York: Syracuse University Press, 1971. Print.

O'Neill, Mark. "Zhou Youguang calls it as he sees it—and is not afraid to offend." *South China Morning Post*. 20 July 2010, Print.

Owen, Stephen. *An Anthology of Chinese Literature*. New York: Norton, 1996. Print.

—. *The End of the Chinese "Middle Ages": Essays in Mid-Tang Literary Culture*. Stanford: Stanford University Press, 1996. Print.

—. "Liu Xie and the Discourse Machine." *A Chinese Literary Mind: Culture, Creativity and Rhetoric in Wenxin Diaolong*. Ed. Zong-qi Cai. Stanford, California: Stanford University Press, 2001. 175-92. Print.

Pollard, David. "Four Examination Essays of the Ming Dynasty: Editor's Introduction." *Renditions* 33 & 34 (1990). Print.

Pu, Kai, and Kun Wei. "Shilun Woguo Gudai Xiuci Yanjiu-De Tedian (试论我国古代修辞研究的特点) (A Discussion of the Characteristics of the Study of Classical Chinese Rhetoric)." *Xiucixue Yanjiu (Studies in Rhetoric)* 2 (1983): 111-24. Print.

Qi, Gong, Zhongxing Zhang, and Kemu Jin. *Shuo Bagu (说八股)(Talking about the Bagu)*. Beijing: Zhonghua Shuju Press, 1994. Print.

Qiao, Gang. *Daxue Xiezuo Xinbian (大学写作新编) (A New Course on University Writing)*. Shanghai: Fudan University Press, 2009. Print.

Ramsey, Robert S. *The Languages of China*. Princeton: Princeton University Press, 1989. Print.

Rawski, Evelyn S. *Education and Popular Literacy in Ch'ing China*. Ann Arbor: The University of Michigan Press, 1979. Print.

Richards, Ivor A. *Mencius on the Mind: Experiments in Multiple Definition*. New York: Harcourt Brace, 1932. Print.

Sacks, Harvey, Emanuel A. Schegloff, and Gail Jefferson. "A Simplest Semantics for the Organization of Turn-Taking in Conversation." *Language* 50.4 (1974): 696-735. Print.

Schleppegrell, Mary J. "Paratactic BECAUSE." *Journal of Pragmatics* 16 (1991): 323-37. Print.

Schoenals, Michael. *Doing Things with Words in Chinese Politics: Five Studies*. Berkeley: Institute of East Asian Studies, University of California, 1992. Print.

Scollon, Ron. "Plagiarism and Ideology: Identity in Intercultural Discourse." *Language in Society* 24.1 (1995): 1-28. Print.

Seeberg, Vilma. *The Rhetoic and Reality of Mass Education in Mao's China*. New York: Edwin Mellen Press, 2000. Print.

Shi-Xu. "Towards a Discourse Studies Approach to Cultural China: An Epilogue." *Discourses of Cultural China in the Globalization Age*. Ed. Doreen D. Wu. Hong Kong: Hong Kong University Press, 2008. 243-253. Print.

Shu, Wu. "The *Baguwen* and the New Literature Movement." *Dushu (Reading)* 8 (1993): 82-85. Print.

Sivin, Nathan. "Ruminations on the Tao and its Disputers." *Philosophy East and West* 42.1 (1992): 21-29. Print.

Smith, Richard J. *China's Cultural Heritage: The Ch'Ing Dynasty 1644-1912*. Boulder, Colorado: Westview Press, 1983. Print.

Suen, Hoi K., and Lan Yu. "Chronic Consequences of High-Stakes Testing? Lessons from the Chinese Civil Service Exam." *Comparative Education Review* 50.1 (2006): 46-65. Print.

Sun, Shaozhen. "Preface: A Landmark of Contemporary Chinese Composition Studies." *Introduction to Advanced Composition Studies*. Ed. Zhengping Ma. Beijing: China Renmin University Press, 2002. 1-9. Print.

Swales, John M. "English as 'Tyrannosaurus Rex.'" *World Englishes* 16.3 (1997): 373-82. Print.

Tai, James H-Y. "Temporal Sequence and Word Order in Chinese." *Iconicity in Syntax*. Ed. John Haiman. Amsterdam, Philadelphia: Benjamins, 1985. 49-72. Print.

Tai, James H-Y. "On Two Functions of Place Adverbials in Mandarin Chinese." *Journal of Chinese Linguistics* 3.2/3 (1975): 154-79. Print.

Tang, Tao. *Wenzhang Xiuyang (文章修养)(Developing Texts)*. Hong Kong: Wenxue Yanjiu Press, 1980. Print.

Tian, Qilin. *Baguwen Guanzhi (八股文观止) (the Complete 8-Legged Essay)*. Hainan: Hainan Publishing, 1994. Print.

Tsao, Ding-ren. "The Persuasion of Kuei Ku Tzu." Diss. University of Minnesota, 1985. Print.

van Dijk, Teun A. *Discourse and Context: A Sociocognitive Approach*. Cambridge: Cambridge University Press, 2008. Print.

Walton, Linda. *Academies and Societies in Southern Song China*. Honolulu: University of Hawaii Press, 1999. Print.

Wang, Chaobo. "Paragraph Organization in English and Chinese Academic Prose: A Comparative Study." Diss. Indiana University of Pennsylvania, 1992. Print.

Wang, Dechun. *Xiucixue Tansuo (修辞学探索)(an Exploration of Rhetoric)*. Beijing: Beijing University Press, 1983. Print.

Wang, Gungwu. *Power, Rights, and Duties in Chinese History*. Canberra: Australian National University, 1979. Print.

Wang, Li. *Hanyu Shigao (汉语史稿) (A Historical Introduction to Chinese)*. Beijing: Kexue Chubanshe, 1958. Print.

—. *Zhongguo Yufa Lilun (中国语法理论) (A Theory of Chinese Grammar)*. Beijing: Zhonghua Shuju, 1955. Print.

Wang, Xiwei, and Huazhen Li. *Xinbian Daxue Xiezuo Jiaocheng (新编大学写作教程) (New Edition of University Writing Course)*. Beijing: Peking University Press, 2008. Print.

Wang, Zelong. *Zhongguo Xiezuoxue Tanyao (中国写作学探要) (An Exploration on Chinese Writing Studies)*. Beijing: Zhongguo Wenlian Chubanshe, 2004. Print.

Wardy, Robert. *Aristotle in China: Language, Categories, and Translation*. Cambridge: Cambridge University Press, 2000. Print.

Watson, Burton. *Han Fei Tzu*. Basic Writings. Trans. Burton Watson. New York: Columbia University Press, 1964. Print.

Wong, Siu-kit. *Early Chinese Literary Criticism*. Hong Kong: Joint Publishing Company, 1983. Print.

Woods, Marjorie C. "The Teaching of Poetic Composition in the Later Middle Ages." *A Short History of Writing Instruction from Ancient Greece to Modern America*. Ed. James Murphy. Mahwah, NJ: Hermagoras-Erlbaum Press, 2001. 123-43. Print.

Woodside, Alexander, and Benjamin A. Elman. "Afterword: The Expansion of Education in Ch'Ing China." *Education and Society in Late Imperial China: 1600-1900*. Ed. Benjamin A. Elman and Alexander Woodside. Berkeley: University of California Press, 1994. 525-60. Print.

Wright, Elizabethada A., and Michael S. Halloran. "From Rhetoric to Composition: The Teaching of Writing in America to 1900." *A Short History of Writing Instruction: From Ancient Greece to Modern America*. Ed. James Murphy. Mahwah, NJ: Lawrence Erlbaum Associates, 2001. 213-46. Print.

Wu, Hanxiang. *University Writing Course (大学写作教程) (New University Writing Course)*. Beijing: Science Press, 1999. Print.

Wu, Hui. "Lost and Found in Translation: Modern Conceptualization of Chinese Rhetoric." *Rhetoric Review* 28.2 (2009): 148-66. Print.

Wu, Yingtian. *Wenzhang Jiegou Xue (文章结构学) (the Construction of Texts)*. Beijing: Renmin Daxue Chubanshe, 1988. Print.

Wyatt, Don J. "A Language of Continuity in Confucian Thought." *Ideas Across Cultures: Essays on Chinese Thought in Honor of Benjamin I. Schwartz*. Ed. Paul A. Cohen and Merle Goldman. Cambridge, Mass: Harvard University Press, 1990. 33-62. Print.

Xia, Gaizun, and Shengtao Ye. *Wenhua Qishierjiang (文话七十二讲) (72 Lectures on Speech and Writing)*. 1st ed. Beijing: Zhonghua Shuju, 2007. Print.

Xie, Yaoji. *Xiandai Hanyu Ouhua Yufa Gailun* （现代汉语欧化语法概论）*(an Outline of Western Grammar in Contemporary Chinese)*. Hong Kong: Guangming Tushu Publishing, 1989. Print.

Xu, Zhichang, et al. *Academic Writing in Language and Education Programmes*. Singapore: Pearson, 2011. Print.

Xu, Zhichang. *Chinese English: Features and Implications*. Hong Kong: The Open University of Hong Kong Press, 2010. Print.

Yang, Busheng, and Dingguo Peng. *Zhongguo Shuyuan Yu Chuantong Wenhua (中国书院与传统文化) Chinese Shuyuan and Traditional Culture*. Hunan: Hunan Education Press, 1992. Print.

Yang, Ling, and David Cahill. "The Rhetorical Organization of Chinese and American Students' Expository Essays: A Contrastive Rhetoric Study." *International Journal of English Studies* 8.2 (2008): 113-32. Print.

Ye, Han. *A Writing Course for College Students*. Zhejing University Press, 2005. Print.

You, Xiaoye. "Alienated Voices in Modern Chinese Rhetoric: Hu Shi and His Transactional Rhetorical Views." Formation and Development of Academic Disciplines in Twentieth Century China Conference. Australian National University, Canberra, 3-5, December, 2007. Reading.

—. "Building Empire through Argumentation: Debating Salt and Iron in Western Han China." *College English* 72.4 (2010): 367-84. Print.

—. "Conflation of Rhetorical Traditions: The Formation of Modern Chinese Writing Instruction." *Rhetoric Review* 24.2 (2005): 150-69. Print.

—. *Writing in the Devil's Tongue: A History of English Composition in China*. Carbondale: Southern Illinois University Press, 2010. Print.

Young, Linda Wai-ling. *Crosstalk and Culture in Sino-American Communication*. Cambridge: Cambridge University Press, 1994a. Print.

—. "Unraveling Chinese Inscrutability." Diss. University of California, 1986. Print.

Yu, Chengkun, Ruiduan Chen, and Renyuan Wu, eds. *Xiandai Yingyongwen Jiaocheng (现代应用文教程) (A Modern Course on Practical Writing)*. Shanghai: Fudan University Press, 2009. Print.

Yu, Daxiang, and Changyong Huang, eds. *Moshi Xiezuo (模式写作) (Schema Writing)*. 1st ed. Shanghai: Shanghai Educational Publishing House, 2009. Print.

Yue, Haixiang, Hongqi Zhan, and Tongqin Zhao, eds. *Mingjia Tan Zenyang Xiewenzhang (名家谈怎样写文章) (Writing Masters on How to Write Papers)*. 1st ed. Beijing: Zhongguo Yanshi Chubanshe, 2009. Print.

Zhang, Dihua. *Hanyu Yufa Xiuci Cidian (汉语语法修辞词典) (A Dictionary of Chinese Grammar and Rhetoric)*. Anhui: Anhui Education Publishing, 1985. Print.

Zhao, Yuanren. *A Grammar of Spoken Chinese*. Berkeley: University of California Press, 1968. Print.

Zheng, Ziyu. *Zhongguo Xiuci Shigao (中国修辞史稿) (A History of Chinese Rhetoric)*. Shanghai: Shanghai Jiaoyu Chubanshe, 1979. Print.

Zhou, Jichang, Baojun Li, and Kefu Lin, eds. *Xiezuoxue Gaojijiaocheng (写作学高级教程) (an Advanced Course on Writing)*. 4th ed. Wuhan: Wuhan University Press, 2009. Print.

Zhou, Youguang. *Xin Shidai De Xin Yuwen (新时代的新语文) (the Language of the New Age)*. Beijing: Sanlian Publishing, 1999a. Print.

Zhou, Zhenfu. *Zhongguo Xiuci Shi (中国修辞史) (A History of Chinese Rhetoric)*. Beijing: Shangwu Yinshuguan, 1999b. Print.

Zhu, Binjie. *Zhongguo Gudai Wenti Gailun(中国古代问题概论) (an Introduction to Classical Chinese Genres)*. Beijing: Beijing University Press, 1990. Print.

Zhu, Zicui. "Baguwen Yanjiu (八股文研究) (A Study of the Baguwen)." *Wenxue (Literature)* 3.1 (1934): 395-408. Print.

Zong, Tinghua, and Jinling Li. "Vol 2: Sui Tang Wu Dai Song Jin Yuan Juan ((隋唐五代宋金元卷). (Vol 2: The Sui, Tang, 5 Dynasties, Song, Jin and Yuan Dynasties.)" *Zhongguo Xiucixue Tongshi (中国修辞学通史) (A Complete History of Chinese Rhetoric)* Ed. Ziyu Zheng and Tinghu Zong. Jilin: Jilin Jiaoyu Chubanshe, 1998. Print.

Zong, Tinghu, ed. *Ershi Shiji Zhongguo Xiucixue-Shangjuan (20世纪中国修辞学-上卷) Twentieth Century Chinese Rhetoric, Part 1*. 1st ed. Beijing: Chinese Renmin University Press, 2007. Print.

—. *Ershi Shiji Zhongguo Xiucixue-Xiajuan (20世纪中国修辞学-下卷) (Twentieth Century Chinese Rhetoric, Part 2)*. 1st ed. Beijing: Chinese Renmin University Press, 2007. Print.

NOTES

1. This chronological division is from Xing Lu, *Rhetoric in Ancient China, fifth to third century B.C.E.,* Columbia, University of South Carolina Press, 1998.
2. See also Kirkpatrick ("Chinese Rhetoric: Methods of Argument").
3. Bo Le and Pao Ding are mentioned by Zhuangzi (360 BCE). Bo Le was a master equestrian and Pao Ding a master chef. When Bo Le was learning about horses, he saw horses in everything. When Pao Ding was learning to butcher cows, he saw all cows as dead cows. The point Wang Chong is making is that seeing ghosts is second nature for the sick. Everything they see becomes a ghost.
4. "Knotting grass" is an expression meaning to repay a favour after death.
5. This comes from Section 10 of Chen Kui's *Wen Ze*.
6. The *Huai Nanzi* is a work of 21 essays on a range of subjects that were presented to the Emperor Wu of the Western Han in 139 BCE.
7. The excerpt is taken from the final part of Chapter 12, *Attack by Fire*, from the translation by R.L. Wing, *The art of strategy: a new translation of Sun Tzu's classic "The art of war,"* New York, Doubleday, 1988.
8. Li Po (Li Bai, 李白) 701-762.
9. The first part of this chapter draws on Andy Kirkpatrick, "Medieval Chinese rules of writing and their relevance today," *Australian Review of Applied Linguistics*, 2004, 27, 1, p1-14. A translation and commentary of *The Rules of Writing* is provided in Kirkpatrick, Andy, "China's first systematic account of rhetoric: an introduction to Chen Kui's *Wen Ze*, *Rhetorica* XX111, 2, p103-52.
10. For example, Liu Yancheng, *Wenze zhuyi, (Commentary on the Wenze)*, Beijing, Shumu Wenxuan Chubanshe.
11. Two Chinese scholars who have expressed this view are Wang Songmao in his *Wen Ze zhuyi bayu (A Postscript to Liu Yancheng's Commentary and Modern Chinese Translation of the Wen Ze)* 1988, 283–295 and Zhou Zhenfu in his *Zhongguo xiucixue shi (A History of Chinese Rhetoric)*

Beijing: Shangwu yinshu guan.

12. Negative rhetoric deals with such aspects of rhetoric as text structure and argument sequencing. Positive rhetoric deals with rhetorical tropes. George Kennedy (1980) makes a comparable division of Classical Western rhetoric into primary rhetoric, the art of persuasion, although this was primarily oral, and secondary rhetoric, the study of tropes and figures of speech.
13. To ensure a clear distinction is made between the examples Chen Kui cites and his own commentary, I have placed the cited examples in italics.
14. The reference to the colour of people's skins reflects the belief that workers and farmers developed dark faces as they worked outside in the sun, while people with white faces were indoor workers (and therefore seen to be of higher class).
15. This is taken from an interview with Zhou Youguang reported in the South China Morning Post newspaper of July 20, 2010 by the journalist Mark O'Neill.
16. 山长 is the Chinese for *Shanzhang* or college president. The Chinese for the other *Shuyuan* positions described here include: 副山长, 助教, 讲书, 监院, 首士, 学长, 副讲, 堂长, 管干, 典谒, 经长, 学长, 书斋长, 引赞, 厨房工役, 门斗, 堂夫, 斋夫, 看司, 看碑, 看书, 更夫.
17. Dao Caoren or Straw Man is a character in Chinese fairy tales.
18. As these are excerpts from discourse, they are relatively long. I therefore only give a literal translation (and, where needed, a more polished one) of the excerpts. A fuller account can be found in Kirkpatrick, "Information Sequencing", "Are they really so Different?", "The Arrangement of Letters".)
19. A quote from the first song in a collection of nine by the Tang poet, Liu Yuxi, entitled "Willow Branch."
20. A reference to the "Two Whatevers" policy articulated by Hua Guofeng, who succeeded Mao Zedong as the chairman of the Communist Party of China upon Mao's death: "We will resolutely uphold whatever policy decisions Chairman Mao made, and unswervingly follow whatever instructions Chairman Mao gave."
21. Note that "counterrevolutionary rebellion" was Deng's term. Note also that the "we" provided in the English translation is not in the original Chinese, so a more accurate translation might be "then his interpretation must be overturned and corrected."
22. Yao Nai's classification: 论辨 (argumentations), 序跋 (prefaces & postscripts), 奏议 (presentations/discussions/petitions to the emperor), 书说 (letters), 赠序 (farewell essays), 诏令 (edicts & orders), 传状 (biographies), 碑志 (epitaphs), 杂记 (miscellaneous writings), 箴铭

(extortations & inscriptions), 颂赞 (odes & pronouncements), 辞赋 (prose poetry & rhapsody), and 哀祭 (condolence & lament writings/elegies).

www.ingramcontent.com/pod-product-compliance
Lightning Source LLC
Chambersburg PA
CBHW030136240426
43672CB00005B/153